T0294236

O Jogo Bonito!

O Jogo Bonito!

Brazil's 1970 World Cup Samba Party

Gary Thacker

First published by Pitch Publishing, 2024

Pitch Publishing
9 Donnington Park,
85 Birdham Road,
Chichester,
West Sussex,
PO20 7AJ
www.pitchpublishing.co.uk
info@pitchpublishing.co.uk

A CIP catalogue record is available for this book
from the British Library.

ISBN 978 1 80150 676 2

Typesetting and origination by Pitch Publishing
Printed and bound in India by Replika Press Pvt. Ltd.

Contents

This book is dedicated to my wife Sue, to Megan
and Luke, Lydia and Gregory, and my precious
grandchildren, Eve, Polly and Benjamin

* * *

It is also dedicated to all those who always
supported and believed in me.
You are my strength.

And to those who only ever doubted me.
You are my inspiration.

Acknowledgements

MANY PEOPLE have assisted in the production of this book. The following have generously agreed to be interviewed directly, by email, telephone or similar, and allowed me to use their wise words:

- Alex Bellos – author of *Futebol: The Brazilian Way of Life*
- Andrew Downie – author of *The Greatest Show on Earth: The Inside Story of the Legendary 1970 World Cup*, and *Doctor Socrates: Footballer, Philosopher, Legend*
- Stuart Horsfield – author of *1982 Brazil: The Glorious Failure: The Day Football Died* and *España 82: A Hazy Shade of Summer*
- Sam Kunti – journalist and author of *Brazil 1970: How the Greatest Team of All Time Won the World Cup*
- Dr Pete Watson – teaching fellow in the Department of Spanish, Portuguese and Latin American Studies, University of Leeds, and author of *Football and Nation Building in Colombia (2010–2018): The Only Thing That Unites Us*
- Aidan Williams – author of *The Nearly Men: The Eternal Allure of the Greatest Teams that Failed to Win the World Cup*

Statistical sources:
- rsssfbrasil.com/sel/national.html
- cbf.com.br/
- fifa.com

Finally, thanks to all at Pitch Publishing for their wonderful professionalism and unstinting dedication.

My sincere thanks to one and all.

* * *

Unless otherwise stated and sources cited, quotes used within the book are taken from my own interviews.

Introduction

AN AIRCRAFT bearing the livery of the Viação Aérea Rio-Grandense (Varig) airline stood waiting on the tarmac. Chartered by the Confederação Brasileira de Desportos (CBD) – the organisation wouldn't change its name to the now more familiar Confederação Brasileira de Futebol (CBF) until 1979 – the flight plan taking it to Rio de Janeiro's Galeão airport had been logged and departure time confirmed. But that allocated slot had passed as the passengers sat waiting mostly patiently, some impatiently, for the call to board. Some wore suits. Many wore tracksuits. Despite the July dateline, the six-word name of their country, emblazoned boldly across their chests, was split asunder – very much as their hopes and aspirations had been torn apart – by the zip fastened up to the neck as protection against the chill London weather. Delayed by 'technical issues', there was plenty of time for reflection and regret as the squad of players and accompanying staff, sent to defend the World Cup won in Chile four years previously, pondered recent events and their fates. Many memories wandered back to a defining moment in Liverpool days earlier.

A dejected and downcast Pelé hobbling from the Goodison Park pitch on 20 July 1966, following Brazil's

3-1 defeat to Portugal, is one of the saddest of the many iconic images illustrating the history of the world's most prestigious football tournament. A blanket loosely draped over his shoulders offered cold comfort and precious little protection, a level somewhat equivalent to that provided by referee George McCabe during the 90 minutes of football that had just been played out. The English official had watched with an inexplicable, negligent disinterest as Portuguese players formed up in disorderly lines to kick and hack at the 25-year-old with what was surely premeditated determination and persistence. João Morais, the Sporting Lisbon defender, was one of the most prominent assailants, and his double foul in a matter of a few seconds, either of which could have warranted his dismissal, effectively relegated the South Americans' star player to the role of limping passenger.

The inevitable defeat eliminated the reigning champions from the 1966 World Cup at the group stage. It was the first time that Brazil had been condemned to endure the indignity of elimination at the initial stage of a World Cup since the truncated initial tournament played out in Uruguay 36 years earlier, when one win, one defeat, and second place in a group of three failed to take them into the next round. At the time of writing, it's also one that has never yet been repeated.

Eight days earlier, with German referee Kurt Tschenscher officiating, Bulgaria had produced the blueprint for the Portuguese team's approach to diminishing the threat of Pelé. Dobromir Zhechev was apparently designated to be the man marking, in more ways than one, the player widely regarded as the best on the planet. The fact that Pelé had given the world champions an early lead had understandably done little to diminish the ferocity of challenges levied against him and, when Garrincha added a second goal to ease Brazil over the line, perhaps it showed that beauty could prevail against the beast. There was, however, a price to pay for the victory. Pelé had recovered from the somewhat less than tender care of the Bulgarians in time for Brazil's second match when, three days later, a game of football broke out, and Hungary put the champions' defence of the trophy in peril with a 3-1 win.

Ahead of the tournament Ken Aston, heading up the Referees Committee, had declared that officials would be instructed to clamp down on aggressive foul play and protect the skilful players. Four years earlier, Aston had been the man in the middle during the infamous 'Battle of Santiago' when hosts Chile and opponents Italy, with an occasional reference to the location of the ball, indulged in a brutal battle more appropriate to a mixed martial arts contest than a World Cup. Ahead of screening the game on the BBC, David Coleman famously described the contest as being 'the most stupid, appalling, disgusting and disgraceful exhibition of football, possibly in the history of the game'. That torrid experience may have influenced Aston's words ahead of the 1966 tournament but perhaps the message got lost somewhere along the way. Neither Tschenscher nor McCabe appeared to have read the script; they seemed inclined to ignore it if they had.

The treatment – and lack of protection – afforded to Brazil's players have rightly been highlighted as one of the reasons for the failure of the two-time world champions to offer anything more than a seemingly token defence of their title. As with most simplistic explanations, however, the oft-quoted reasoning that 'futebol força', as Carlos Alberto later described it, doomed Brazil only takes you so far. Pelé himself suggested when reflecting on the contest against Portugal, 'The physical nature of the game doesn't explain our defeat. We just failed.'[1]

Such failure had not only occurred during the tournament. Several events preceding it had hardly contributed towards a successful defence of the trophy. As the dying embers of Brazil's ambition for a hat-trick of World Cup triumphs faded into ash, and England took possession of the Jules Rimet Trophy, other consequences would follow. Largely because of the brutal treatment meted out to him, and the lack of protection offered by referees, Pelé declared that he would never play in another World Cup. Brazil had lost the brightest star in their firmament, and regaining the titles won in 1958 and 1962 seemed like a distant dream. The 1966 World Cup experience had been a chastening one, and there were fears that another would be awaiting the team's return to Brazil.

The 'technical issues' were eventually 'resolved' and the aeroplane carrying Brazil's team and supporting entourage eventually took off many hours later. The true reason for the delay would come to light afterwards. Those 'technical issues' were, in reality, camouflage for officials deeming that a landing back in Rio in the middle of the night was far less likely to be greeted by angry fans than the earlier scheduled arrival. Whether there would have been any greeting committee is less than clear. Suffice to say that all was quiet as the flight touched down.

---

1   do Nascimento, Edson Arantes, *Pelé – The Autobiography* (London: Simon & Schuster UK Ltd, 2006)

As the players disembarked, some to catch other flights to far-flung locations across the vast area of Brazil, others with less distance to travel, the next World Cup, taking place in Mexico in 1970, held out little promise of success. There would be no Pelé. They were no longer defending champions and, for the first time since 1958, they would have to go through a qualification process to even be present. An inflated confidence born of successive tournament victories had been punctured by the experience in England. Like a deflated balloon, it lay on the floor, apparently beyond repair and consigned to its fate.

And yet, the glorious celebration of the greatest team ever to win a World Cup was just four short years away. *O Jogo Bonito* would light up Mexico with incandescent colour. It would be Brazil's 1970 World Cup Samba Party and, with global colour television coverage, all the world was allowed to join in. Arriving at the party was anything but simple, however. In the 20 years between 1950 and the 1970 tournaments there were both glorious triumphs and dispiriting defeats for Brazil, on the long road to success.

Across the following pages, we'll follow that road, look at the trials, tribulations and triumphs on the way to Mexico, and how the political backdrop of Brazil influenced events. We'll look in detail at the Mexico World Cup, Brazil's reaction to the victory and then consider the legacy left by Zagallo's victorious team, and how the national team's identity of *O Jogo Bonito* became more myth than reality. In June of 1970, the *Seleção Canarinho* claimed a place among the ranks of sporting legends. This is their story.

Part 1 – The Long and Winding Road[2]

---

2   'The Long and Winding Road', *Let It Be*, the Beatles (Apple & EMI, 1970)

Years of Sorrow

To look at Brazil's performance at the 1970 World Cup in isolation would only be telling a part of the story. As with so many outstanding sporting successes it isn't something that can be reduced to the events of a few weeks. There were years of sorrow to be endured before the years of joy that followed and, even then, a roadblock to be negotiated. After a couple of frustrating failures, the first step was taken in 1958, but there was still a long way to travel before Brazilian football hit its zenith with *O Jogo Bonito*. It was a triumph a dozen years in the making.

1950 and the *Maracanazo*

Following the end of World War Two, FIFA were keen to resurrect the World Cup and, at their 1946 congress, invited countries to bid for the hosting rights for the proposed 1949 tournament. In the aftermath of the conflagration that had cost millions of lives across the previous half a dozen years, however, few countries saw this as an opportunity to grasp, especially those whose infrastructures, economy and social structures had been ravaged during the conflict. Ahead of the war, Brazil and Germany had been competing to host the subsequently cancelled 1942 finals and, with a defeated, demoralised and largely destroyed Germany in no fit state to resurrect its ambitions, a resubmitted Brazilian bid to host was hastily accepted by FIFA. With so many European countries focusing solely on rebuilding and recovery as their overwhelming priorities, and the previous two tournaments held first in Italy and then in France, South America was a logical choice, with Brazil as the host.

A truncated tournament, denuded by withdrawals, boycotts and absentees, was eventually reorganised to comprise a pair of groups with four teams each, one with three and a final one of just two. It required a sole game to decide who would top that group and move forward into the second stage of four group winners, and was a cobbled-together solution, but at least it got things moving. From there, each of the four top teams emerging from the groups would play each other with the team topping the final group declared as the new world champions. It was a format scheduled not to have a deciding final, but the fates conspired to compromise that plan.

The games in the final group would take place on 9, 13 and 16 July, with the matches of the last day set to be Sweden facing Spain and Brazil facing Uruguay. In the earlier games, Uruguay had first drawn with Spain thanks to a late goal by their captain, Obdulio Varela, before squeezing past Sweden 3-2 after twice trailing the Scandinavians, when Óscar Míguez netted twice in the final dozen minutes. Meanwhile, Brazil had slalomed through their games, defeating Sweden 7-1 and Spain 6-1. The hosts only needed a draw in the final rubber to become world champions and, with the game played at Rio's intimidating Estádio do Maracanã, in front of an official attendance of some 199,000, while unofficially the figure is regarded to have breached the 210,000 mark – equivalent to around ten per cent of Rio's total population – anything but a Brazilian triumph was surely inconceivable. It was seen to be more of a coronation than a contest. The man who would later break Brazilian hearts, Alcides Ghiggia, later recalled that ahead of kick-off, 'Their supporters were jumping with joy as if they'd already won the World Cup.' For the first time, but hardly the last, a large fee would be demanded for Brazilian hubris.

It was not to be. In a game that was later to gain infamy in Brazil as the *Maracanazo*, despite the hosts taking an early second-half lead through Friaça, Uruguay rallied against all expectation and the fervour of the Brazilian crowd. Juan Alberto Schiaffino, who would later become the world's most expensive footballer when he moved from Peñarol to AC Milan for 52m Lire in September 1954, equalised on 66 minutes after capitalising on a cross from Ghiggia. And when another Uruguayan strike, this time from Ghiggia 13 minutes later, gave the visitors the lead, Brazilian dreams were buried. Ghiggia would later remark that he was one of only three people ever to have silenced the Maracanã. 'Frank Sinatra, the Pope and me,' he recalled during an interview with the BBC.

People broke down in tears in the stadium and Pelé later recalled that it was the only time he had ever seen his father cry. He wasn't alone. In his book telling the story of the World Cup's bridesmaids, those who so nearly reached the crowning glory but fell tantalisingly short, Aidan Williams painted the picture of the enduring effect of that defeat, 'For all of Brazil's footballing grandeur, all of those glittering prizes, those moments when their canary-yellow shirts dazzled as the sun shone on their crowning glories, it is a moment of sporting tragedy that remains the most morbidly fascinating to Brazilians.'[3] The trauma was woven into the social fabric of Brazil, and there it would stay entangled, enmeshed, eternally haunting.

Watching in the stadium was a young 18-year-old soldier, who would grow up to deliver three of those 'glittering prizes' alluded to by Williams, in World Cup triumphs for Brazil – two as a player and one as a coach. His name was Mário Zagallo and in 1970 he would be the coach of the greatest team ever to win the World Cup. Not far from the stadium there's a museum, and in a darkened room there, a flickering newsreel retells the story of that fateful game. As Ghiggia scores the goal that turned Brazilian dreams into nightmares, the commentary quietly intones with solemn finality, 'Two-one Uruguay. The heart of Brazil stops.' Up until this point, the *Seleção Canarinho* was yet to be born, as Brazil played in white, with blue collars. The trauma and dread spectre of Brazil wearing white would haunt the team for many years to come, not least ahead of the 1958 World Cup Final.

Following the *Maracanazo*, with the white shirts now deemed to be both unlucky and lacking in patriotic links to the country and its culture, Brazilian newspaper *Correio da Manhã* sought permission from the CBD to run a competition inviting readers to submit designs for a new kit for the *Seleção,* which would incorporate the colours of the national flag – yellow, green, blue and white – offering a new start for the national team and wiping away the memories of the *Maracanazo*. The competition was won

---

3   Williams, Aidan, *The Nearly Men: The Eternal Allure of the Greatest Teams that Failed to Win the World Cup* (Worthing, England: Pitch Publishing Ltd, 2022)

by 19-year-old Aldyr Garcia Schlee, who would later go on to become a celebrated writer, journalist, translator, illustrator and professor. His drawings depicting a yellow shirt, trimmed in green and blue shorts edged in white would later become a world-famous icon of Brazilian football, and adopted by the CBD in February 1954, when the *Seleção Canarinho* took to the field against Chile in Santiago's Estadio Nacional in a qualifying game for the upcoming World Cup.

1954 and the Battle of Berne

Four years after the *Maracanazo*, with a 100 per cent win record across all four of their qualifying games, Brazil arrived in Switzerland to compete in the 1954 tournament. With a squad containing the likes of Djalma Santos, Nílton Santos and Waldyr Pereira – forever known as Didi – they were placed into Group 1 alongside the other seeded team, France, and the two non-seeds, Mexico and Yugoslavia. Presumptively, FIFA had decided who the eight seeded teams – two being in each of the four groups – would be before the qualification process had been completed. Austria, Brazil, England, France, Hungary, Italy, Spain, and Uruguay were selected. Turkey threw a spanner into the works when they eliminated the Spanish, but FIFA merely moved the seeding spot to them instead.

Following a strange format, the two seeded teams would not play each other and a thumping 5-0 win over Mexico and a 1-1 draw with Yugoslavia was sufficient to see Brazil qualify along with the eastern Europeans. Officially Brazil finished top of the group, but this had little to do with their massively superior goal difference over the runners-up. That factor was deemed to be irrelevant, with the drawing of lots bizarrely considered to be a better option of deciding prominence.

Topping the group sent Brazil into a quarter-final with the Magical Magyars of Hungary. After the demolitions of England, Gusztáv Sebes's team were widely considered to be the best on the planet and strong favourites to win the trophy, especially as the location surely favoured a European side over those from South America. In this contest, however, the scintillating play that the cherry red-shirted Hungarians had displayed across recent years was absent as the game degenerated into the infamy of the 'Battle of Berne'. Three players were dismissed, and that number could have been much higher. Even after the final whistle, the teams continued their running battles into the tunnel and dressing rooms.

As with the debacle in the Chilean capital four years later at the Battle of Santiago, again an English referee, this time Arthur Ellis, was the arbiter of fair play, if any could be found. Hungary prevailed 4-2 after twice taking a two-goal advantage, and being pegged back, before Sándor Kocsis put the game beyond the reach of Brazil with a couple of minutes to play. Ellis would later find fame on television as a 'referee' in the slapstick knockabout antics of *It's a Knockout!* and *Jeux sans Frontières*. The contest in Berne was certainly a game without frontiers, and ended up as a knockout for Brazil.

After the traumatising defeat to Uruguay in what was a de facto home World Cup Final in the Estádio do Maracanã four years earlier, Brazil's prospects of becoming world champions barely seemed to have progressed. A quarter-final defeat, albeit in such a tempestuous game, hardly suggested that things were moving in the right direction and, with the next tournament taking place in

Europe again – Sweden the hosts – the prospects were far from dazzlingly bright.

At such times, it's understandable to cast around for the right man to put things back on track, and across the next four years the CBD took to such an exercise with copious amounts of zeal, and equal measures of apparent indecision. Coach Zezé Moreira would not survive in post for long, and returned to his club side Botafogo. Vicente Feola took charge on the first day of July 1954 and would be in charge of the team for precisely two years. The São Paulo coach had a pedigree of success with his club, securing the Campeonato Paulista title in 1948, and retaining it the following year. His time with the *Seleção* was brief but he would take charge again, both three years and 13 years later, with hugely differing amounts of success. Flávio Costa had been the man at the helm of the Brazil team in the 1950 tournament and, had the result been different on that fateful 4 July day in Rio, his fame would have been assured. Following the *Maracanazo*, however, his doom was assured. A brief return after the departure of Feola offered little in the way of redemption for Costa and he was replaced by Corinthians coach Osvaldo Brandão. The new man would flit in and out of contact with the *Seleção* across the next 24 months, before remarkably returning two decades later for a two-year spell in charge.

Teté took over in 1956, but didn't stay long before Flávio Costa returned. His third term with the national team, perhaps significantly, began on 1 April 1956. The wisdom, or otherwise, was confirmed by the fact that just four months later he was again on the move, this time to European club football, taking over at Porto. Sylvio Pirillo had scored six goals in his five games for the *Seleção* and he was the man drafted in to take charge following Costa's third exit. As with so many others, in the few years since the World Cup elimination in Switzerland, his time was brief, but as well as guiding Brazil to qualification for Sweden his tenure was marked out by one hugely significant event.

With three slots allocated to CONMEBOL, the South American federation, and nine teams seeking qualification, it was a fairly simple matter to produce three groups, each comprising three teams, with the group winners making the trip to Scandinavia. Feola's team were placed into a group alongside Peru and Venezuela, with their task being made easier when the latter decided to withdraw from the competition. A 1-1 in Lima's Estadio Nacional on 13 April 1957 set things up for Brazil to complete the job eight days later back in Rio. The team that faced Peru in Lima had no Pelé – his international debut was still a few months away – but, with Gilmar in goal, both Djalma Santos and Nílton Santos in front of him, plus Didi in midfield and Garrincha in the forward line, the team that would take Brazil to the summit of world football the following year was taking shape. Sure enough, a goal by Didi 11 minutes into the return fixture confirmed Brazil's passage to Sweden.

Three months later, with qualification confirmed, the coach could turn his mind to looking at players likely to be travelling to Europe the following year. On 7 July 1957 Brazil faced Argentina in a Roca Cup game in Rio. The trophy had been donated in 1913 by General Julio Argentino Roca, a former president of Argentina and ambassador to Brazil, to be awarded to the winner of games between the two countries, and this version would mark the debut of a precocious talent. Edson Arantes do Nascimento had made his first appearance for Santos as a 15-year-old on 7 December 1956, and just ten months later the player who would become universally known as Pelé entered the international arena. He was just 16 years and nine months old. Argentina would win 2-1 but, on 76 minutes, the Brazil goal was netted by the teenager. Across the course of a further 91 appearances for the *Seleção* he would add another 76 to his total. The second was not long in coming. Three days later the teams met again, this time in São Paulo. Pelé opened the scoring after 20 minutes and Brazil went on to win 2-0.

The teenager was a sensation, although no one knew that he would grow up to be regarded as the best player in the world, and few realised how thankful they should be for Pirillo giving the skinny tyro his debut. Pedrinho took over from Pirillo, before Feola was appointed to lead the team into the 1958 World Cup.

* * *

Years of Joy

1958: The First Step on the Journey

Officially, Feola's appointment began on 7 June 1958, the day before the tournament began and Brazil began their opening game against Austria. His first term heading the *Seleção* had hardly been a runaway success. Of his 16 games, he had won eight, drawn five and been defeated in three, averaging just a single goal per match. When the tournament got under way, that record would improve dramatically both in terms of victories and goals scored. A total of 16 strikes in their six matches in Sweden is impressive enough. Throw in the fact that the sequence includes a goalless draw against England, and a single-goal victory against Wales, and the average in the other games rises dramatically.

Feola's squad was a mixture of youth and experience, although only a couple of the 22 players had passed their 30th birthdays. Goalkeeper Carlos José Castilho, who had reached that mark just eight months earlier, was the second eldest, behind the vastly experienced Nílton Santos, who was 33 and had 46 caps to his name. At the other end of the scale, Pelé – still only 17 – had five caps, Vavá had four, Didi and Zagallo just three each, and Orlando a single one. All five would feature in the World Cup Final triumph over Sweden, with Pelé, Zagallo and Vavá sharing the goals.

In the previous two tournaments, Brazil had lost in what was the final – in everything but name – to Uruguay eight years earlier, and had then suffered defeat to what was probably the best team in the world in 1954 as they were eliminated by Hungary. As such, placed in a group with the Soviet Union, England and Austria, they were considered by many to be favourites to progress. On paper, however, the task was perhaps not as easy as some may have thought. The Soviet Union, playing in their first finals, were the reigning Olympic champions and many of the gold medal winners had made the squad for Sweden. Austria had collected the bronze medal in that same competition and, despite England being denuded of some star names following the tragedy of the Munich air disaster, they still had a strong squad, witnessed by the fact that they were the only team throughout the tournament to both deny Brazil a goal and, consequently, victory. It was the first time a game in a World Cup finals had ended goalless.

Brazil started the tournament in confident fashion, disposing of Austria with some comfort. A brace from Altafini, sandwiching Nílton Santos's goal, was more than enough to carry them to victory. Three days later, with Vavá replacing Didi, they faced a much more resilient opponent as England battled to a 0-0 draw in Gothenburg. The Soviet Union had also beaten Austria and drawn with England, meaning that the final rubber of the group would decide who topped the table and, depending on other results, who would finish in the runners-up spot.

Following his team's failure to find the back of the net against England, Feola made three changes to his starting 11. Zito replaced Sani in midfield with both Garrincha and the teenage Pelé joining the attack in place of Joel and Altafini. The team that would play in the final was taking shape. More than 50,000 fans crowded into the Ullevi stadium to watch the contest and Vavá's two goals saw Brazil top the group. Despite his tender years, and a failure to score, Pelé marked his entrance into World Cup competition with a performance full of skill and promise. Feola's team had prevailed without conceding a goal and the Soviet Union edged England out of second place, and qualification, in a play-off after both teams had finished with four points and matching goals records.

Despite his brace in seeing off the Soviet Union, Vavá was missing against Wales as Altafini replaced him in an otherwise unchanged team. Playing just his second match in a World Cup, Pelé began to deliver on the promise he had shown in the previous group game, and scored the winning goal as the Welsh stretched the eventual champions in what was probably their toughest contest of the tournament.

Joining them in the final four were Sweden, France and West Germany. Brazil were the only non-European team remaining in the competition and, as no team had ever won the World Cup outside of their own hemisphere at that time, there was plenty of opinion that thought the winners would come from one of the other three sides, who all had good reason to consider themselves worthy of the title.

The hosts were coached by George Raynor, who would go on to be the first Englishman to take a team to the World Cup Final, beating Sir Alf Ramsey by eight years and two tournaments. The Swedes were also fired by a crop of exciting forwards, with some of them making a significant impact in Italy's Serie A, including Gunnar Gren, Kurt Hamrin and Nils Liedholm.

West Germany were the reigning champions, following their defeat of the overwhelming favourites, and conquerors of Brazil, Hungary in Switzerland. A less-than-impressive progression to the semi-finals had seen the Germans win one and draw two of their group games, before edging past Yugoslavia thanks to a goal by Helmut Rahn, who had netted the decisive goal in the final four years earlier.

France not only had the tournament's top goalscorer, Just Fontaine, in their team, but also the brilliant Raymond Kopa who had played for Stade de Reims in the first European Cup Final, when the French club lost to Real Madrid, but then returned to the final the following year, this time wearing the all white of the Spaniards. *Los Blancos* had been so impressed that they paid handsomely to take him to the Spanish capital where he would be part of their European domination for the next three years. Albert Batteaux's team also had the man often regarded as one of the most accomplished defenders in Europe as part of their team, in Robert Jonquet. While Sweden faced West Germany in front of nearly 50,000 fans in Gothenburg, Brazil would travel to Solna's Råsunda Stadium in the other semi-final where an injury to Jonquet would be key in deciding the outcome.

Feola had restored Vavá to his forward line and, just two minutes into the game, he opened the scoring. A sliding challenge by Jonquet broke up a Brazil attack but the ball ran free, and an astute pass to Vavá set him free around the penalty spot with just goalkeeper Claude Abbes to beat. A low powerful shot completed the job. The lead was short-lived though, and seven minutes later an incisive pass from Kopa set Fontaine through on goal. Confidence high, the forward skipped around Gilmar and the scores were level, despite the efforts of Bellini and Nílton Santos to get back and block the shot. With the patterns of play now as level as the scoreline, the game, and the consequent place in the final, were in the balance. Ten minutes before half-time, however, an inadvertent collision between Vavá and Jonquet swayed the contest heavily in favour of the *Seleção*.

A seemingly innocuous clash left the France captain holding his right shin and clearly in distress; the attentions of the attendant doctor to apparently bring comfort by rubbing the affected area unsurprisingly failed to offer any solace. Jonquet was forced to leave the field, in pain, struggling with an injury that was later diagnosed as a fractured fibula. The loss of their skipper and defensive keystone understandably rattled the French and Didi took advantage to put Brazil back in front, firing in from distance as Abbes flailed forlornly at the ball. Jonquet would later valiantly return but, no more than a limping shadow of his former self and shunted out to the left flank, he was at best a passenger. Trailing 2-1 at the break and with their captain incapacitated, France looked a beaten team, and in the second period Pelé confirmed that status by notching a hat-trick.

Seven minutes after the restart, a low cross from the left was spilled by Abbes and the teenager fired home from a couple of yards. The game was surely finished but Pelé certainly was not. On 64 minutes another French defensive error delivered the ball to his feet inside the area. This time the range was around ten yards, but the result was the same as he unerringly found the back of the net again. The hat-trick was completed, and the *coup de grâce* – ironically against the French – was delivered with 15 minutes to play. A pass from Garrincha on the right found Pelé on the edge of the area. An instant control brought the ball under his spell and a second touch fired it low past Abbes's dive. A late goal from Roger Piantoni was anything but a consolation of any measure. In the other semi-final, Sweden had recovered from being a goal down against West Germany to record a 3-1 win and the hosts would face Brazil in the final.

On 29 June, the two teams lined up at the Råsunda Stadium with around 50,000 fans watching to see if Sweden would become the first postwar hosts to win the World Cup, or whether Brazil could be the first South American country to triumph in Europe. With both teams' first-choice colours being yellow shirts and blue shorts, there was the need for a hasty solution for the Brazilians. The initial plan was for the team to return to their previous colours of all white. Many of the players rejected this out of hand, as the dreaded spectre of the *Maracanazo* still haunted the nation, and especially the players who had been involved in that game. Eventually, a delegation was sent to buy up a package of blue V-necked and collared T-shirts, and members of the coaching staff hand-stitched the CBD badges in place. Sweden wore their traditional colours and Brazil played their first World Cup Final in blue shirts with white shorts. As the fates would have it, the difference between that and the white kit worn for that fateful 1950 game against Uruguay was sufficient to assuage any perceived curse. Although, with just four minutes played, that didn't look to be the case.

Nils Liedholm was now reaching the veteran stage of his career and had played for AC Milan since moving there from IFK Norrköping in 1949. Almost a decade's experience in the defence-dominated world of Serie A had honed the forward's skill to a fine point and, when a pass from the right found him in space on the edge of the Brazil penalty area, the result looked inevitable. He coolly avoided two challenges before placing the ball beyond the reach of Gilmar. At the age of 35 years and 263 days, the Sweden captain became the oldest scorer in a World Cup Final. Had that goal remained the only strike, his global fame would have been assured. In this game, however, a different record-breaker would take possession of that mantle.

The lead, and Liedholm's time in the sunshine, was to be short-lived and just five minutes later Brazil were level. A low cross from Garrincha on the right inexcusably evaded several defenders. Pelé touched the ball on and, with goalkeeper Kalle Svensson fatally exposed, Vavá bundled home. As with France's first goal against Brazil in the semi-final, the equaliser brought a broad balance to the game, but with the South Americans looking the more dangerous.

Despite a shot from Pelé that struck Svensson's post before bouncing clear, and Vavá firing straight at the goalkeeper after a slipped pass from Pelé put him in with a clear chance, the deadlock looked likely to be maintained heading towards the break. Just past the half-hour mark, however, a carbon copy of their first goal restored Brazil's lead as Vavá again converted from close range following a low cross from the right. Sweden had threatened in patches but Brazil had done so much more consistently and the goal reflected the flow of the game. At half-time, though, there remained just the narrowest of margins between the teams, with all to play for, and the hosts left the field believing they were still in with a chance of being crowned world champions.

Sadly for Sweden, those aspirations were severely dented ten minutes after the restart when Pelé snatched the limelight from Liedholm. A cross from the left was floated towards the teenager and, isolated in the box, he was surrounded by three towering Swedish defenders. Leaping to gently nod the ball forward and into space, he slipped past his first opponent, then lifted it over the second as he closed to challenge. As the ball dropped, Pelé's eyes never left it before he stabbed it home with his right foot. The occasion now not only had the oldest player to score in a World Cup Final, it also had the youngest. Pelé was 17 years and 249 days old. Unlike Liedholm whose song was now sung, Pelé would deliver sweet music in World Cups across the next dozen years, culminating in the Samba Party of 1970.

At 3-1 the game was surely up and when Zagallo added a fourth, after cutting in from the left and powering through a weary challenge to drive the ball home through Svensson's legs, it eliminated any doubt. Agne Simonsson cut the deficit with ten minutes to play, but any dreams of an unlikely recovery were consigned to the whims of fantasy when Pelé headed home a fifth as time ebbed away.

Moments later, Nílton Santos raised the Jules Rimet Trophy. Brazil were champions of the world for the first time in their history and were about to embark on 12 years of unprecedented domination of the global game. After the disappointments of 1950 and 1954, Brazil had discovered a national pride in the success of its football team, as Mario Rodrigues Filho illustrates in his book *O Sapo de Arubinha: Os Anos de Ouro do Futebol Brasileiro* (The Arubinha Frog: The Golden Years of Brazilian Football), 'Brazilian football was doubted, and thus Brazil was doubted. And you swept away that doubt, elevating Brazil in the eyes of the world. Not only are we brilliant, not only are we acrobats, not only are we circus artists: we are world champions.'[4]

There was even a song written to celebrate the triumph, 'A Taça do Mundo é Nossa' (The World Cup is Ours).[5] It contained a line that not only described the essence of Brazilian football, but set in place a story that would reach its celebratory conclusion with the country's third World Cup victory in 1970. Translated into English, it explained, 'The Brazilian has shown off true football abroad; he has won the World Cup dancing the Samba with the ball at his feet.' With both Pelé and Zagallo having scored in the final, two of the key participants in Brazil's 1970 World Cup Samba Party – the team's coach and star player – had RSVPed their party invitation. The long and winding road of a 12-year journey was under way.

1962: With and without Pelé

Brazil arrived in Chile with a new coach. Feola had left the *Seleção* in 1960. There's an old showbusiness saying that you should always leave the audience wanting more. Feola had delivered the Holy Grail of the World Cup for Brazil, and gifted the precocious talents of Pelé and the other tyros who

---

4   Filho, Mario, *O Sapo de Arubinha: Os Anos de Ouro do Futebol Brasileiro* (São Paulo, Brazil: Companhia das Letras, 2015)

5   'A Taça do Mundo é Nossa' – Wagner Maugeri, Lauro Müller, Maugeri Sobrinho and Victor Dagô

played in the 1958 final to the wider footballing world. He had won 20 of his 26 games in charge, drawing three and suffering just three defeats. When the final game of his second term in post ended with a 5-1 hammering of fierce rivals Argentina, he had fully delivered on that piece of advice. Rubén Sosa had put the visitors ahead in the sixth minute but, by the break, Brazil were 3-1 up. That lead had extended to 5-1 at the final whistle, with the fans at the Maracanã roaring their approval. Although that victory followed hot on the heels of a 1-0 defeat to Uruguay, sure enough Feola would be asked back in order to reprise his success for the 1966 World Cup, but his third term would be much less successful.

The new man at the helm was Aymoré Moreira, a former goalkeeper who had played 32 times for the *Seleção*, and coached multiple Brazilian club sides after hanging up his gloves in 1946. He was also the brother of Zezé Moreira who had briefly led the national team in 1952. Aymoré Moreira took control of his first game on the last day of April 1961, just 13 months before the World Cup in Chile would begin.

As reigning world champions, Brazil were exempted from the qualification process and Moreira's team played a series of friendlies, allowing the coach to hone his squad and tactics before the serious business got under way at the end of May 1962. Given the demands of the domestic season in Brazil, however, these games were all condensed into a packed two-month period, with the first four – two in Paraguay, and two in Chile – played across a period of a dozen days, before Paraguay visited Brazil on 29 June.

The first match, away to Paraguay in Asunción's Estadio Puerto Sajonia, brought an encouraging 2-0 win. Few would have taken much note at the time, but one of the substitutes given a debut that day was Botafogo's forward, Amarildo. Three days later Brazil repeated the win, this time prevailing 3-2, despite trailing by two goals with just 15 minutes played. Once more, Amarildo joined the action from the bench. He would do the same in the second game in Santiago, but miss out entirely at home to Paraguay. Nevertheless, those cameo performances and others in pre-tournament games would convince Moreira to go out on a limb and include Amarildo in his World Cup squad. Despite the young forward only having half a dozen caps to his name at the time, that limb the coach went out on would bear such sweet fruit when Pelé was injured and put out of the World Cup during the group game against Czechoslovakia.

After leaving Asunción, Brazil moved on to Chile and two more victories were secured, at the Estadio Nacional in Santiago where, the following year, Moreira would repeat Feola's success. A 2-1 win on 7 May was followed by a single-goal triumph four days later. The Chilean excursion was particularly significant for a 21-year-old Flamengo midfielder who made his debut in the first of those two games and scored his first international goal in the second. Gérson wouldn't make Moreira's squad for the 1962 World Cup due to a serious knee injury, but he was already being lined up as the natural successor to Didi who was a decade older. He would travel to England four years later, making his sole appearance that summer in the team that lost 3-1 to Hungary, and would be a key element of the *Seleção*'s success in Mexico, where they would come face-to-face with Didi as an opponent. Finally, on 29 June, Paraguay visited the Maracanã and a much-changed Brazil laboured to a 3-2 win. Pelé had been unavailable for all five of these games and Brazil won them all despite that. No one knew it at the time, but Moreira would face a similar task in the World Cup.

Pelé was back in the line-up as Brazil opened up their 1962 campaign with retaining the World Cup as the only target. On 21 April Paraguay were once more the visitors at the Maracanã, and a 6-0 victory did nothing to dampen down expectations for success in the coming tournament. Four days later the teams met again as Brazil added four more goals, and further fire to the hopes of success in Chile. In a move that proved to be portentous for the future, after Pelé had scored the second and third goals, he was substituted for Amarildo.

Early in May, the *Seleção* faced a non-South American team for the first time in over 12 months of official matches, as Portugal, who had failed to qualify for the World Cup, offered their services to provide experience of European opposition for two games. In a tight first encounter Brazil eventually prevailed 2-1, and then they triumphed again 1-0 three days later. Rolling over Paraguay with a feast of goals was all well and good, but the hard-fought matches against Portugal were probably of greater benefit in preparation for what awaited Brazil in Chile. There was now just one more double-header to play before the squad left to cross the Andes. Wales provided the opposition in two meetings at the Maracanã across three days in May, losing 3-1 both times. Moreira had led Brazil in 11 matches since his appointment just over a year earlier, and won every one. The world champions appeared to be in fine fettle heading towards Chile.

The quality bristling in the squad of 22 players despatched by the CBD to retain the Jules Rimet Trophy benefitted greatly from the one that Feola had taken to Sweden. Many of the younger players who blossomed in 1958 were now not only tournament-hardened, but also had accumulated four years of additional experience of international football. Whereas only two players had celebrated their 30th birthdays in the 1958 squad, no fewer than eight had passed that landmark in 1962. Pelé now had 30 caps, Zagallo 21 and Pepe 25, while the experienced defensive solidity of Djalma Santos and Nílton Santos had 140 between them. The balance was ideal.

The wisdom of Brazil facing European opposition as the latter part of their preparations made perfect sense as they were placed into a group alongside Mexico and both Czechoslovakia and Spain from the other side of the Atlantic, with the opening game to be played against *El Tri* on 30 May. Given that Brazil were reigning world champions, it was perhaps surprising that this match attracted less than 10,500 fans, but it set a precedent for much of the other group fixtures across the tournament. Other than those played in the group involving Chile at the Estadio Nacional, where crowds averaged more than 50,000, even when the hosts weren't involved, attendances at all of the other three groups' games were low. Only Brazil's group, played at Viña del Mar's Estadio Sausalito in the Valparaíso region, had crowds consistently topping 10,000, and even then they still failed to hit 20,000.

Pelé and Zagallo had marked their cards for the future in the final of the 1958 tournament when both scored against Sweden. They would pick up in this game where they had left off four years earlier. After a goalless first period dominated by Brazilian attacking and resilient Mexican defence in which Pelé struck an upright direct from a free kick, the breakthrough came ten minutes after the restart. Pelé drove into the right-hand side of the Mexico penalty area, skipping past two challenges before being bundled out of possession. The loose ball ran on to another Brazilian who fed it back to the young star. Escaping one more challenge, he glanced up to see Zagallo running in from the opposite flank. A clipped cross found the Botafogo winger, who dived to head past Antonio Carbajal in the Mexico goal. Brazil had the breakthrough.

The flow of the game had suggested there was little likelihood of Mexico staging a fightback, but any such thoughts were cast to the winds anyway with 17 minutes to play when a virtuoso dribble by Pelé took him past four defenders, and ended with him slipping the ball past Carbajal to double the lead. It had been a more-than-efficient performance and, with Pelé already looking likely to be the star player of the tournament, Moreira had every reason to look forward with confidence. Ahead of the World Cup there had been concerns that a niggling groin injury could, at the very least, limit Pelé's audacious skills. For Moreira, however, not taking him to Chile would have been unthinkable and, after his performance against Mexico, such concerns were eased. Little did the coach know that his forward would only actively contribute around another 20 minutes to Brazil's defence of the world crown.

Three days later, a confident Brazil returned to the Estadio Sausalito to face Czechoslovakia for their second game. Three years earlier the eastern Europeans had given prior warning of the difficult opposition they could provide when Dukla Prague faced a Santos side including Pelé as part of a South American tour for the club from the Czechoslovakian capital. After falling two goals down in no time at all, Dukla Prague fought back to win 4-3. The game in Chile would not have as many goals, but would probably be even more disappointing for Pelé and fans of the *Seleção*.

Garrincha had already struck a post with a shot from distance when the key incident occurred with 25 minutes played. Hitting in an effort from outside the penalty area, there were gasps of hope then disappointment when Pelé's effort was partially deflected by goalkeeper Viliam Schrojf. The ball struck the post but bounced clear. Disappointment rapidly turned to concern, though, at the sight of the *Seleção*'s star man gesturing towards the Brazil bench with one hand raised in the air and the other holding the top of his left thigh, hobbling and visibly in pain. There was precious little chance of any on-pitch medical attention solving the problem and, with their most important player now shunted out to the right flank and overwhelmingly inactive, Brazil's task of breaking down their stubborn opponents became even more difficult. Inevitably, the game drifted to a goalless draw. The jaunty stride with which Brazil had begun had now turned into a dejected and concerned stumble. Moreira still had the likes of Zagallo, Vavá and Garrincha to call upon, and the latter would become a key weapon, but Pelé would take no further part in the tournament.

The following day, a last-minute goal from Atlético Madrid's Joaquín Peiró edged Spain over the line to victory against Mexico. The result meant that if Brazil could defeat Spain in their final group game, both they and the Czechs would advance to the quarter-finals, regardless of the eastern Europeans' fate in their last match against Mexico. With Spain now in contention to qualify themselves, however, even if Pelé had been in place, it would not be an easy encounter. Without him it would be even tougher. Moreira needed to choose wisely when selecting the player with the thankless task of filling the cavernous gap left by that torn thigh muscle.

Amarildo Tavares da Silveira, simply known as Amarildo, was a month shy of his 23rd birthday when Moreira decided that the player with six substitute appearances for Brazil, and still yet to find the back of the net in international football, was the man to replace Pelé. The apprentice thrust into the limelight may have been lacking experience on the international stage but, alongside team-mate Zagallo, his Botafogo side had secured back-to-back Rio State Championships in 1961 and 1962. Whether Moreira said something along the lines of 'I know it's your first start, and this is the World Cup, but go out there, replace Pelé, and don't let anyone notice the difference' is not known, but that was the size of the task in front of Amarildo. He would later recall thinking, 'Pelé was considered irreplaceable … so I was the replacement for the irreplaceable. For me the responsibility was enormous.' He later added, 'Pelé was always a star and I was called in to replace him in the game against Spain.'[6] It was the only change to Moreira's team.

Despite being beaten by that late Czechoslovakian goal in their opening game, Spain, under legendary Argentine coach Helenio Herrera, had a formidable array of talent, including Luis Suárez who Herrera had taken from his former club Barcelona to be part of his *Grande Inter* team that would dominate Italian football and win successive European Cups. Alongside him were Francisco Gento and

---

6   https://account.miamiherald.com/paywall/subscriber-only?resume=1965353&intcid=ab_archive

Luis del Sol of the all-conquering Real Madrid side, plus the co-opted talent of their *Los Blancos* team-mate Ferenc Puskás. Victory would need to be hard-won, and so it was the case.

Understandably, with their talismanic forward absent, Brazil initially seemed hesitant, with Spain dominating early and looking the more likely to score. The goal came with ten minutes of the first half to play. From well outside of the area, Adelardo's low, powerful shot arrowed past Gilmar and found the bottom corner of the net. Brazil's grip on the Jules Rimet Trophy was slipping and, had Chilean referee Sergio Bustamante been more up with play when Nílton Santos clumsily bundled Spain captain Enrique Collar to the ground inside the penalty area ten minutes after the restart, it may well have fallen totally from their grasp. Fortunately for the defender, Bustamante, unsure of the precise location of the offence, erred on the side of caution and awarded a free kick outside the area. Even then, the danger was not over. Puskás clipped the free kick into the area where a weak defensive error only succeeded in dropping the ball towards Joaquín Peiró. The Torino midfielder's acrobatic bicycle kick flew past Gilmar. Brazil's fate looked to be sealed, but Señor Bustamante would again spring to their rescue by identifying an offside that had escaped everyone else. Even a review of the incident on video reveals little to justify the official's decision. Brazil were on the ropes and in need of a hero. Pelé wasn't there, but their salvation came from the man selected in his place.

Inside the last 20 minutes of the game, with Spain still having the better of the play, the understudy took to centre stage. Driving in from the left flank, Zagallo arrowed a low cross towards his Botafogo team-mate arriving from the right. The ball exploded from Amarildo's boot and ripped into the net past a helpless José Araquistáin. Against the run of play Brazil were level, but Amarildo was not finished yet. With time running down, both teams, knowing the next goal would surely be decisive, began to sink back in fear of conceding. It opened up rare spaces. Seizing on one of them out on the right, Garrincha teased and taunted two Spanish defenders, first jinking this way, and then that, before reaching the dead-ball line and lifting a cross towards the far post for a waiting Amarildo to convert. 'My history changed that day,' he would later unnecessarily confirm.[7] Brazil progressed, Spain were eliminated and, despite losing their last game 3-1 to Mexico, Czechoslovakia slipped quietly into the quarter-finals as well. Fate still had things in store for the *Seleção* and eastern Europeans.

The last-eight games paired Brazil with England, who had scraped through their group with three points after losing to Hungary, defeating Argentina and drawing with Bulgaria. The final table showed England to have progressed at the expense of the South Americans who were gifted the unwanted distinction of being the only team ever to be eliminated from a World Cup by the weird calculations of goal average. As with Spain, England too had some star names in their line-up; a young Bobby Moore was at the centre of defence and a forward line containing Jimmy Greaves, Johnny Haynes and Bobby Charlton promised to carry plenty of threat to Brazilian aspirations.

Moreira selected the same 11 as had come through against Spain and the teams met on 10 June back at the

---

7   https://account.miamiherald.com/paywall/subscriber-only?resume=1965353&intcid=ab_archive

Estadio Sausalito. Perhaps encouraged by the progress of both teams, the crowd had now grown to more than 17,000. They would watch a game in which Brazil, possibly emboldened by the success against Spain and Amarildo's brace, would largely dominate in Walter Winterbottom's last match in charge of England.

So far, apart from providing the cross for Amarildo's second goal against Spain, Garrincha had enjoyed a fairly low-key tournament, but he would step up in this game, scoring two and having a hand – or more accurately a foot – in the third of Brazil's goals. There was a bizarre incident when, ahead of kick-off, Zagallo called his team-mates and two photographers to surround him while he knelt in the centre circle for a few seconds before they all dispersed and the game began. The mystery was later solved when Zagallo confessed that he had forgotten to urinate before leaving the dressing rooms, and had needed to relieve himself before the match started. Such actions have been linked to desperately unsuccessful attempts to lift curses in the past but, if there were any incantations at work in this incident, it certainly favoured Brazil – and Garrincha.

Pelé's absence had allowed the winger much more freedom to cut inside to develop a freer role in attack and, against England, it delivered great benefits for Moreira's team. With half an hour played, however, it was a rare header from Garrincha that put Brazil ahead as he nodded home from a corner. England rallied and were level before the break when Gerry Hitchens profited from a rebound after Greaves had looped a header against the crossbar. It was a brief respite, and by the hour Brazil were two goals clear. First Vavá headed home from a Garrincha free kick, then the winger hit a curling *folha seca* shot into the top corner of Ron Springett's net, with the goalkeeper impotent. The name relates to the course of a 'falling leaf' never following a straight line. In Pelé's absence, first Amarildo delivered. Against England it was Garrincha's turn in what was one of his finest games for the *Seleção*. Bereft of their star player, Brazil were proving that they had a team capable of retaining the World Cup, with or without Pelé.

After playing four games in the relatively quiet surroundings of the Estadio Sausalito, for their semi-final they would need to travel the 100km or so to the Chilean capital. The reason being they would now be facing Chile in the Estadio Nacional on 13 June, with a place in the 1962 World Cup Final, back at the same stadium four days later, at stake. Whereas the game against England had seen the largest crowd Brazil had played in front of so far in the tournament, that figure would almost quadruple against the hosts.

Compared to Chile's tournament experiences, Brazil's progress had been almost serene. The infamy endured as Chile played against Italy had been considered a price worth paying for the 2-0 win that, alongside a 3-1 victory over Switzerland, had been enough to get them into the knockout stage despite losing 2-0 to West Germany, and a closely contested 2-1 win over the Soviet Union had taken them in to the final four. If Brazil had the better team, there's little doubt that the passionate 76,000 fans in the stadium would do all they could to take up any slack in terms of quality on the pitch.

As is often the case when two South American teams face each other in continental or global tournaments, there's often some recent club history at play, feeding into the narrative. This was the case here with Chilean hard man Eladio Rojas having memories of Garrincha running rings around him and his fellow Colo-Colo defenders when the Brazilian winger was wearing Botafogo colours. Even without the insistent baying of the hyped-up fans in the stadium driving him on, Rojas was not minded to suffer a similar experience wearing his national colours. As soon as the game started, kicks, trips, not a few elbows and even a poke in the eye were delivered, but Garrincha took it all and still delivered a man-of-the-match performance as Peruvian referee Arturo Yamasaki, doubtless intimidated by the crowd, chose not to see the catalogue of offences committed by Rojas.

Nine minutes in, Garrincha delivered his own kind of justice, firing home left-footed to put Brazil ahead, and then doubled down on the punishment by notching the second goal with a header on the half-hour. A goal by Jorge Toro just ahead of the break offered Chile hope but, when Garrincha opened up the defence for Vavá to score Brazil's third, their hopes of a comeback were dented. A highly debatable penalty awarded by Yamasaki was converted by Leónel Sánchez, briefly rekindling hopes, but a second from Vavá poured cold water over them again.

With just six minutes left, and the game surely won, Garrincha's patience with Rojas's intimidation – which had now migrated from intended deterrence to malicious spite – was finally exhausted. Another foul sent Garrincha to the floor once more. Rising to his feet, he walked over and planted a knee into his intimidator's back. Eschewing his hard-man image, the half-hearted retaliation was apparently sufficient to send Rojas to the floor in apparent agony. Following a quick conversation with his linesman, Yamasaki decided that, despite all of the earlier provocation going the other way, a clear penalty denied to Garrincha and chalking-off a seemingly perfectly good goal by Vavá, this incident demanded justice – and Garrincha was sent off.

Trudging slowly from the pitch, howls of derision and fury rolled down from the Chileans in the stadium. Moreira rushed over to accompany his player just as a stone hurled from the crowd struck Garrincha on the head and he fell to the ground. The game ended in a few minutes of heated over-physicality before Yamasaki blew for full time without any further goals. Brazil were through to the final to play old foes Czechoslovakia, but what of Garrincha? At the time, a ban was not mandatory, and his fate would be decided by the seven members of the FIFA Disciplinary Committee, based on the referee's report. Brazil lobbied hard in favour of their man, citing the provocation he endured, and even the country's government got involved, pressuring the Peru administration to lean on Yamasaki to soften his report.

Despite politics and football not being easy bedfellows, they are often far more entwined than anyone would care to concede, and perhaps the inter-governmental approaches bore some fruit. Other issues were also at play though. Cold War tensions were being ramped up, with the world just a few months away from the Cuban Missile Crisis and, in the west, the prospect of an Eastern Bloc country winning the World Cup was hardly to be welcomed. Brazil would be without Pelé regardless but if FIFA took Garrincha away from them too, it would only aid Czechoslovakia and, therefore, ran the logic, Communist hopes of triumph. Also, Brazil had bailed FIFA out by hosting the 1950 tournament when candidates were difficult to find after the war. It was time to call in a few markers.

When the committee convened, the referee's report stated that he had not seen Garrincha's offence, but had been alerted to it by his linesman, who was not present but left a note for his colleague in which he described the offence as 'a typical response' with clear reference to earlier intimidation. The reports gave Garrincha's lawyer sufficient ammunition to manoeuvre the committee into a place where they could deliver the verdict they had wanted to anyway. Garrincha was absolved by five votes to two and cleared to play in the final. Given his brutal treatment by Rojas before the relatively tepid act of retribution, it was surely an equitable decision. The way it was reached, however, was less so. That mattered little to Moreira, Garrincha, the *Seleção* and all of Brazil. Their chances of retaining the World Cup had received an enormous boost.

After edging into the knockout stage of the tournament on the coat tails of Brazil, Czechoslovakia had faced two other eastern European teams, defeating Yugoslavia 1-0 in the quarter-finals and then reaching the final by disposing of Hungary 3-1 to set up a rematch against Moreira's team in the final. At 2.30pm on 17 June, the city of Santiago was basking in balmy summer conditions, with the hot sun persuasively counselling against any ideas of strenuous activity. Except for, that is, on the pitch of Estadio Nacional, where Brazil, as overwhelming favourites even without Pelé, would seek to retain their title as world champions. By 2.45pm, however, that aspiration looked in peril.

As was the case four years earlier, Brazil conceded the first goal. Gaining possession in the Brazil half of the field, Sokol OKD Ostrava outside-right Tomáš Pospíchal drove forward and across the field, eluding challenges, before jinking right towards the opposition penalty area, some 25 yards from goal. Glancing up as he did so, the sight of a team-mate making a forward run arrowed into his vision. Stabbing the ball into the gap that would soon be filled by Josef Masopust, he watched as the white-shirted midfielder collected the pass ahead of Gilmar and defender Zózimo before driving his shot under the goalkeeper and into the corner of the net.

Czechoslovakia were ahead and with a defence that had only conceded four goals in the five games played in the tournament so far – with three of them coming in the dead group rubber against Mexico after qualification had already been assured by Brazil's victory over Spain – there was understandable confidence that the pendulum of fate had now swung in their direction. Sadly for the eastern Europeans, their dreams of glory would last for a mere 100 seconds before a speculative shot from a tight angle by Amarildo, on the left, somehow eluded the previously reliable goalkeeping of Viliam Schrojf and Brazil were back on level terms. The Czechoslovakians' moment of glory had been deliciously savoured but was all too ephemeral. Further goals from Zito and Vavá would follow after the break as, despite the enforced absence of their star player, Brazil dominated the remainder of the game. As Soviet Union referee Nikolay Latyshev brought the final to an end, the task of retaining the Jules Rimet Trophy, which had assumed a whole new level of difficulty after the loss of Pelé, had been accomplished with some measure of ease. For only the second time in history, following Italy's successes in 1934 and 1938, the world champions had successfully defended their title.

The *Seleção* were now indisputably the best team in the world. They had won the World Cup in 1958 with the ebullient teenage talent of Pelé to the fore and four years later they had proved that they could do so without the brightest star in the Brazilian firmament, as others – Garrincha, Amarildo, Zagallo among them – stepped up to prove their worth. The 1966 tournament would be played in England but, having already proved that a South American team could triumph in Europe following the 1958 success, that situation held little concerns for a Brazil side that had comfortably beaten the next tournament's hosts on their way to retaining the trophy, as well as defeating Spain and Czechoslovakia. Confidence can be both a seductive and treacherous mistress though, often only being hubris in disguise, and while Brazil basked in their glory as kings of international football other teams were focusing on how to dethrone them.

* * *

Paradise Postponed
1966: The School of Hard Knocks

The Brazil of 1962 and 1966 were very different – not only the football team, but also the country itself. In 1961, following the resignation of President Jânio Quadros, vice-president João Goulart, a member of the left-of-centre Labour Party, was elected to take his place. After some political power-wrangling and constitutional mangling, by 1963 it was clear that Goulart sought to introduce measures aimed at increasing social equality, including land reform, nationalisation of some of the country's larger enterprises and a reduction in the established power of the land-owning aristocracy. Perhaps most dangerously of all was his espoused desire to adopt a more neutral stance in relations with the USA. Already considered to be something of akin to a communist by the church, right-wing parties of Brazil and the armed forces, these moves caused alarm to the established order as well as deep concern in Washington, where the government was obsessed by the threat of encroaching Communism and defending its self-perceived geographical spheres of interest.

On 1 April 1964, with the acknowledged support and encouragement of the USA government, the Brazilian armed forces struck and launched a *coup d'état*, enjoying almost complete support across the military as well as from the church and landed classes fearful of the threat to their property and privileges from the supposed Communist regime. It swept Goulart from power and installed a military dictatorship headed by General Castelo Branco. Aware that the coup not only had the overwhelming support of the military, but also the USA, any attempts by Goulart to resist would only have led to a pointless, bloody and ultimately futile civil war, and he fled to Uruguay. The military assumed power.

Brazil was no stranger to such events. Three decades earlier the military had stepped in to support Getulio Vargas's attempts to take control of the government and, by 1937, that support had helped to establish him as Brazil's dictator, before also removing him from power in 1947. As is so often the case, the initial claim of the dictatorship was a determination to first restore order, secure national defence, and then deliver a swift return to constitutional government. It ensured that the coup enjoyed considerable initial support. The regime was also quick to recognise the importance of success in sport, particularly football, as an aid to its aims, and intervened to exploit the opportunities it presented.

As well as promoting sporting successes for internal political propaganda contributing to an improved optimism and confidence among the Brazilian people, there were also external benefits. Sporting triumphs were seen as a measure of the country's progress and development as a major player in both hemispheric and global matters. Two successive World Cup triumphs were an ideal starting point and, should a third be achieved two years after the establishment of the dictatorship, the positives for the regime were clear. Convinced of its own ability to make this outcome more likely, government involvement in the CBD and, consequently, the *Seleção* was inevitable.

One of their first moves was unlikely to endear the players to the new regime. At the time, payment of income tax in Brazil had been largely theoretical, rather than enforced, but the military would change all that. Many of Brazil's World Cup heroes were pursued for payment of back taxes, with Garrincha, for example, reckoned to owe an estimated 44m cruzeiros in back payments. Players such as Didi and Zagallo ended up emptying their bank accounts to clear their names, but for the hard-living Garrincha, that was hardly an option. Eventually he was bailed out by the then president of the CBD, João Havelange. It was a less than totally philanthropic gesture. Havelange was a political animal and saw great importance in Brazil winning a third successive World Cup as part of his drive to become head of FIFA. He therefore considered that clearing Garrincha's debt, and enabling him to travel to England for the World Cup, was an investment. Politics and football in Brazil were inextricably linked.

The national motto of Brazil, 'Ordem e Progresso' (Order and Progress), is carried on its flag and, at least publicly, espousing these ideals was sufficient for the dictatorship as it assumed power. Whether there was ever any real intent to return the country to constitutional government is a moot point. If there was, the resolve was short-lived. By 1967 the dictatorship's possession of power was formalised by a new, far more restrictive constitution, with political opposition limited and freedom of speech largely curtailed. The *Seleção*'s efforts to deliver a hat-trick of World Cup triumphs in 1966 were influenced by a backdrop of increasing political pressure and oppression.

With the successful retention of their title in Chile, Brazil were, once more, excused the requirement to qualify, and played their first game of 1963 on 3 March in a friendly away to Paraguay. It took place a week ahead of the start of the South America Championships to be held in Bolivia. Of the 15 players Moreira used, only one, Guarani's Ílton Vaccari, had previously appeared for Brazil. The game ended in a 2-2 draw. For the championships the coach kept faith with much of the team that had played against Paraguay. Brazil finished fourth as Moreira's young side won their first two games, but then drew one and lost three of the remaining four.

Moving into April, it was a far more familiar team that faced Argentina in a Roca Cup encounter at the Estádio do Morumbi in São Paulo. Despite this return to the colours for many of the team that had triumphed in Chile, the game ended in a disappointing 3-2 loss. Three days later, revenge was swift as Brazil triumphed 5-2 at the Maracanã in what would be their last home match of the year. Just five days after leaving the field following victory over their neighbours, Brazil were lining up to face Portugal in Lisbon's Estádio Nacional, in the first leg of what would be a whistlestop tour around Europe which also took in fixtures in Israel and Egypt. Altogether, including some unofficial games against club teams, the tour comprised a crushingly intense schedule, with incessant travelling and PR obligations in between.

Some reports suggest that, ostensibly, the tour was promoted as allowing the coach to build a new team and the players to better understand European conditions ahead of the upcoming defence of their title in England. In reality it was more akin to an exercise in proving that money-driven tours, touting the *Canarinho* shirt, are nothing new. As double world champions there was a burnished golden tinge to the now-famous yellow shirt and, in Pelé, the *Seleção* had the world's most celebrated footballer. European football was enamoured by all things Brazilian, and the continent's various associations were prepared to pay handsomely for the stars to visit.

Facing Portugal so soon after the Argentina encounter was hardly ideal preparation, and a 1-0 defeat was probably not unexpected. Worse was to follow, however. Three days later the circus was in Brussels facing Belgium in the Heysel Stadium. In his book on the 1970 World Cup, Sam Kunti detailed that the Belgian FA laid out 'about 1.25m Belgian francs in match fees and guest appearances' to get the *Seleção* to play their national team.[8] At the time, Belgium were hardly one of Europe's footballing powerhouses, despite being the first team to defeat West Germany after they had won the 1954 World Cup. In normal circumstances a win for the world champions would have been widely anticipated. These were hardly normal circumstances.

---

8 Kunti, Sam, *Brazil 1970: How the Greatest Team of All Time Won the World Cup* (Worthing, England: Pitch Publishing Ltd, 2022)

Although the prospect of watching their team take on the double world champions was a magnetic draw for fans, it may well have been outweighed by the opportunity to see Pelé in action. It would, therefore, have been a huge disappointment when, less than half an hour before kick-off, an announcement was made that, due to an injury sustained in the Portugal game, the great man would be absent from the team selected by Moreira. The delayed release of the information was clearly timed to ensure any likely deserters from the paying fans in attendance were already in the stadium, and any opportunity to withhold their financial support was negated. Twenty-one minutes after the game started, that mood would have massively lifted as Belgium led 4-0. It eventually finished 5-1 and the *Seleção* suffered their worst defeat since 1940.

It was the lowest point of the tour, as far as results were concerned, but other defeats would follow. On 26 April, despite fielding a largely inexperienced second-string team, a 2-0 reverse to Racing Paris was hardly likely to raise spirits. In mitigation, the game only lasted for 60 minutes with 30 minutes played for each half, and was largely considered to be a training occasion. Two days later, the same couldn't be said for the 3-2 win over France as Pelé marked his return to the team with a hat-trick. The next stop was in the Netherlands, and another 1-0 loss on the second day of May, before another second-string encounter, and a 1-0 win over PSV Eindhoven.

Two days after the last match Brazil faced West Germany in Hamburg's Volksparkstadion. A 2-1 win was followed, three days later, by a draw with England at Wembley. By this stage the continual process of travel, training, PR and playing must have been taking its toll on the Brazilian party and a 3-0 defeat to Italy in Milan on 12 May at least had the benefit of drawing the European leg of the tour to a close before the *Seleção* crossed the Mediterranean.

Victories in Egypt and Israel, 1-0 and 5-0 respectively, were decent enough, but a record of just two wins, a single draw and four losses in the official games in Europe suggested that retaining the World Cup against such opposition may be more of a challenge than had been expected. Although playing a total of 11 matches, including those unofficial ones, in just one day over a month, with all the inherent travelling involved, may not have been the best way to replicate a more settled World Cup experience. The final fixture of the tour took place in Berlin on 22 May as Brazil faced a Berlin Select XI. It ended 3-0 in favour of the world champions and, although he would return briefly in the future, it marked the end of Moreira's role as coach of the *Seleção*.

The tour had offered little of real benefit for the players' development and, as it dragged to a weary conclusion, it left them increasingly bedraggled, wrung dry by its mangling effects on fitness and form, plus formations and teams being constantly changed. Several of them considered the performances and outcome of games as seriously as the CBD had. For them, this was no World Cup and, if the CBD were treating it merely as an exhibition tour, why shouldn't they? The fortunes of CBD's bank account may well have offered comfort to the organisation to the tune of around a quarter of a million US dollars in profit from the enterprise. It was gold in the bank but, on the field, that bright sheen on the *Canarinho* shirt had lost a little of its golden glistening.

Among the lessons from the tour, one was largely overlooked. Portugal, Belgium, the Netherlands and Italy had all overcome any inferiority complexes they may have harboured before playing the world champions. Whatever extenuating circumstances of fatigue or form, both Belgium and the Italians had delivered comprehensive beatings to the *Seleção*. At least in Europe, where the next World Cup would be held, the Brazilian myth of invincibility had been diminished.

When questioned about potentially detrimental effects of the 1963 European tour, and whether it helped the European teams more than Brazil and exposed them as vulnerable, author and journalist Sam Kunti was in little doubt, 'It did. That tour and Brazil's defeats signposted the demise of Brazil's golden generation of Garrincha and Didi and the rise of northern European football. Amarildo called that tour a stroll where the Brazilian players were mainly interested in buying transistor radios – and that will have been true to an extent as these were friendlies – but amid all the tourism, the Brazilians failed to notice that the game was moving on – Belgium, Italy and Netherlands all bit Brazil in different ways, but they were all physically more fit and more athletic. From an organisational point, that tour was modelled after Santos's famous excursions around Europe, cramming in as many matches as possible. It was an endless journey from airports to hotels, stadiums and back. It didn't benefit Brazil's performance at all but just the coffers of the CBD. This tour also foreshadowed the disorder and confusion that so dominated the preparations for the 1966 World Cup, which the hosts England won, confirmation that (northern) European football was indeed on the rise.' The worldwide hawking of the *Canarinho* shirt in pursuit of financial advancement, rather than progressing the team, is hardly a new phenomenon.

In 1964, Brazil would play just three games, with Vicente Feola returning to take charge. On 30 May England visited the Maracanã and were crushed 5-1, despite going in level at the break. A few days later it was Brazil licking their wounds as Argentina won 3-0 in the same stadium. Finally, revenge of sorts was exacted on Portugal with a 4-1 victory. The game was notable for the scoring debut of a teenage Botafogo winger named Jairzinho, who would be an integral part of the 1970 World Cup team.

If the previous year had delivered a mixed bag of results, 1965 suggested that Brazil were now on course for a determined defence of their title. In nine games they won six and drew the other three. At the turn of the year, there was a little over six months before the 1966 World Cup got under way. In April, under temporary coach Carlos Froner, a young Brazil team played two games against Chile. They won the first 1-0 in Santiago, but lost the second 2-1 in Viña del Mar. With Feola then returning to take charge, they played a series of seven home friendlies. If that reads like an organised preparation for the World Cup, it is far from being the reality. Andrew Downie is an expert of Brazilian football and the author of two books on the subject, *The Greatest Show on Earth: The Inside Story of the Legendary 1970 World Cup* and *Doctor Socrates: Footballer, Philosopher, Legend*, and has little doubt how significant the disorganised approach ahead of the World Cup was complicit in the *Seleção*'s loss of their title in England, 'When Brazilians talk about the 1966 defeat, they are also very aware of the poor preparations. They often mention the 44/45/46 players who were called up, meaning that they did not have a settled team going into the tournament. That led to confusion.'

As Downie suggests, preparation for the tournament had been far from ideal, and squad selection damagingly erratic at best, catastrophically indecisive at worst. At the end of March no fewer than 46 players were named, including Amarildo who, now playing for AC Milan in Serie A, became the first player selected for a Brazil squad while playing club football outside of the country. The hero of 1962 would eventually miss out due to injury. Training camps had been set up in different locations across the vast area of Brazil, requiring extensive and exhausting travelling between the centres, as the CBD sought political favour and financial advantage from local politicians keen to have the *Seleção* visit their districts. It was almost like the CBD were taking the team on a lap of honour around the country before they had even travelled to England.

Vicente Feola, the triumphant coach from the 1958 World Cup, had returned to take charge of the team, albeit with the added complication of having to deal with a Technical Commission that was often at odds with the man supposedly in charge. The prominent, often strident, voice of the commission was Carlos Nascimento, who had been appointed by the government as head of the delegation travelling to England. Alongside Havelange, Nascimento would be an increasingly influential figure in both team selection and tactics. From the outside, restoring Feola seemed the perfect appointment, but eight years on he was a different and much less authoritative figure, a worsening heart condition hardly helping matters, especially when in conflict with Nascimento – which was often. Pelé recalled that Nascimento 'would even come to the senior players to ask us to mediate'. It hardly made for a harmonious group, as Pelé confirmed, [it] 'put us in a very awkward position'.[9]

Too many cooks potentially spoiling the broth was also a factor with the initial squad selection. The over-large group of players would have facilitated four full teams, with substitutes to spare, and in the following months they played countless games between themselves, and against club or representative teams. Legend has it that, such were the options available and the combinations to be tried, the same starting 11 never played twice. Unsurprisingly, a settled team and formation was elusive.

Even when the plane left Brazil on 27 June for the final practice games against Scotland and Sweden before heading to England, there were 27 players on board, with five of them to be cut from the final selection. Those days before the World Cup squad was confirmed were filled not by team harmony but by suspicion, intrigue and the urgent need for self-preservation to avoid the cruellest of last-minute chops. Throw in the change of climate, food and an over-confidence that defence of the trophy was going to be a stroll in the park, and the champions were hardly in an ideal situation when they arrived in England. Even when the tournament got under way, those selection issues were not left behind.

The final squad selection suggested that Feola, aided and abetted – or hindered – by the Technical Commission, depending on your view, had more of an eye to the past than the future. There was a hint that some of those players included provided a warm comfort blanket of the tried

---

9   do Nascimento, Edson Arantes, *Pelé – The Autobiography* (London: Simon & Schuster UK Ltd, 2006)

and trusted, capable of writing one more glorious chapter in the history of Brazilian football. But, for others, that simply wasn't the case. For example, Garrincha, now 32 years old, was a pale shadow of the dancing demon of the touchline that teased and taunted defenders with his tricks and explosive pace. Age, chronic knee injuries, and self-inflicted abuses of his body and fitness meant he was very much yesterday's man. As Sam Kunti described, 'Garrincha was the sad symbol of a generation in steady decline, one that shouldn't have been considered for reselection. Feola's insistence on dragging the veterans and their star power along hastened Brazil's own doom.'[10]

Brazil's squad was the oldest of any competing nation. They also had the tournament's most senior player in 37-year-old Djalma Santos. He remained the oldest player in Brazilian World Cup history until 39-year-old Dani Alves travelled to Qatar in 2022. The squad contained an abundance of experience, to be sure, but for the likes of skipper Bellini, goalkeeper Gilmar, and Garrincha, as well as Djalma Santos, 1966 would be a step too far for their ageing limbs and minds. This wasn't 1958, or even 1962. The football world had moved on and the old masters had been left trailing in its wake. A group made up of Bulgaria, Hungary and Portugal would have been comfortable fare for this group of Brazilian players at their peak. For many of those selected, however, their peak had passed some time previously.

On the surface, the 2-0 victory over Bulgaria, despite the fearful battering of Pelé in Brazil's opening game of

---

10 Kunti, Sam, *Brazil 1970: How the Greatest Team of All Time Won the World Cup* (Worthing, England: Pitch Publishing Ltd, 2022)

the 1966 World Cup on 12 July, suggested that perhaps the confidence espoused by the champions was more than mere hubris. The eastern Europeans were coached by Rudolf Vytlačil, who had led Czechoslovakia to the World Cup Final four years earlier, before seeing his side succumb to Brazil despite taking an early lead. That experience had emphasised the importance of subduing the attacking flair of the *Seleção*, and led to the robust approach he deployed. Brazil would win out with goals from Pelé and Garrincha, the last time they appeared in the same international side, but it was hardly an inspiring performance, and for the remaining group games there was a clear template marked out as to how to combat Brazil.

Victory, however, offered comfortable reassurance, and it was easy to mark down the stuttering performance as merely an inevitable consequence of kicking off the rust of non-competitive matches in a tournament's opening game. Three days later the loss to Hungary, with Pelé absent thanks to the less-than-tender care offered by Zhechev, placed the possibility of an unthinkable failure, and elimination from a tournament they believed was theirs for the taking, front and centre. If ferocity had been the sword used against them in the Bulgaria game, facing Hungary offered a far more cerebral challenge.

Somewhat distant from the Magical Magyar era of the mid-1950s, this latest flaring of the cherry red-shirted Hungarians still had purpose, polish and pace aplenty. Ferenc Bene and Gyula Rákosi ran riot on the flanks and the subtle play of Flórián Albert, delivering an acceptable homage to the great Nándor Hidegkuti, pulled the *Seleção* defence this way and that, directing the Hungarian orchestra with flair. They were the harsh reality of what

Brazil thought they themselves would be. That reality bit hard and bit deep.

The 3-1 defeat could have been worse, but it was bad enough to shake the belief and confidence of the world champions. With the final game to play against a Portuguese side who had already secured qualification by winning their previous two games, a steady hand on the tiller was required of Feola. Instead the coach veered off course, reverting back to the frantic and often chaotic team changes of the preparations back in Brazil. Even before the game there were signs of disquiet in the Brazilian camp. Representations were made to FIFA from both Havelange and Nascimento regarding refereeing standards, particularly in the way Bulgaria had been allowed to deliver numerous and malicious fouls with impunity. They demanded that an improvement was delivered, but received little redress. Rumours also spread about how much say Feola was now having in team selection and tactics. The threat of elimination at the group stage, a humiliating prospect for the double world champions, only increased the power of the Technical Commission, primarily Nascimento, and gnawed away at the coach's credibility and authority. Some suggest that the team against Portugal was far from being Feola's choice, with decisions compromised by the demands of Nascimento. The old saying that a horse designed by a committee resembles a camel may well be apposite here. The outcome certainly gave all Brazilian football fans the hump.

A half-fit Pelé was brought back into the fold – leaving him out was unthinkable – as one of no fewer than nine changes to the team that had lost to the Hungarians, including the goalkeeper and entire defensive unit. Only teenage winger Jairzinho and midfielder Lima retained their places. Even then, Jairzinho was changed from the right flank to the opposite side of the field. Only Lima's position was unchanged. Even 19-year-old Tostão, who had scored against Hungary, was sacrificed on the bonfire of panic.

Only three players – new captain Orlando Peçanha, Rildo and Pelé – had appeared in more than 20 official games for Brazil. Other than for dead rubbers, it's questionable whether any coach in a World Cup before or since has been seen to gamble so wildly and make so many unforced changes – and certainly not while being in charge of two-time world champions. Vicente Feola led Brazil in 74 games, losing only six times. Two of them occurred in the 1966 World Cup. The final one was the 3-1 defeat to Portugal, when the minimum requirement for the *Seleção* to progress was a three-goal winning margin.

Following the lead from Bulgaria, whether at coach Otto Glória's instigation or inspired by their own design, the Portuguese players dealt with the returning Brazilian talisman with brutal intensity, led by Morais. Just past the half-hour mark another attack on Pelé proved to be the breaking point. The player earmarked by many to be the star of the tournament was reduced to a shuffling, limping figure, later to be so disgusted by the treatment he had received with little protection from the officials that he vowed never to play in another World Cup. Pelé was a forlorn figure, and Brazil were a beaten team, in more ways than one. And yet with the likes of Eusébio, who would end as the tournament's top goalscorer, José Torres and Mário Coluna in their side, there was every reason to think that Portugal could have achieved the sort of triumph achieved by Hungary, rather than follow the Bulgarian template. It was Feola's final game in charge of the *Seleção*.

With hindsight, the defeat and loss of their title looks inevitable and the logic of the panicked team changes – whether driven by Feola, Nascimento, or given life as the bastard son of both men – was unfathomable. Yes, the brutality of the treatment meted out to Pelé and others in the famous *Canarinho* shirt hardly helped their cause but, as Pelé alluded to, that hardly tells the full story. Preparation before, and divided leadership during, the tournament also contributed, as Andrew Downie would attest to, 'They changed goalkeepers, there were nine changes between the second and third games. The sense is that while violence was a factor, they were complacent and unprepared, especially when compared to '58 and '62.' The European tour of 1963 had exposed the CBD as utilising the *Seleção* as a tool for financial gain, regardless of the fate of the team itself and its results, with nothing tangible learned from the defeats, especially the humiliation of losing 5-1 in Belgium. In 1966, the fallout of such an approach was hammered home as a party woefully underprepared, and yet conversely over-confident, was brought low by teams no longer in awe of Brazil.

It would have been easy, and far less disruptive, for the chastened Brazilian football authorities to adhere to the widely expounded narrative of the time – that the team had been brutalised, kicked out of the World Cup by some kind of European conspiracy determined to tear the crown of world champions from their heads by whatever means necessary. To be fair, even to this day, that version of football history still holds sway with many followers of the game.

As with almost all reductionistic or deterministic analyses though, its beguiling simplicity is merely the seduction that persuades, rather than informs. Sam Kunti has little truck with such assessments. 'They were not kicked out,' he said when canvassed for his thoughts on the matter. Very much in line with the above analysis, he continued, 'Rildo, Antonio Lima and some of the members of that team that I interviewed [for his book] never emphasised that the tournament had been brutal. Yes, Portugal were nasty, but Brazilian players were used to playing against opponents who'd play hard. Remember that protection of players was also limited back then. Ultimately, multiple factors contributed to Brazil's early elimination: the preparation for the tournament was disastrous, with endless friendlies against insignificant teams in insignificant towns to please local Brazilian politicians. So Feola never settled on a single team. Brazil effectively had four teams during the preparation.

'At a personal level, it was purgatory for the players as they were never sure whether they were in or out of the first team. If you were playing alongside Pelé, then you were safe. But in all those towns, the team were celebrated by locals and fans as if they had already won a third world title. It almost seemed a formality – Brazil simply had to show up in England and the Jules Rimet Trophy would be theirs. It was hubris. And then of course there was the team selection of Feola who, once Brazil did depart for England, selected veterans who had their best years well behind him. Garrincha was the prime example. He never really recovered from his knee injury. He was limping on one leg and in training. Full-back Paulo Henrique sometimes took pity on him and played along as if this was still the great Garrincha. The man with bent legs became a sad symbol of the generation that should no longer have been around in 1966. So, Brazil's downfall in 1966 was predictable given the circumstances, a toxic mix of bad preparation, cronyism, hubris and the belief that world champions would always remain world champions.'

The Varig plane that landed at Rio de Janeiro's Galeão airport in late July 1966 returned a chastened *Seleção* to Brazil leaving the Jules Rimet Trophy, that they had come to consider as their own property, still in London. A few days later it would be lifted by England captain Bobby Moore as Alf Ramsey's 'Wingless Wonders' claimed the title of world champions. The 1970 World Cup in Mexico, and a chance of redemption, seemed a million miles away, but the lessons of the disaster of 1966 would be learned and would feed into a dazzling future, as yet hidden from the passengers on that plane.

On the last day of August 1969, General Costa e Silva, the erstwhile head of Brazil's military junta, suffered a stroke and was replaced as president by General Emílio Garrastazu Médici. His accession began what came to be known in the country as the 'Years of Lead'. The new man was an avowed hardliner and visited upon the people of Brazil the greatest human rights abuses of the time. Political opponents were either 'disappeared', persecuted or arrested and submitted to torture in order to extract unconvincing confessions of treason. Any semblance of a free press was extinguished, and censorship vigorously enforced. Dissent led to closure, and was accompanied by the inevitable arrests and detention.

But less than 12 months after the jackboot of Médici's rule stamped down, as the country cowered under the yoke of the oppressive regime at home, on the football field things could hardly have been more different. In Mexico joyous freedom of expression would lead to *O Jogo Bonito* and the Samba would be danced in celebration.

Part 2 – Long Way to Mexico[11]

---

11 'Long Way to Mexico', Roger Creager (Dualtone, 2003)

Recovery, Qualification and Preparation

With a disenchanted Pelé declaring himself retired from international football following the loss of their title, Brazil were compelled to confront the task of qualifying for the 1970 World Cup without the player widely regarded to be the best in the world. Fortunately, the qualifying tournament wouldn't begin until the summer of 1969 and, by that time, more reflective counsel had prevailed. The first task facing the CBD was to select the man to take over from Vicente Feola. Undeterred by the failure of reappointing a previous World Cup-winning coach, the CBD initially doubled down on the logic and returned 1962 hero Aymoré Moreira.

The first official *Seleção* games of the post-world champions era came across three days when Brazil visited Uruguay. First, however, there were two matches played in Porto Alegre. The first was against a combined Grêmio-Internacional team on 21 June. Two days later, Moreira's men faced a Grêmio side. The first game resulted in a 2-1 loss, the second a 1-1 draw. Taking a young and largely inexperienced team to Montevideo for the Copa Rio Branco, Moreira would have been broadly satisfied with two draws in the Estádio Centenario, and returning to Brazil unbeaten.

In goal, for the first of the two games, was Portuguesa's Félix, playing his second game for the *Seleção*, not only taking the number one jersey as Gilmar's heir apparent but also making his mark for the future.

A third game had been scheduled in the Uruguayan capital but, for this encounter, it was former double World Cup-winning winger Mário Zagallo taking charge of the team. Just half a dozen weeks short of his 35th birthday, Zagallo had missed out on selection for the 1966 World Cup and retired from playing after 14 years split evenly between his only two clubs, Flamengo and Botafogo, before taking over as coach at the latter. He would stay in that post until 1970, on occasions sharing his time coaching *A Estrela Solitaria* with games in charge of the *Seleção*.

The third game, in Montevideo on the first day of July, was such an occasion and the first step on what would become a glittering career on the international stage. As with Moreira, he would select a young team and also earn a draw. Two months later, in Brazil's last match of the year, he would go one better. Visiting Chile, Zagallo's team won 1-0 to give the young coach his first win in the stadium where he had been part of the triumphant Brazil team in the 1962 World Cup Final. If 1967 had been fairly truncated for the *Seleção*, comprising just four games, the following year would more than compensate for that small number as Brazil played no fewer than 20 official internationals.

The first games were against Uruguay. On 9 June a 2-0 victory at São Paulo's Estádio do Pacaembu set things off on a positive note, which was then reinforced by a convincing 4-0 rout back in Rio's Estádio do Maracanã three days later. In a foretaste of what was to follow a couple of years down the road, Tostão scored in both games, with both Gérson and Jairzinho finding the back of the net in the second. With Pelé absent, Tostão was charged with pulling the strings for the *Seleção* attack as he did for club side Cruzeiro. In Mexico, with Pelé back in the *Canarinho* fold two years later, Tostão would demonstrate his versatility by playing a more forward role. But that was yet to come.

Four days after the triumph in the Maracanã, Brazil were in West Germany to face the 1966 World Cup runners-up in Stuttgart's Neckarstadion. German coach Helmut Schön still had the nucleus of the team that had taken the Wembley final to extra time and added some emerging talent, such as Bertie Vogts. Facing a largely inexperienced Brazil, the Germans would run out 2-1 winners with Tostão hitting the only goal for Moreira's team. It was the first game of a hectic two-week European tour that also included matches in Poland, Czechoslovakia and Yugoslavia, before finishing with an encounter against Portugal staged in Mozambique. Two of Brazil's goals in the 6-3 win in Warsaw were scored by Rivellino, his first two international goals in his fourth outing. Alongside the other young rising stars of Gérson, Jairzinho and Tostão, the Corinthians forward would become an increasingly important part of the Brazil team on the way to Mexico. In this game, however, he would be forced to leave the field with an injury two minutes before full time.

Wrapping up the European leg of the tour, before travelling to Africa to face Portugal, Tostão and Carlos Alberto scored in a 2-0 win over Yugoslavia. The man who was destined to lift the World Cup in Mexico had been a controversial absentee from the Brazil squad in England, when Feola had opted instead to retain the services of the veteran Djalma Santos. It had epitomised the backward rather than forward-looking approach of Feola, as the younger man, who had played consistently and outstandingly ahead of the tournament, and featured strongly in the elongated preparation games, was jettisoned. Moreira had quickly reinstated him, and Carlos Alberto captained the team throughout the European tour, and would do so in Mozambique too as another 2-0 win ended the *Seleção's* travels on a high. Goals from Rivellino and Tostão sent the team back to South America with plenty of momentum behind them and a handful of young stars making a play for a berth in Mexico.

Leaving Europe and Africa behind hardly signalled an end to the travelling for Moreira and his team, as they visited Mexico, Peru and Paraguay, playing pairs of games in each country. After winning the first match in Mexico City's Estádio Azteca on 7 July, Brazil were beaten 2-1 three days later. A shade under two years from that date they would triumph in a much more significant encounter in the same stadium.

The team then moved on to Peru, winning both games in Lima – the first a closely contested 4-3 success, the second a more comfortable 4-0. A victory by the same score against Paraguay in Asunción a few days later was followed by a 1-0 defeat in the same city as Gilmar returned to play in his 92nd international just a few weeks short of his 38th birthday. Ahead of Gilmar's return to goalkeeping duties in that second Asunción fixture, another player had made his comeback in the 4-0 victory. Gilmar would play just two more games for Brazil but the other returnee would be much more significant for their aspirations of World Cup glory in Mexico.

Pelé's sad exit from the 1966 tournament had led to him retiring from international football. Two years later, however, he felt in a position to reverse that decision. His break from the rigours of the international game had fed into spectacular form at Santos where he was their leading scorer and enjoying a rejuvenated love for football. He had also developed an increasing belief that the CBD had learned from the debacle of haphazard preparation for 1966, and that the tournament in Mexico held out the promise of something special. On top of that, there was a feeling that the World Cup was unfinished business for him. After the despair of 1966, the prospect of leaving finals as a loser was unpalatable. Despite now having registered more than 1,000 goals across his career, he felt that there was still something to prove. Winning the World Cup for a third time, and ensuring that the Jules Rimet Trophy would belong to Brazil in perpetuity, could provide the perfect finale to his illustrious career with the *Seleção*. Making himself available for selection again was an enormous boost for the team and its hopes of World Cup glory two years later. The four-goal triumph in Asunción was a celebration of the return of the Prodigal Son.

For the Paraguayan leg, the team had been taken over by Antoninho, and it was the former forward, who had made his name winning both the Coppa Italia and UEFA Cup Winners' Cup with Fiorentina in the 1960/61 season, who would, in the first of his only two games in charge of the team, welcome Pelé back. When Brazil returned home to face Argentina on 7 August, it was Zagallo back in charge of the team. A 4-1 win allowed the home fans to bask in the relief of having Pelé back in a *Canarinho* shirt, although he was absent for this game, with the coach offering chances to a few younger options. One of those benefitting was

Waltencir, who opened the scoring on his debut. Sadly for the Botafogo player, it would be his only international appearance.

Three days later in the second game, staged at Belo Horizonte's Mineirão, the combined coaching talents of Biju, Carlyle Guimarães and Jota Júnior briefly led another experimental side to win 3-2. Moreira returned to take charge for the home game against Mexico on the last day of October. It began a run of five matches that would round out the year's fixtures, six days ahead of Christmas Day. A 2-1 defeat to the Mexicans at the Maracanã, despite Pelé's return to the starting line-up, was followed three days later with a victory by the same score in the Mineirão. In both games, Moreira had fielded his strongest sides and the performances were disappointing, despite victory in the second match.

The following week, back in Rio, a 2-1 win over a FIFA Select XI was very much more of the same. It was another victory but came against a scratch team which, although admittedly containing world-renowned players such as Lev Yashin, Franz Beckenbauer and Hungary's 1966 World Cup star Flórián Albert, had little time to develop a coherent strategy or tactics. A visit to Coritiba's Estádio Belfort Duarte to play the local club brought another stuttering 2-1 win and, with the World Cup qualification process due to swing into action in the middle of the following year, concerns were being raised. Was Moreira the right man to take the *Seleção* to Mexico? Reappointing Feola had suggested that going back to a coach who had delivered in a previous World Cup was hardly a guarantee of continuing success, and yet the CBD seemed to be backing the same horse, in the same race, again.

The return of Pelé had given the team a boost, but had the momentum fuelled by his comeback quickly run out of steam? In his absence, Tostão had played the role that he had abdicated. Now he was back in the fold, there was little chance that the Cruzeiro forward would keep Pelé out of the team. If he wanted to be part of the starting line-up in Mexico, rather than merely a reserve option to Pelé, Tostão would need to change his game and become the fulcrum of the attack, leading the line, albeit often dropping deeper – precursing the oft-highlighted false nine role of modern times. Tostão was an abundantly skilled and hugely intelligent player but such changes at the highest level would inevitably take time – and they did. The plan wasn't helped by a serious injury that would occur in a domestic game during September 1969, just weeks after Brazil's qualification for Mexico had been confirmed.

Entering December 1968, there were three more matches to play before ending the year. West Germany visited the Maracanã on 14 December. A 2-2 draw was barely acceptable, especially after leading 2-0 at the break. The final two games would both be against Yugoslavia, firstly on 17 December in Rio and then two days later in Belo Horizonte. After seeing a team broadly consisting of his first-choice players labour to a 3-3 draw after twice falling behind to the eastern Europeans in the first encounter, the game was largely up for Moreira. Flamengo coach Dorival Knippel – universally known as Yustrich – took charge for the second match, selecting a largely inexperienced team that won 3-2. It meant that, in their last seven home games, Brazil had only won four times and, aside from the 4-1 win over Argentina each of those had only been by the odd goal. Going into 1969, with the World Cup qualification fixtures now looming into view, the *Seleção*'s prospects of getting to Mexico, let alone pursuing glory in the tournament itself, were looking decidedly shaky, and the press weren't slow to let the CBD know.

João Havelange's plans to use a Brazil World Cup hat-trick in the 1966 World Cup as a springboard to the FIFA presidency had been thwarted by the team's early exit – his speculative investment in Garrincha proving to be a busted flush. The tournament in Mexico offered another chance to complete the treble, and kickstart his plans, but with the team less than totally convincing Moreira was suddenly looking like a tired and old man with his best days a long way behind him and the press were raging against the team's performances. Havelange decided to act. Returning to a World Cup-winning coach in 1966 with Feola had failed and, with a nod towards the old maxim – often attributed to Einstein – of the definition of insanity as applying the same process over again and expecting a different result being the height of folly, a new man at the helm was required. The dilemma was highlighted by author Sam Kunti, 'Brazil's football boss needed a coach who could prove that the chaos and complacency of the 1966 World Cup hadn't destroyed Brazil's reputation. He wondered who could bring new impetus, rebuild the team, navigate the World Cup qualification and, above all, satisfy the fans?'[12]

In early 1969, Moreira was removed from post and replaced by João Saldanha. It was an action somewhat akin to the FA dropping a net into Fleet Street to select the next England manager – well, perhaps not quite – but the

---

12 Kunti, Sam, *Brazil 1970: How the Greatest Team of All Time Won the World Cup* (Worthing, England: Pitch Publishing Ltd, 2022)

selection of Saldanha was from left field in more ways than one. After retiring from playing, he had made his name as a sports journalist, described by Alex Bellos, author of *Futebol: The Brazilian Way of Life*, as 'a brilliant writer – one of the best sportswriters Brazil has ever produced'.[13] Forthright and often provocative, Saldanha's writing pulled no punches and gave no quarter in any disputes, be it with officials, clubs or players. He wrote like a fan, for the fans. In 1957 he was seduced away from his typewriter by an invitation to coach his old club. Botafogo were in decline at the time and bordering on crisis. Yet, despite having no previous experience, Saldanha performed a Lazarus-like resurrection of their fortunes and won the Campeonato Carioca in his first season.

In typically controversial fashion, however, he would leave the club just two years later and return to journalism. He was also a member of the Partido Comunista Brasileiro – the Brazil Communist Party – an organisation at the time declared illegal by the military junta; a fact that would later count strongly against him when he was removed from post. This was the man to whom Havelange turned. It may seem strange to consider, but it's been widely acknowledged that one of the considerations for the appointment was that, if the man in charge of the team was a journalist, others of his profession may be less inclined to be critical. It's difficult to throw stones at the tent if one of your family is sitting inside it. When asked for his thoughts on the appointment of Saldanha, Sam Kunti expressed clear appreciation of Havelange's logic, describing it as, 'Daring but, above all,

---

13   https://web.archive.org/web/20070929141357/http://
     www.futebolthebrazilianwayoflife.com/AskAlex.
     aspx?year=2003&month=June

a masterstroke. He wanted to take the sting out of the criticism by the press and did so by handing the managerial role to one of their own. Saldanha also enjoyed immense popularity. Once a manager of Botafogo, mostly a journalist, he had some credentials in the game. His main task was to rejuvenate the *Seleção* and he did so with flying colours as Brazil breezed through the qualifiers. That's where Saldanha's merit lies: the *Seleção* was popular again.'

If the appointment was a gamble and, for many at the time, it certainly seemed to be, Pelé's initial reaction to the new man was encouraging, describing how the upfront and no-nonsense approach of Saldanha was a refreshing change for a squad who had grown weary and become increasingly uninspired by Moreira. The new coach was a big man in many ways. As well as being tall and erect, despite suffering from pulmonary emphysema which meant he only had the use of one lung, being a smoker and drinker, he was a strong swimmer and during training would goad his players by telling them that despite his health and lifestyle, he was still fitter than all of them. Pelé also liked Saldanha's approach to team selection which had been 'a little bit all over the place', under Moreira of late.[14] 'Santos and Botafogo are the best teams in Brazil,' Saldanha declared to his players after calling them together for an early meeting. 'So, the base of the national team will be Santos and Botafogo. That's that, you can say what you like but I'm not changing my mind.'[15] Playing for the former of those two clubs, that was hardly an issue for Pelé. Saldanha also decided that his team

14   do Nascimento, Edson Arantes, *Pelé – The Autobiography* (London: Simon & Schuster UK Ltd, 2006)

15   do Nascimento, Edson Arantes, *Pelé – The Autobiography* (London: Simon & Schuster UK Ltd, 2006)

would play in a 4-2-4 formation, with wide players on each flank, usually Jairzinho and the teenage Santos winger Edu – who would eventually convince Saldanha to look at a 4-3-3 formation instead – to stretch the opposition defences, creating more space for Pelé and Tostão.

Impressing your players with strong opinions and a forthright approach is one thing, but the true test of a coach's mettle is on the field, especially in competitive games, and that was where Saldanha's worth – at least in the short term – would be measured. Brazil's bid to qualify for Mexico wouldn't begin until 6 August when they were placed into a four-team CONMEBOL group alongside Colombia, Paraguay and Venezuela, with just the top team progressing to the finals. Before that, there were three home friendlies to play, two against Peru in April and one against England in June. No one knew at the time but both of those teams would later be opponents for the *Seleção* in Mexico.

With the World Cup qualification competition starting later in the year, playing South American opposition in the first couple of games under the new coach was ideal preparation for what was to come. Peru visiting Porto Alegre's Estádio Gigante da Beira-Rio on 7 April and then travelling north up the coast to play the second game in Rio's Estádio do Maracanã two days later fitted the bill perfectly. The visitors would be anything but a pushover for Brazil, however, due to the man now coaching Peru, for whom the Brazil team would hold few surprises.

Saldanha wasn't the only coach debuting in the game – Peru had a new man leading their team too. Didi was a former Brazilian playmaker and part of both the 1958 and 1962 World Cup-winning teams, and was the first non-Peruvian to take charge of the national team. In the

1958 triumph, despite the scene-stealing performances of the teenage Pelé, it was Didi who was awarded the player of the tournament accolade. After spending his coaching apprenticeship with Sporting Cristal, Didi had then taken charge of Peru, declaring that he would play a brand of attacking front-foot football broadly akin to that displayed by Brazil in Mexico. His approach would be hugely rewarded as, across the next couple of years, and especially during their time in Mexico, Peru forged an image that would endear them to all football hipsters for years to come.

Both games were keenly contested. In the first, a second-half strike by Gérson settled things after Jairzinho's early goal had been levelled by Alberto Gallardo. The leggy Sporting Cristal wide man was developing a penchant for scoring against Brazil. It was something he would carry forward to Mexico the following year. If the first game was testing for Saldanha's team, the second was even more so as with just eight minutes played they trailed 2-0. First Gallardo reprised his goal from the first match with just four minutes on the clock, then Julio Baylón doubled the advantage after a further four minutes. Brazil would quickly strike back and, inside 60 seconds, Pelé halved the lead.

The equaliser would have to wait until ten minutes ahead of the break, when Tostão netted. Shortly afterwards, both teams were reduced to ten men when an altercation between Gérson and the Peru defender Pedro González saw both men dismissed by Peruvian referee Alberto Tejada. Just over a year later, those events would have echoes for Peruvian team selection in Mexico. A goal 15 minutes from time by substitute Edu, on the field to replace Dirceu Lopes, finally settled the game in Brazil's favour.

It was interesting to note that, despite Saldanha's forthright intention to have players from Santos and Botafogo dominate his teams, that had hardly been the case in these two games. In Porto Alegre, only skipper Carlos Alberto, Rildo, Pelé and substitute Edu were Santos players, with Gérson and Jairzinho from Botafogo contributing to half a dozen players from those two clubs among the squad of 12 who took part. In the second game, that increased to eight of 14. Joel Camargo brought the Santos contingent up to five and Paulo Cézar joined the other two Botafogo players. If there were doubts that Saldanha had weakened his stance, however, any such assumption would be cast aside by the team selected for the *Seleção*'s next match, at home to England on 12 June, back at the Maracanã.

As reigning champions, England were in the position enjoyed by Brazil for the previous two tournaments and had no need to qualify for Mexico, as was also the case for them ahead of the 1966 World Cup when they were hosts. In preparation for the tournament, Sir Alf Ramsey had taken a squad on a brief tour of South America to both help the players who would be defending England's title better appreciate the conditions they would be playing in, and also gain some idea of the sort of opposition they would face in Mexico. On the first day of June they played out a goalless draw against Mexico in the Estádio Azteca, before defeating Uruguay 2-1 a week later in Montevideo. The tour was rounded out on 12 June with the game against Brazil. This would be Saldanha's last chance to see his players perform in an official game before qualification for Mexico began, although there would be four more unofficial games against state or club teams before the serious business got under way.

As well as offering both coaches an insight into how their teams would fare against opposition from the other side of the Atlantic, the game was also billed as a 'Farewell Curtain Call' for Gilmar who was winning his 93rd cap. The veteran was just a couple of months short of his 39th birthday and, with Félix now established as the first-choice goalkeeper, a swansong in the upcoming World Cup was not on the cards. Offering him a starting place in this prestige friendly, however, not only gave him the chance to play his last game against the reigning world champions, but also allowed Saldanha to fulfil his earlier stated commitment to focus on Santos and Botafogo as the main source of players for the team. Whether the selection was intended as a justification for his earlier commitment to concentrate on those two clubs is unclear, but in consequent matches that duopoly dominance would be watered down.

Gilmar's brief return, and other changes, meant that almost all of the 12 players who saw action were selected from those two clubs, save for Cruzeiro's Tostão. One of the players to benefit from the two-club addiction of the coach was Clodoaldo, who was granted his debut in the game. Just 19 at the time, the midfielder would become a key element in Brazil's success in Mexico and had a hand in probably the most famous World Cup Final goal of all time. The iconic moment when Pelé almost paused before rolling the ball to Carlos Alberto to drive the fourth goal home has come to symbolise the *Seleção*'s entrancing majesty in the tournament but wind the clock back a few seconds and there's an extravagant piece of play by Clodoaldo that is just as representative of *O Jogo Bonito* as anything else that happened during the times of that Samba Party in Mexico. Receiving the ball in his own half of the field, he twists and turns, this way, then that, eluding no less than four challenges in a display of self-belief that speaks of the *joie de vivre* that was coursing through the veins of all of the Brazilian players at the time, before rolling off a simple pass.

That epic final was more than 12 months away though, and in this game Brazil would be forced to fight to the end to earn victory. With 15 minutes played a Martin Peters cross from the left eluded all of the Brazilian back line as Bobby Charlton threw himself at the ball but failed to connect. With confusion in the defensive ranks, the ball drifted through to Colin Bell on the far post, who stretched to drive past a scandalously exposed Gilmar.

There was a chance for Saldanha's team to get level before the break when a clumsy Brian Labone challenge on Gérson, as he latched on to a through pass from Pelé, saw the prematurely balding midfielder – still only 28 at the time – tumbled to the ground inside the penalty area. Looking supremely confident, Carlos Alberto picked up the ball and placed it on the spot, even while his team-mate was receiving medical attention. Eventually Gérson was helped to his feet and the captain stepped up, driving low to Gordon Banks's right-hand corner. The goalkeeper had guessed correctly and dived to smother the shot. England's lead was preserved and would remain so until around 11 minutes from time.

Perhaps affected by the heat and humidity of the Rio summer evening, an understandable tendency to protect what they had, a compelling requirement demanded by Brazil's increasing pressure for an equaliser or a combination of everything, England dropped deeper into defence as the game wore on towards the final dozen minutes or so. Just when Ramsey's team could see the finishing line of a memorable victory homing into view, Brazil broke through.

A sliced clearance as Clodoaldo challenged was ballooned into the air. On the edge of the area, it was flicked on by Pelé towards the England goal, and Tostão challenged Labone for the ball as it dropped. Neither player got anything like the contact they were looking for and, as both fell to the floor with the ball dropping between them, the Cruzeiro forward reacted fastest, driving past Banks as he advanced.

The game was now level but the wind was very much billowing out the Brazilian sails and the winning goal followed just two minutes later. Substitute Paulo Cézar, on for Edu, swept the ball wide to the right where it was collected by Carlos Alberto. Playing the ball forward and then running past a tiring Keith Newton, Carlos Alberto caught the ball before it ran out of play and pulled it back into the England penalty area. Whether by intention or just good fortune, the ball ran directly to Pelé's feet and he swept it into the far corner of the net, eluding Banks's despairing dive. Brazil had won 2-1 and Saldanha's team had shown not only the resilience and self-belief to come back from being a goal down with time running out, but they had done so against the world champions. The coach was also ready to acknowledge that his team had peered over the precipice and into the depths of defeat. 'We were lucky in the end,' he admitted when speaking to Geoffrey Green of *The Times*. 'If Charlton had scored just after half-time to put you two up we should have been finished, although we missed a penalty at the half hour plus one or two other chances as well.'[16] Twelve months later the teams would meet again and, with a different coach in charge of the *Seleção*, the respect earned

---

16 'Late Brazilian win should not disguise benefits of trip', *The Times*, 13 June 1969

on that Rio evening would feed into Brazilian tactics when facing Ramsey's team.

Ramsey may well have agreed with his opposite number, and went home convinced that a more concentrated defensive performance would have seen England over the line to victory. Brazil moved on increasingly convinced that however many goals their opponents may score, they could always score more. Both analyses would colour the way each team played when they met the following July in Mexico. There were now just half a dozen weeks until the qualification competition for the World Cup began, and Saldanha planned another four games for his players to hone his squad, and take them to peak match fitness and preparedness. Three would be in Brazil, and the fourth in Colombia. This wasn't a return to the chaotic preparation pre-1966 however. Saldanha would use the matches to tweak his team rather than make countless wholesale changes, and try out different combinations before settling on the 11 players he wanted to kick off qualification against Colombia on 6 August.

Precisely one month before that day, Brazil played a team from the Bahia club in their home ground of Estádio da Fonte Nova in Salvador, running out 4-0 winners. Two days later, an 8-2 victory over a Sergipe State XI in the Estádio Lourival Baptista kept the goals coming. Finally, a 6-1 triumph in Recife over another state select side, this time from Pernambuco, rounded things out in Brazil. After the game, Saldanha took his squad to Colombia to ensure the players were acclimatised to the conditions where they would begin their qualifying campaign for the World Cup.

With the opening qualification match taking place in Colombia, playing a friendly in that country a few days ahead of the qualifier was ideal preparation, especially with the game against the Millonarios club being staged in Bogatá's Estádio El Campín, where the *Seleção* would face the Colombian national team five days later. A 2-0 win kept the team's 100 per cent record of wins bubbling along, with the increased confidence it brought, but just as valuable to the coach was the time he and his players had together.

By the time they reached Bogatá, Saldanha's planning was almost complete and of the 11 that started the game against Millonarios, only one would miss out when the team was named to face Colombia on 6 August to begin the campaign for World Cup qualification, Brito making way for Djalma Dias in defence. That preference would remain in place throughout the qualification competition. When Brazil opened their World Cup finals campaign in Mexico a year later, however, the Vasco de Gama defender had reclaimed his place and Djalma Dias wouldn't even make the squad.

Colombia had already completed two of their fixtures by the time they entertained Brazil, defeating Venezuela 2-0 at home and then drawing 1-1 in the Caracas return. The game against Saldanha's team would complete the full set of possible results for the hosts as two first-half goals from Tostão settled things. The first was prodded home from short range after a cross from the right, and the second saw him profit from an error by Deportivo Cali goalkeeper Luis Largacha, as he fumbled a save from a free kick. With the other two teams in the group, Paraguay and Venezuela, being lesser-fancied than the Colombians, travelling to your perceived biggest rivals and winning in the group-opening game was the ideal start.

The next couple of games, as the *Seleção* completed their away fixtures in the group, underscored the relative strength, or lack of it, of the other teams, and yet in their next match things were going far from smoothly by half-time. Four days after the victory in Colombia, the *Seleção* were in Caracas facing Venezuela. Following their games against Colombia, *La Vinotinto* had succumbed to a 2-0 home defeat against Paraguay and were hardly considered likely to offer much resistance against Saldanha's team. With 45 minutes completed though, the score remained goalless. The coach was furious and, in a move infamously repeated many years later by Hull City's Phil Brown, Saldanha refused to allow the players to seek the sanctuary of the dressing room, hurling the key away and berating them about their performances. Although it took another 15 minutes after the restart to break the deadlock, the message had clearly been received loud and clear. Tostão netted a hat-trick and Pelé grabbed a brace as Brazil accelerated to a 5-0 victory.

Seven days later, another clean sheet and strikes by Jairzinho, Edu, plus an own goal from Mendoza were comfortably sufficient to overcome Paraguay in Asunción, and the value of that result would be brought into sharp focus for the final game of the group. With all three away games played, three wins recorded, ten goals scored and not a single one conceded, qualification from there looked to be a canter.

Four days after the win in Paraguay, Brazil returned home to face Colombia, easing to a 6-2 win. Venezuela were punished with another six of the best three days later, before Brazil completed the perfect programme by beating Paraguay. Ahead of the game, with the *Seleção* on ten points and *Los Guaraníes* having eight – the home defeat to Brazil being the only blot on their otherwise perfect copybook

– there was still a chance that an away victory could deny Saldanha's men qualification, although a huge swing in goal difference would also be required. It never looked likely to happen. A single Pelé goal secured victory and confirmed qualification, in front of 183,341 fans. It was the highest officially recorded attendance at a football match in the game's history.

Six wins out of six, 23 goals scored and a paltry two conceded was a hugely impressive record. In fact, across all three of the qualifying groups – the others would see Peru and Uruguay also book their tickets for Mexico, where both would be eliminated by the *Seleção* – the three top goalscorers in the qualifying competition were all Brazilian. Tostão had scored ten goals in the six games. Pelé had added six and Jairzinho three. Saldanha had been in charge for nine competitive matches and four friendlies. He had won every one.

Havelange's gamble looked to be paying out mighty dividends and yet, on the same day that Brazil had completed that 100 per cent record, events elsewhere in the country were sowing the seeds of Saldanha's exit. Across the city, General Artur da Costa e Silva, head of the military junta, suffered a severe stroke. During the previous year he had delivered the Fifth Institutional Act, by which the regime granted dictatorial powers to the president – in effect the head of the junta – suspending constitutional rights. It had been expected that, when Costa e Silva relinquished power, it would be his vice-president stepping up to assume power. Instead, the junta chose General Emílio Garrastazu Médici.

If the time under Costa e Silva had been repressive, Médici's reign would take that to a whole new level. He would also use football, and the national passion it engendered, as a sedative for any restless resistance that escaped the heightened levels of arrest, kidnapping, torture and assassination that quickly became normal during his period leading the military junta. He reportedly authorised the construction of 13 new football stadiums across the country and began attending Flamengo's games, with some suggesting that he even sought to influence team selection. His dedication to the club was questionable at best, at least outside its political advantages, but while his tactical acumen and personnel suggestions were probably of little value his presence doubtless helped the *Rubro-Negro* by intimidating the opposition, whether the club wanted it or not. It was, however, with the national team that Médici's interference would be most strongly felt. Saldanha was not only an avowed communist, he was also ferociously independent and hardly one to be swayed by gentle, or not so gentle, persuasive suggestions from on high. Although when it happened, there were other factors involved as well; despite the team's success on the field, it was surely inevitable that this toxic cocktail would lead to a parting of the ways for Saldanha and the *Seleção*.

It may have been a portent of what was to follow but after the run of success and confirming qualification for Mexico, Brazil played a further four games before the end of Saldanha's reign. They would only win once. Three days after the victory over Paraguay, the coach took his team to Belo Horizonte to play Atlético Mineiro in a friendly that carried the overly grandiose title of the *Taça Prefeito Luís Sousa Lima*. The official label of the opposition is perhaps questionable. Despite all of the players coming from Atlético Mineiro, and the game taking place in that club's home stadium, the team actually wore the shirts of the Minas Gerais State FA. Regardless of any identification issues of their opponents, or potential fatigue, a win was surely to be expected, and Saldanha selected a team largely similar to the one that had completed the clean sweep of wins in the qualifying tournament.

Things didn't pan out as expected. On a day when Carlos Alberto was sent off for the first time wearing a *Canarinho* shirt, Pelé's equalising goal after an early strike for the home team by Amaury was insufficient to sway the game in the *Seleção*'s favour. A winning goal by Dário condemned Brazil to their first defeat under Saldanha, albeit in a friendly. Dário had joined Atlético Mineiro from Campo Grande during the previous year, after a difficult and sometimes traumatic childhood and a truncated career in the army. The 23-year-old striker was now forging a growing reputation as a goalscorer with the *Alvinegro*. His winning strike wouldn't be the last time he would feature in the thoughts of Saldanha. Less than 12 months later, he would travel to Mexico as part of the Brazil squad, but under a different coach after his goalscoring prowess may have, inadvertently, contributed to the dismissal of Saldanha. The defeat would end the year on a flat note for the coach and his squad, and they would have to wait until March of 1970, just a couple of months ahead of the World Cup, before they could look to get things back on track with a couple of games against Argentina. Before then though, a meeting of an entirely different kind would prove invaluable to Brazil's prospects of success in Mexico.

Saldanha's appointment and his impact on the team's performances were unarguably positive, but it was far from being the complete answer, as Sam Kunti suggested when asked, 'The first-round exit in England forced Brazil to rethink – it was the end of a generation but that World

Cup was also clear proof that European football was now superior. So, if Brazil wanted to be a serious competitor again four years later, change was needed. For two years, the CBD and the *Seleção* wasted time, with few games in 1967 and the appointment of Aymoré Moreira, a coach of the old guard.'

Saldanha's appointment was a step along that road, but there was still a distance to travel. Kunti continued, 'But perhaps the answer to Brazil's problems lay off the pitch. The 1968 Olympics in Mexico City provided a window for scientists to explore questions of altitude and heat in relation to athletic performance and the improvement thereof. Those studies were also fundamental for how teams would approach the 1970 World Cup. It's a stretch to say a science war ensued, but there was a bit of fetish about altitude. Brazil and England were the two teams that took altitude preparations the most seriously and did it most thoroughly. Brazil had professor Lamartine DaCosta to thank for that. He set out in 1967 to explore the altitude and corresponding heat in Mexico. He discovered Guanajuato [later an important base in Brazil's preparation for the 1970 World Cup] and drew up plans for Brazil's Olympic delegation and then later the *Seleção* of '70. DaCosta was a technocrat and in that sense Brazil's preparation for the 1970 World Cup reflected that.'

In the autumn of 1969, Saldanha met with DaCosta. Although hardly a football fan, DaCosta's expertise would be key to ensuring that if Brazil had the best players, having a fitness programme in place to deal with the issues of playing at high altitude in Mexico would give them the best chance of winning the World Cup. At first Saldanha was sceptical of Da Costa's revolutionary ideas, but he was eventually won over after a meeting in a bar where the professor, then a commander in the Brazilian Navy, laid out a plan for how the players could be put through a series of training camps, with regular testing and medical checks. Scribbled on the back of a table napkin, DaCosta proposed his plan for ensuring that if Brazil failed to return from Mexico with the World Cup, it wouldn't be because of lack of preparation. The lessons of 1966 were being drilled home. Beginning in February 1970, if the plan was followed the *Seleção* would move to various different locations, training and building up their tolerance to the effects of high altitude before arriving in Mexico.

Historically, Brazilian football had succeeded on the ethos of inspiration and outstanding ability. Now there was a chance to add science to the arsenal. Fortunately for Brazilian football, Saldanha was wise enough to eventually be persuaded and DaCosta's plans were put into practice. Looking back, Carlos Alberto Parreira, who joined the national setup as a coach under Saldanha's successor, recognised the importance of taking up DaCosta's plan. 'We came to the conclusion,' he recalled, 'that we still had the best players; a team that has Jairzinho, Gérson, Rivellino, Pelé, Tostão, Carlos Alberto has to play well. So, then something was missing and it was concluded that thing was, perhaps, better tactical organisation and, above all, better preparation to manage Mexico's altitude ... Brazil was the only team at Mexico's World Cup that acclimatised to the altitude as prescribed by scientific data.'[17] Apart from the hosts themselves, the Brazil squad would be the best-equipped to deal with the conditions.

---

17 *CHAMP10NS*, Netflix

While the coach was contemplating revolutionary approaches that would help his team, the availability of one of his key players was thrown into massive doubt. Tostão had proved himself to be an invaluable member of the Brazil team and looked destined to continue to be so, albeit in an amended role in Mexico. However, an incident in a Brazilian Championship game at Corinthians' Estadio Paulo Machado de Carvalho Municipal, in São Paulo in October 1969 threw his World Cup participation into serious doubt. Inadvertently, a ball struck by Corinthians' Ditao smashed into his left eye, the impact detaching the retina. With fears about losing the sight in his eye, and the consequent end of his footballing career, the Cruzeiro forward was flown to Houston for surgery. He would spend months in rehabilitation, cautiously avoiding sudden head movements lest they upset the delicate work of the surgeons, and was unable to run and train, much less head a ball. He would be missing from the *Seleção* until April of 1970, just two months before the World Cup got under way.

Following such a prolonged absence, and so short a time before the tournament began, there were obvious concerns about whether he would be able to compete at the highest level. In Tostão's absence, initially his Cruzeiro team-mate Dirceu Lopes was tried out as a replacement, then Roberto Miranda of Botafogo, followed by Dário; each was selected to play alongside Pelé. Only the latter would journey to Mexico though, as Tostão recovered in time, convincing his coach that he was not only fit to play, but was emotionally ready too. There would be a scare along the way, and doubts remained right up until the final days before the tournament, but following a practice game against a Mexican club side the decision was made, and Tostão, playing in his adjusted role ahead of Pelé, would begin the World Cup. There is a sad postscript to the story, however. In 1972, after moving to Vasco de Gama, the problem reappeared and, despite attempts at corrective surgery, he was forced to retire from the game, aged just 27. Understandably disillusioned, Tostão left the world of football and trained to be a doctor. He would return as a television pundit and journalist a few years later. All of that was for the future though. At the end of 1969, now bereft of one of their key forwards, Brazil needed to pick up the pace again.

In February, players under consideration for the squad were called to a meeting, and the DaCosta schedule was laid out. Taking on board the lessons learned both from 1966 and the physical travails of the games played recently in Mexico, training schedules, they were informed, had been developed using the experience of NASA's aerobic requirements for astronauts to ensure the team arrived in Mexico for the first match in June at the peak of fitness and stamina. The errors of the 1966 World Cup would not be repeated. The logic was simple. The *Seleção* squad that landed in Mexico would be a wildly talented group. If they were also among the fittest of teams competing there, it would give them the best chance of winning the tournament. Gérson recalled the intensity of the programme, 'We were in a training camp for about two months. You'd get a few hours to go home while in Brazil and then were away for ten weeks for the World Cup.'[18]

Preparations went beyond mere fitness. The shirts that the players would wear would not only be made to measure for each of their different physiques, but were made of a

---

18   Donald, Michael, *Goal!* (London: Hamlyn, 2017)

fabric that would absorb sweat draining from the players in the heat of the Mexican sun, keeping them cooler and more comfortable. Andrew Downie considered that 'the preparation was absolutely key'. Pelé had a similar opinion, 'After the disaster of 1966 we would only lose this one by being beaten by a better team, not for lack of preparation or consideration of our tactics.'[19]

Despite Argentina not qualifying for Mexico, any games between the two neighbouring countries are fiercely contested and, after the late defeat in September of 1969, a win for Brazil against their neighbours and fiercest rivals was considered to be just as important as preparations for the World Cup. However, in the first game, staged in Porto Alegre, Saldanha chose to experiment a little with his line-up, bringing in the Corinthians goalkeeper Ado and Palmeiras defender Baldocchi for their debuts. He also selected the Cruzeiro defender Fontana for just his fourth official *Seleção* game. With some Brazilian players keenly aware of the danger of injury and potentially missing out on the trip to Mexico, and the Argentines free of any such concern about upcoming fixtures and keen to put a dent into Brazilian confidence, perhaps a 2-0 defeat was less surprising than might otherwise have been the case.

Back in Rio three days later, and following on from a second successive defeat, anything other than a win was unthinkable, especially with the World Cup looming ever larger on the horizon. Still, Saldanha experimented with his goalkeeper, offering a debut to Leão of Palmeiras. Fortunately for the packed Maracanã crowd, in a game

---

19   do Nascimento, Edson Arantes, *Pelé – The Autobiography* (London: Simon & Schuster UK Ltd, 2006)

largely dominated by Brazil, with Pelé to the fore, a measure of revenge was enacted and pride was restored by a 2-1 win. Jairzinho opened the scoring before Miguel Brindisi levelled for the visitors, leaving Pelé to notch the winner. Interestingly, all three debutants across the two games would make the squad for Mexico, albeit for Leão it would be as a late replacement. None would get on to the pitch. Fontana, however, would play in the final group game against Romania.

Just under a week later in the much smaller surroundings of the Estádio Moça Bonita, the home to Rio club Bangu, the *Seleção* played what was, in effect, a glorified training game against the hosts. The unofficial nature of the event was illustrated by both the copious use of substitutions on both sides, and Saldanha's team playing in unnumbered training tops rather than their traditional *Canarinho* shirts. Unofficial or not, it would be Saldanha's last game in charge of the *Seleção*. Generally, results on the pitch had been encouraging. Off the pitch, however, Saldanha's character had begun to grate with several players, coaches and administrators – not to mention the military junta and especially the newly anointed president, General Emílio Garrastazu Médici.

The success of the *Seleção* was a double-edged sword for Médici. Should Brazil win, the junta could trumpet their success, citing it as a positive consequence of the order restored, and the progress achieved by the military takeover, and wrap themselves in the flag, basking in reflected glory. The downside was that given Saldanha's political leanings, very much to the left and far away from that of Médici, if he was acknowledged across the country as the man who delivered the third World Cup triumph to Brazil, the coach would potentially have a national platform to proclaim his beliefs. Hardly a shrinking violet, it was surely a stage he may well have availed himself of.

Eight years down the road, the Argentine military junta then in power had a similar issue to consider with the left-inclined César Luis Menotti leading *La Albiceleste* into the 1978 World Cup. Perhaps not as outspoken as Saldanha, Menotti was certainly not shy about his political convictions, once declaring, 'There's a right-wing football and a left-wing football. Right-wing football wants to suggest that life is a struggle. It demands sacrifices. We have to become of steel and win by any method … obey and function, that's what those with power want from the players. That's how they create retards, useful idiots that go with the system.'[20] One would imagine that such oratory was sufficiently incendiary to fire up the junta's ire. Menotti, however, was clearly the man most likely to deliver success and with the tournament held in Argentina, that was the lifejacket that kept him afloat. He was allowed to progress to the finals with his team and the junta were rewarded when *La Albiceleste* became world champions for the first time. What may have happened had Argentina not won is open to conjecture. After the victory, Menotti maintained his political independence, but was level-headed enough not to rock the boat too much. The same was less likely to be the case with Saldanha. Then there was also the matter of Dário.

Médici had attended a match between Atlético Mineiro and Internacional, when Dário had scored a hat-trick, and

---

20 Wilson, Jonathan, *Inverting The Pyramid: The History of Football Tactics* (London: Weidenfeld & Nicolson 2018)

a rumour quickly followed that the head of the military junta was now a confirmed advocate of the forward and was convinced he should be in the national team. There's no material evidence that Médici held such an opinion, let alone voiced it, or even that he was impressed by Dário at all. The problem is that, wherever the speculation came from, the press grabbed hold of it and ran. Rumours can be halfway around the world before truth gets its trousers on. This was certainly the case here, and the concern over Tostão's eye injury was the perfect opening.

Dr Pete Watson is a teaching fellow in the Department of Spanish, Portuguese and Latin American Studies at the University of Leeds and author of *Football and Nation Building in Colombia (2010–2018): The Only Thing That Unites Us*. In an interview with the author, he offered his opinion on the veracity, or otherwise, of the rumour, 'It's certainly widely reported, so you assume there is some truth in it. What we can certainly say is that Saldanha responded in the way he did through the press regarding rumours and gossip in the newspapers that Médici wanted Dário to play. Médici did not say it to Saldanha directly. The report about Médici wanting Dário in the team, or at least to be in the squad, apparently began from an article by a sporting journalist called Armando Noguiera, in the *Jornal do Brasil*. Médici was a football fan and did go to games. He was also a gaucho so had loyalties and affiliations.'

Dr Watson also referred to an online article from the BBC that quotes an interview from a TV programme called *Roda Viva* on which Saldanha appeared in 1987, once censorship was over. [21] It suggests Médici may not have been Dário's

---

21 https://www.bbc.com/portuguese/brasil-57398513

only influential advocate. Dr Watson recounted, 'Saldanha appears to say that João Havelange also was advising him to select Dário, given the new president's views.'

Ahead of the two games against Argentina in March 1970, the press presented Saldanha with the rumour that had now achieved stone-certain status. 'Médici wants Dário to replace Tostão,' they announced to the coach. They asked for his thoughts on the president's idea. It wasn't quite a 'no win' sort of question, when any answer can condemn, but it was getting there. The usually brusque Saldanha replied with calmness and a rare smile. It wasn't the time to pick a fight with an enemy that literally had all of the guns. He acknowledged the president's right to have an opinion, as do all Brazilian football fans. He even commented that he and Médici had things in common, such as both being *Gremistas*. Even the pay-off line, after he addressed the question, carried a polite ending. He didn't select members for the president's ministry, he declared, and the president didn't select the Brazil team. 'You can see we get along well,' he concluded. Regardless, it was Dirceu Lopes, Tostão's team-mate at Cruzeiro, not Dário, who wore the number nine shirt for both games against Argentina, and in the subsequent friendly against Bangu, Saldanha's last game in charge of the *Seleção*.

Saldanha's reply to the heavily loaded press enquiry was hardly controversial. Nevertheless, it has often been painted to be so since, and is regarded by some as the first step in the eventual, and inevitable, removal from his post. The reality may be less clear. Dr Watson suggests that, as with the fogs surrounding the origin of the rumours, the same may apply to its consequences, 'Equally, this is hard to really establish in terms of whether it would damn him or not.' He then went on to explain, 'Médici, however, was not used to being disobeyed or criticised, and certainly not by someone who had Communist Party membership, was widely known to hold those political opinions, and had been arrested on various occasions to boot.' He recalled that far more aggressive comments were delivered at other times, especially when the coach was speaking to members of the European press, when his distaste for the dictatorship was often given clear voice, 'Saldanha had used his position and popularity to criticise the arbitrary imprisonment, torture and death of opposition activists, most openly in an interview with *Le Monde,* that he gave, when in Mexico to participate in the drawing of teams into the groups.[22] I would suggest that these comments and this openness would potentially have angered Médici and the army more than selection issues centring on Dário. If he had been prepared to use his platform there and give that interview, then he could easily have used it in a similar way given any triumph in Mexico, potentially positioning the World Cup win as a victory for the people against the regime, rather than a victory for the regime.'

There were other more immediate issues to address. The momentum that the *Seleção* had created through their victorious qualification campaign had begun to run out of steam. The 2-0 reverse to Argentina in the first of the double-header played in Brazil only added to the mounting pressure. The 2-1 win in the second fixture, four days later, was an improvement, if only a marginal one and the 1-1 draw with Bangu suggested there were still problems. Saldanha's position was hardly helped when he looked to

---

22 https://www.bbc.com/portuguese/brasil-57398513

shift blame for the team's struggling performances on to the players, targeting Pelé in particular. It was an easy way to turn allies into enemies and offered fresh ammunition to those already aligned against him.

News reached Saldanha that Yustrich, who had coached the team for that single game against Yugoslavia after Moreira was removed, and before Saldanha had been appointed, had been critical of his handling of the *Seleção*. Impetuous as always, Saldanha visited the club's training ground to challenge him. Some reports even suggested that he had taken along a gun to ensure that his point was forcibly delivered. If that seems a little over the top, other reports suggest that it was hardly a novel situation, with talk of another 'shoot-out' occurring with a former Botafogo goalkeeper years before. Reports suggest that, apparently convinced that the goalkeeper was guilty of match-fixing, Saldanha stood in front of the player and fired off a round of bullets into the air from a revolver that he was frequently accused of carrying around with him. Such matters can be written off as exaggerations and mere unsubstantiated rumour but, with Saldanha's dogged independence of spirit also bringing him into conflict with the military, selecting your enemies with care was perhaps a talent that the abrasive coach lacked. It was only going to end one way.

It was the Ides of March that saw Caesar's demise as his enemies crowded around him. For Saldanha, the knife was plunged in two days after the middle of that month. Called to the offices of the CBD for a meeting with Havelange, the coach was astute enough to realise the purpose of the summons. Fifteen minutes after arriving at the office he was on the way out again – in more ways than one. The matter had become an increasing concern for Havelange who wanted success for the team, plus the acclaim of press and fans to further his own aspirations, but was a canny enough political operative to appreciate that keeping on the right side of the junta was required as well. A solution eventually presented itself when Saldanha's assistant coach resigned claiming that it was impossible to work with him. Seizing the opportunity, Havelange announced that he was disbanding the coaching structure and, when the new team was announced, Saldanha's name was absent.

At such times it's difficult to tease apart the different threads of a situation and clearly identify which is the most important, the most demanding of action. Saldanha's politics were always going to be an itch that the junta would eventually be compelled to scratch, and the Dário issue, whatever the merits of it, hardly helped. Even if Médici had never expressed any thoughts about the player, there was a clear 'turf' issue couched within the coach's response to the matter when questioned by the press. It was hardly likely to defuse a potentially explosive situation. Neither did the offhand comments made about the junta's oppression. An official line was, as Dr Watson related, that 'the reasons given for his sacking were to do with coming into conflict with Antonio do Passo who was the football director of the CBD'.[23] Throw in the stumbling performances and disappointing results of the team and Saldanha's reaction to them, and it was a toxic cocktail that made his dismissal almost inevitable. The volatile Saldanha may only have ever been a short-term solution in Havelange's mind anyway, someone to lift the gloom that had settled over the *Seleção* and its performances. When the rain had stopped, had he

---

23 *Jornal de Brasil*, 18 March 1970

decided that it was time to put the umbrella away? Sam Kunti pondered the possibility, 'Had Havelange's intention been to use him and then discard him once Saldanha had served his purpose? Possibly, but with Brazil under a military dictatorship it was always going to be unlikely for a communist coach to lead the team at the World Cup.'

No one was surprised when Saldanha declined to accept the decision with good grace. Immediately returning to his old hunting ground of the press room, he let it be known that the team, and some of its biggest stars, were in big trouble. Pelé, he alleged, had serious issues with myopia, often could not detect the location of the ball during matches, and should be kept out of the team. Gérson was said to have mental problems that often stopped him playing at his best and goalkeeper Leão had short arms. It all reads like tantrums being voiced through a mouth full of sour grapes. Pelé would later retort sarcastically that perhaps if he hadn't been so short-sighted he would have 2,000 goals. Now outside the tent once more, Saldanha hurled rocks at the *Seleção* and would continue to do so while reporting on the Mexico World Cup for TV Globo.

Ousting Saldanha was only one side of the coin. Who would replace him? There were just a couple of months until the World Cup and the team didn't have a coach. Behind the scenes though, even before the decision to remove Saldanha, moves had been afoot at the CBD. Born in Rio de Janeiro, Otto Glória had proven his worth with Benfica, winning four league titles. He had also led Portugal against his native country in the key game that confirmed Brazil's elimination from the 1966 World Cup, before taking the Portuguese to an impressive third-placed finish in the tournament. Havelange wanted a more local option though. Top of the list was Dino Sani, but talks with the Corinthians coach hadn't gone well and on 18 March the post was offered to Botafogo's Mário Zagallo, who readily accepted.

Zagallo had taken up a post at the club he had played for since 1958, leading Botafogo's junior team, before being handed the role of head coach in 1967. The man now selected to take charge of Brazil's dreams of World Cup glory had then delivered early success for the *Estrela Solitária*, winning the Rio de Janeiro State Championship in 1967 and 1968, and adding the Campeonato Brasileiro Série A in the latter of those two years. A young coach, already carrying the respect of many of the players due to his experience with the *Seleção*, Zagallo seemed the ideal antidote to Saldanha. Calm and understated, he coached like he played – diligent and dedicated, with little time for the fripperies of fame. He wanted success and was used to achieving it.

If Havelange had seized an opportune moment to move Saldanha out, the Brazilian military junta were also motivated to act. Wrapping their arms around a country's sporting success is no stranger to governments, especially authoritarian ones. The Argentine junta following the 1978 World Cup being a clear example. With results on the decline, a dispute between the former coach, Havelange and members of the team being played out in the media, and the World Cup only months away, the decision was made that Brazil's fortunes on the football field were simply too great a matter of national importance to be left to others. The military were stepping in.

Brazil's minister for education and sport, Jarbas Passarínho, was called to meet with Médici. The newly self-anointed football expert instructed the minister to demand that Havelange produce a full report on the crisis, to be submitted to him by the middle of the following week. Passarínho also ordered that an impartial commission should be urgently set up to undertake medical examinations of some of the players. If the team were to underperform in Mexico, the junta now had the cover of saying that they did all they could to solve the problem. If, on the other hand, Brazil succeeded, the glory could be grasped by the government, as their very own, for rescuing the team from a crisis. When invited to consider how invested the government were in the fate of the *Seleção*'s Mexican adventure, Dr Watson was in little doubt, 'I think they were very interested indeed, as they needed a national unifying cause, given some disquiet and rising opposition during the Costa e Silva presidency … The presence of Brigadier Jerônimo Bastos as head of the delegation [to Mexico] is indicative of how much the military was focused on a successful tournament … I can't think of many other occasions when the military was so close to the team, certainly not in Brazil. There was some proximity in Argentina in 1978, but mostly just assuring that the best players that Menotti wanted were all available to be trained together all the time.'

For all the bile that followed his removal, it would be wrong to downplay Saldanha's influence on the team that arrived in Mexico and his input into the way they played. The decision to implement DaCosta's ideas was key, and looking at the team he selected for his last game in charge – the 2-1 victory over Argentina – and comparing it to Zagallo's starting 11 in the opening match of the World Cup offers sound evidence. Of the outfield players who appeared against Czechoslovakia, only three didn't take part against Argentina. Rivellino and Tostão were both unavailable to Saldanha and would surely have played had that not been the case, leaving just Everaldo as the only true 'first-choice' difference, a player Saldanha had already capped three times in the previous year. Perhaps he should have been selected more often though. He certainly had an enviable record in international football. Across his 24-game career with the *Seleção*, the Grêmio defender would be on the losing side just once, in the 2-1 defeat to Mexico in October 1968.

Initially, Pelé had welcomed Saldanha's appointment and he may well have been the right man at the right time as Moreira's reign drifted away. Now, however, despite much of the team being in place, a different approach was needed, a calmer hand on the tiller, and Brazil's brightest star welcomed the arrival of his old team-mate from the triumphs of 1958 and 1962. It's a view that Andrew Downie recognises, commenting, 'The Brazilian players all say that Zagallo changed the team. He gave them greater balance.'

The new man at the helm had already led the team for a couple of games, but now in full charge he could set things up his own way. Building on the professionalism of the preparations already taking place with regard to player fitness, he added Cláudio Coutinho and Carlos Alberto Parreira to the coaching roster, both of whom would go on to lead the team at World Cups in their own right in later years. His first test would come in a friendly against Chile at the Estádio do Morumbi in São Paulo on 22 March. A good performance and result would be the ideal start to his reign, and with braces from both Pelé and Roberto Miranda – wearing the number nine shirt temporarily vacated by Tostão's absence – and a goal from Gérson, that's precisely what Zagallo got with a comfortable and reassuring 5-0 victory – a situation helped by the dismissal of Colo-Colo's Carlos Caszely. It was something of a false dawn, however.

Three days later, back in the Maracanã, things were more than a little different. A largely unchanged *Seleção*, with Félix returning in goal to replace Leão, fought to a 2-1 victory. Goals from Carlos Alberto and Rivellino more than wiped out Osvaldo Castro's opening strike. The game, however, was marred by four players, two from each side, being dismissed by Brazilian referee Airton Vieira de Moraes. Roberto Miranda and Jairzinho left Brazil down to nine men and Moisés Silva together with Gustavo Laube did the same for Chile. They were two rumbustious matches, but at least Zagallo had seen his team come through in difficult circumstances, as they headed into a hectic programme of five fixtures in April – including two on the same day – before heading out to Mexico.

Zagallo had inherited Saldanha's 4-2-4 formation, but it was far from being his preferred mode of play. As a player he had nominally been a left-winger, and that was certainly the case as Brazil attacked. When out of possession and defending, however, he would drop deeper to supplement the midfield, making the formation more of a 4-3-3. Saldanha's team had zipped through the qualifiers, and in Paulo Cézar and Edu had two young left-wingers who suited 4-2-4. If the new coach was to evolve his team into his preferred way of playing, either of those two would need to adapt their game, or he would have to manufacture a new 'Zagallo' in the image of his playing days. It wasn't the only change that would be required.

In the first of those five games, four of which would be on consecutive Sundays, Zagallo took his players into the north of the country to the capital of the state of Amazonas, the city of Manaus. On 5 April they would have successive matches at the Estádio Vivaldo Lima, first facing an

Amazonas state 'B' team, before then playing the 'A' team. While both were deemed as unofficial friendlies, the first was barely more than a practice game, with no fewer than four local players – Catita, Evandro, Pretinho and Pompeu – slotting into Zagallo's team, allowing him to save more players for the second game. That Brazil won 4-1 is hardly of relevance. What was significant, though, is that it marked the first tentative steps back towards a return to the *Seleção* for Tostão.

In the second match, a more recognisable Brazil team repeated that score with Carlos Alberto, Paulo Cézar, Rivellino and Pelé finding the back of the net. This game also marked the return of another player who had been absent for a while, with Everaldo given a starting berth on the left of the defence. The Grêmio defender hadn't been selected in the starting 11 for the *Seleção* since December 1968 and, despite a substitute appearance in the final warm-up game before the World Cup, wouldn't do so again until the tournament's opener against the Czechs. In 1969, Marco Antônio of Fluminense had replaced the established Rildo in the left-back slot, signalling the end of the Santos defender's international career, and looked set to be first choice in Mexico, after he started all of the remaining games running up to the tournament's opening. He was included in the squad, and made a couple of substitute appearances, but when Zagallo announced his team for the opening game it was Everaldo, not Marco Antônio, at left-back. Perhaps Zagallo was aware of the defender's record as a lucky charm for the *Seleção*, only having suffered defeat once while wearing the *Canarinho* shirt. The coach kept him in the team throughout the tournament, and that record remained intact.

Zagallo had also used the opportunity of playing two games to deploy each of the two strikers seemingly vying for a place alongside Pelé in the forward line. Atlético Mineiro's Dário started in the first game and Roberto Miranda in the second. With eight goals coming across the two there were encouraging signs but, with tougher tasks ahead, neither would prove to be the answer in the longer term.

A week later on 12 April, the *Seleção* took to the field at the Maracanã to face Paraguay in a friendly, with two players making their debuts. Rogério had his first taste of international football and in the coming weeks would do enough to convince Zagallo to select him in the squad for Mexico, before a late injury scuppered his dreams. The other player involved for the first time was Dário. Roberto Miranda had played consecutive games alongside Pelé without convincing Zagallo that it was the pairing to take to the World Cup. Now Dário would have his chance. Whether that opportunity came at the behest of Médici or even the persistent rumours about the president favouring the forward is unknown but, given that Médici would surely have been invited by Havelange to sign off on Saldanha's replacement, a certain pliability in receiving advice may well have been something important on the new coach's CV.

The game ended goalless but, seven days later, Dário would justify his opportunity as the *Seleção* returned to Belo Horizonte and the Mineirão, the forward's home ground, to face a Minas Gerais State XI. Perhaps it was the familiar surroundings, or maybe a less than overly conscientious opposition, eight of whom played for Atlético Mineiro, the same club as Dário, but the forward notched a brace of goals to add to Gérson's opener before substitute Natal reduced the arrears to 3-1.

On 26 April Brazil played their penultimate match before flying to Mexico, facing Bulgaria in São Paulo's Estádio do Morumbi. Again, the status of this game is questionable. Although the CBD rated it as a full international, the Bulgarian FA record it as being a 'B' team selection, while other records denote the eastern Europeans as being an under-23 team. Whatever the merits of that, as with the game against Paraguay, it ended goalless. Regardless of the correct classification for their opponents, the fact that Brazil had failed to find the back of the net, as had been the case in their previous international against Paraguay, there was plenty to concern Zagallo.

There was a bright spark for the *Seleção*, however, as Tostão returned to the starting 11. He had completed his convalescence following eye surgery, and after the gentle run-out against the Amazonas state 'B' team three weeks earlier, it was time to get him back into action if there was to be any chance at all of being included in the World Cup squad. After being cleared to return to the squad, initially there was an understandable reluctance to get involved in anything over-physical and a noticeable caution about heading the ball. Confidence slowly returned though and, with the tournament so close, Zagallo had to test whether the forward was going to be both fit enough and confident enough to offer his best for the team. Tostão's return wasn't as a partner to Pelé, however. Both he and Dário were omitted from the starting team with Roberto Miranda playing alongside the returning Cruzeiro forward. Pelé would enter as a substitute, but it was to replace, rather than join, Tostão.

Three days later the team was back in the Maracanã, with Tostão retained in the starting 11, this time with Pelé alongside him. Austria provided the opposition for Zagallo's last game before leaving Brazil, and a Rivellino goal sent the team off to the World Cup with the momentum of a win behind them, albeit a narrow one. Paulo Cézar had started in each of the games since Zagallo replaced Saldanha. With Edu only offered a brief substitute appearance against the Minas Gerais State XI, and just a single game to play before flying out of Brazil for preparation in Mexico, the Botafogo wide man looked to have nailed down the left-wing role. It wasn't to be.

Despite the consistency of selection, on the left of Brazil's attack, Paulo Cézar had failed to convince Zagallo that he could fulfil the role required of him under the coach's system. The ploy of adapting a dedicated left-winger into someone who could also function in midfield, as Zagallo had done himself, had palpably failed. Another plan was required but with precious little time remaining.

Rivellino had excelled as an attacking midfielder for Corinthians in a role similar to that performed by Pelé for both Santos and the *Seleção*. In that position, however, the chances of Rivellino establishing himself in the Brazil team were severely limited, with Pelé an immovable obstacle in front of him. Zagallo had granted Rivellino just a single starting appearance, alongside Clodoaldo in midfield against the Amazonas state 'A' team, before being replaced by Piazza part way through the game. That, and a couple of substitute appearances in similar roles, had offered precious little evidence that Rivellino would be a key player in the World Cup. However, he would play every minute of every game, save for the final group match against Romania, when injury offered Paulo Cézar a brief chance to regain the position that, for so long, had appeared to be his, but had been lost.

Against the Austrians, Zagallo placed Rivellino on the left flank, with instructions to drop back into midfield when the team were defending, not so much a 'false nine' but more of a 'false 11'. Naturally left-footed, it looked like a good fit, but nothing can be taken for certain until it is proven. He had neither the speed or guile of a Paulo Cézar, but his tendency to drift inside would open up channels of attack for Everaldo in Mexico. Initially, the player was both nervous and excited, knowing the high stakes he was playing for, later describing it as the most important game of his life. If he could make the role work then the position was his; if not, then a place on the plane to Mexico wasn't even guaranteed. Rivellino wasn't the only player to be offered a chance to prove he could make a different position his own.

Wilson Piazza had made a career from being a dedicated defensive midfielder. He was a dogged and hard-working holding player in front of the back line, with a sweat-drenched shirt after the game proving to him that he had delivered a good performance for both Cruzeiro and in his 16 full internationals up to that point. With the emergence of Clodoaldo as the ideal foil for Gérson, though, his chances had been limited to a single substitute appearance under Zagallo. The experienced Brito was established at the heart of the defence, having played every minute of every game since Zagallo's appointment, but the question of who should fill the position alongside the Flamengo defender was far from settled.

In the games since taking control of the *Seleção*, Zagallo had mixed and matched several options without being totally convinced by any of them. Joel Camargo of Santos had been the man in possession when Zagallo took over from Saldanha, alongside Cruzeiro's Fontana and Baldocchi of Palmeiras, but Zagallo, despite the latter two being in the final squad for Mexico, was unconvinced. For the game against Austria, not only was Rivellino dropped into an unaccustomed role, the same was true for Pizzaro, as Zagallo placed him in the back line.

Further forward, Tostão and Pelé were united in the front line for the first time since the 1-0 win over Paraguay on the last day of August 1969. Both Roberto Miranda and Dário were accomplished goalscorers, although the latter would never find the back of the net in any of the official international games in which he appeared for the Seleção, but Zagallo wanted more than that. Both forwards would go to Mexico but Dário would never set foot on the pitch for match action, and Roberto Miranda's involvement was limited to a couple of substitute cameo appearances. He replaced Tostão for the final 22 minutes against England and was sent on for Jairzinho after 80 minutes in the quarter-final against Peru. Much as Clodoaldo and Gérson complemented each other, Tostão did the same for Pelé. Intelligent and prepared to sacrifice a part of his game to create more space for Pelé, Rivellino's requirement to drop deeper when required also created space for Tostão to exploit on the left.

Brazil would win 1-0 as Rivellino celebrated his return to the team with the goal. The performance was hardly impressive though. Playing at home against an Austrian team who had only finished above Cyprus in a qualifying group that also included West Germany and Scotland did nothing to convince observers that Zagallo had managed to find the perfect blend. And yet the team that would entrance the world in Mexico just over a month later was nearing completion. Marco Antônio would maintain his place at left-back across the remaining preparation games in Mexico, before Everaldo took over as the tournament began. The only other change would be that the unfortunate Rogério, who started on the right flank against the Austrians ahead of Jairzinho, would miss out on playing at the World Cup due to a late injury. It was unlikely that he would have displaced the Botafogo winger when the real action started, and a place on the bench with a late entrance into a game was probably the best he could have hoped for.

A single win, and just a single goal, in their last three internationals had injected more than a measure of caution into the hopes of Brazilian fans. Unlike in 1966 when confidence – even overconfidence – chased the team across the Atlantic to England, four years later there were doubts, and even pessimism, as Rivellino confirmed, 'We left the country with everyone thinking Brazil wouldn't even get through their group.'[24]

The draw for the groups of the 1970 finals had taken place on 10 January 1970 in Mexico City's grand Maria Isabel Hotel, where FIFA would house their headquarters for the extent of the tournament. In both 1962 and 1966, a seeding system had been employed to keep the top teams from eliminating each other until the latter stages. It had been widely assumed that this would also be the case in Mexico, but disagreements as to which teams should be seeded, in which order, eventually ruled that out and, on the day of the draw, FIFA announced that the teams competing would be placed into four different pots, defined geographically. The more-favoured European teams were

---

24 Downie, Andrew, *The Greatest Show on Earth* (London: Arena Sports, 2021)

placed in Pot 1, labelled 'European 1'. This comprised England, as holders, West Germany, the beaten finalists from four years earlier, the Soviet Union, who had been losing semi-finalists in England, plus the reigning European champions, Italy.

In Pot 2, 'Americas' were Mexico, Brazil, Peru and Uruguay. Pot 3, 'European 2', contained the assumed-to-be lesser lights of European qualification – Belgium, Bulgaria, Czechoslovakia and Sweden. Finally, Pot 4 was labelled as 'Rest of the World'. It was made up of El Salvador, Israel, Morocco and Romania, with the eastern Europeans apparently deemed less worthy of geographical accuracy than the members of Pots 1 and 3.

There was also a political dimension, as always, to this particular method of grouping, as it eliminated the possibility of Morocco facing Israel in a group game. The North Africans had withdrawn from the Olympic football tournament two years earlier rather than face Israel, and had threatened to do so again. With neither team likely to progress from the group stages, placing them in the same pot largely eliminated this potential danger.

Each of the four groups would contain a team from each pot with the locations for the groups defined before the draw. Group 1 would play in Mexico City's cavernous Estadio Azteca. Group 2 would be split between Puebla and Toluca. Group 3 teams would play in Guadalajara's Estadio Jalisco, and Group 4 would be placed in León. The only pre-draw decisions were that, as holders, England would be placed in Group 3, playing in Guadalajara and, as hosts, Mexico would have the honour of playing in their own capital city, as the ten-year-old daughter of Guillermo Cañedo, president of the Mexican Football Federation and chief of the FIFA

Organising Committee, repeatedly dipped her hand into four silver cups to decide the composition of the groups.

When all was completed, Brazil had been placed in Group 3 alongside England, Czechoslovakia and Romania. Covering the draw on British television, Brian Moore somewhat optimistically declared to the watching millions that an England v Brazil final 'was possible'. Such optimism would later be exposed as hubris, but the groupings did draw a sharp focus on how Brazil would complete their preparations for the tournament.

With just over a month before the start of the World Cup, the squad took off from Rio and travelled to their base in Guadalajara, landing there on the second day of May. The plan was to stay there for five days, acclimatise to the conditions, settle into their hotel and play a friendly against local club Chivas Guadalajara. The game would not only give the team a chance to introduce themselves to the local fans, but also play in the Estadio Jalisco where their group fixtures would take place. The initial five days in Guadalajara were merely the prelude to what Zagallo asserted would be a much longer stay in Mexico, as Sam Kunti related in his book, with Zagallo claiming that Brazil 'was the first team to arrive but would be the last to leave'.[25] DaCosta's scheduling had meant they were the first team to land in Mexico, and the coach was convinced an extra seat would be required on their flight home – for the Jules Rimet Trophy.

On 7 May they would then move on to Guanajuato, and play against another local club, Deportivo León. They would

25 Kunti, Sam, *Brazil 1970: How the Greatest Team of All Time Won the World Cup* (Worthing, England: Pitch Publishing Ltd, 2022)

stay there for just short of three weeks. As well as playing the game, they would endure gruelling fitness sessions designed to harness the advantages of the higher altitude and fine-tune their physical levels, before finally travelling to Irapuato on 27 May and a final warm-up match against the local team there, and more fitness work. Each of these destinations were at a higher altitude above sea level than Guadalajara's 5,400ft. The schedule allowed the players to benefit from what was, in effect, a few weeks of altitude training before returning back down to Guadalajara fully prepared for the opening game. DaCosta's schedule was being followed. Altogether, they would be away for several weeks. It would allow sufficient time for the benefits to remain in the players' systems all the way through the tournament, and to still be there if they reached the final in Mexico City's 7,300ft above sea level. It was another element of the meticulously planned preparation that would deliver the team in the best physical shape possible, despite playing all of their matches, up to the final, at sea level in Guadalajara.

The game in the Estadio Jalisco brought a 3-0 win for the *Seleção*, and a third successive start for the returning Tostão, but Zagallo was careful to ease him back into the action. In the previous two games he had been substituted, first by Pelé against Bulgaria and then by Dário against Austria. The same thing would happen against Chivas, with Dário again taking his place, and perhaps offering up a dilemma for Zagallo. The president's assumed favourite was a genuine frontman rather than a player adapting to a new role to avoid being a second option to Pelé as was the case with Tostão. It wasn't as simple as that though. As well as playing their own role, an ability to mesh with the players around them, Pelé, Gérson, Rivellino and Jairzinho would also weigh heavy on Zagallo's mind. There were a couple more games for the coach to make his decision.

Before he could do that, however, fate would take a hand in ruling out one player and putting the participation of another in serious jeopardy as the squad moved up to the higher altitude of Guanajuato. This was business, pure and simple, and far from being a luxury excursion, as Rivellino later recalled, 'It was endless boredom. Our resolve to win that World Cup was tested. The food was awful, it was hot as hell and every night we had to check our rooms to see if there were scorpions. Everyone complained but Pelé. He was fired up because in 1966 he got an injury against Portugal, Brazil were knocked out and many people in Brazil said he was finished.'[26]

Less than two weeks before the start of the tournament, Zagallo was forced into a change from his intended squad. Right-winger Rogério, who had made his third appearance for the *Seleção* against Chivas in Guadalajara, was injured during a training session and declared unfit for the tournament. The unfortunate Botafogo player was distraught to miss out at such a late stage but, rather than send him home, Zagallo retained him in the party as a scout for the tournament. Although his career still had six years to run, Rogério's two outings up to that point would never be added to. His scouting for Zagallo provided important information to the coach, however, and given he was surely destined for only cameo appearances at best in the tournament, the injury may well have increased his contribution to Brazil's triumph. The early introduction

26 https://www.dailymail.co.uk/sport/football/article-8444069/Im-not-dead-Pele-inspired-Brazil-redemption-1970-World-Cup-Mexico.html

to elements of coaching didn't influence Rogério's longer-term thinking. After retiring from playing, his life took a different direction and he later became a Reverend of the World Messianic Church of Brazil.

The obvious solution would have been for the coach to select a like-for-like replacement. Instead, Zagallo selected a third goalkeeper, Leão, having originally decided to just take two – 32-year-old first-choice Félix, and backup Ado. Astutely, the coach turned the loss of Rogério into an opportunity to boost the confidence of Jairzinho, as the winger later recalled. 'Zagallo would often talk to the players individually,' he explained. 'He took me aside and said, "Jair, I have total confidence in you, and because of this I'm not going to call up another player to play on the wing [following Rogério's injury]. We're going to count on you." I thanked him for putting his trust in me. It meant a lot.'[27] Zagallo would be richly rewarded in Mexico, not only for that decision, but also for the way he delivered it to Jairzinho, and his investment in man-management.

The FIFA deadline for finalising the squads was eight days before the tournament started. So, even though it was unlucky to lose Rogério, at least the timing meant that Brazil would still go into the World Cup with a full complement of players. As fate would have it, adding the extra goalkeeper had no tangible merit on the field. Félix would play in every game and Ado would end his career with just three caps. Leão, however, would represent the national team on 80 occasions, featuring in the World Cups of 1974 and 1978, and achieve the distinction of being the first goalkeeper to captain the *Seleção*, in the latter tournament.

––––

27 Donald, Michael, *Goal!* (London: Hamlyn, 2017)

While in Guanajuato, Brazil played against Deportivo León, with Zagallo's plans now being nicely tuned. Of the starting 11 that eased to a comfortable 5-2 win over the Mexican club side, ten would also take the field against Czechoslovakia a couple of weeks later. Only Everaldo, who displaced Marco Antônio, would elbow his way into the team. When asked for his opinions on why Zagallo eventually settled on the Grêmio defender rather than the more experienced Marco Antônio, Sam Kunti offered an explanation for the coach's decision, 'Ultimately, Zagallo thought of Marco Antonio as too attacking – and I don't think Marco Antonio has ever forgiven him for it! With Carlos Alberto Torres pushing up on the right, his team would perhaps be too exposed. Zagallo always wanted balance – [as a player] he personified 4-3-3 shuttling up and down the wing in 1958 and he used that same success formula again in 1970, discarding Saldanha's more open 4-2-4 for a 4-3-3 with Rivellino in the false-winger role. Zagallo was much more conservative and firmly believed that Brazil would have no chance against the European teams in a 4-2-4.'

The victory was sweet enough but, afterwards, renewed concern about Tostão's eye threatened to throw the coach's plans into disarray. The forward appeared to have convinced Zagallo that not only was he fit enough to play, both physically and mentally, but having tried out other options with Dário and Roberto Miranda, Tostão – in his more advanced position – looked the best team option. After the game against Deportivo León, the coach confirmed as much to the player but a couple of days later things were back up in the air. A haemorrhage appeared in Tostão's eye, which had been operated on in Houston, and Dr Roberto Abdalla, the surgeon involved, was brought in to assess the situation. Fortunately, after a day-long drive up to Guanajuato, the good doctor was able to deliver the required words of calming reassurance. Everything concerning the operation was fine and there were no adverse effects from playing, and no danger in continuing to do so. A simple case of conjunctivitis was diagnosed, and the green light to continue playing was delivered.

Having gone through so much since that fateful game back in October, Tostão was understandably massively relieved to be given the all-clear by the doctor to play in the World Cup. The previous months had seen times of great concern, 'There was a risk I wouldn't get my sight back. Then I had to convince the [ophthalmologists] to clear me to play. Then I had to convince the *Seleção* doctors. I hadn't done anything except read books – my other eye worked – for six months. I had to get my fitness and rhythm back. Saldanha, who believed a lot in me, left. Zagallo didn't know me and was sceptical over my injury. Plus, the *Seleção* had been in training for the World Cup for a while. I only returned just before the World Cup began and then a hemorrhage appeared in my eye. Think about all that!'[28] Tostão obviously did. For the final, the doctor was invited to attend the game as a guest of the *Seleção* and, when the team finally escaped from the chaotic scenes of victory on the pitch, back in the sanctuary of the dressing room, his former patient passed his World Cup winner's medal to Dr Abdalla. The debt for the successful surgery, that urgent journey and the day-long drive was paid in full.

---

28 https://www.fifa.com/fifaplus/en/articles/tostao-interview-brazil-fifa-world-cup-pele-maradona-cristiano-messi

A week after beating Deportivo León, the *Seleção* played their final fixture before the World Cup began, in the Estadio Irapuato, against the local Mexican club team. It was decision time for Zagallo and it clearly showed as he made seven substitutions throughout the game. One of the few players to stay on the pitch for the full 90 minutes, however, was Tostão. His inclusion for the World Cup was now surely sealed, but there would be disappointment for Edu. The teenage Santos winger had featured regularly in Saldanha's teams but convincing Zagallo of his merits was proving to be a tougher nut to crack, having made just one substitute appearance during the new coach's short reign. That would be the case in this game as well as he took to the pitch to replace Jairzinho. His efforts would come to nought. When shortly afterwards Zagallo's squad was confirmed, Edu's name was in the 22, but he would only have a 15-minute role in Mexico. The young flyer had excelled under Saldanha's tactics but Zagallo's approach made him a square peg, unable to fit into the round hole that the coach's drill required. Brazil would win 3-0 with goals from Paulo Cézar, Roberto Miranda and Rivellino. Nine days later, the man who scored the last goal in Brazil's preparation for the World Cup would also open their account when the tournament got under way.

Part 3 – Down Mexico Way[29]

The Squad – Finalising the Guest List

When Mário Zagallo confirmed his squad of 22 players for World Cup duty to FIFA, he had been in charge of the *Seleção* for just ten games, only half of which had been internationals, and one of them had even been downgraded to a 'B' game by the Bulgarian FA. It was hardly a CV ringing with comforting experience having, by necessity, been established in a few short months on the international stage. The three goalkeepers were the first-choice Félix, established backup Ado and the late arrival of Leão who, somewhat appropriately, was given the number 22 shirt. Neither of the latter two would feature in the tournament as the Fluminense custodian played every minute of every game.

As with the goalkeeper, the Brazil defence of 1970 lived in relative shadow compared to the spotlight that shone so brightly on the team's forward players, illuminating their brilliance. Two of the now first-choice back four were well established. The remaining pair were much less so as part of an international back line. Leading the defence, as well as the team, was skipper Carlos Alberto. Although just 25 years of age, the Santos defender had played 55 times for the *Seleção*, 42 of them in official internationals. The right of Brazil's defence was well served. Inside of him for much of the tournament would be Brito and Piazza. Although slightly less experienced than the team's captain in terms of appearances for the *Seleção*, Brito was well established in the middle of the defence. Now 30 years old, this would be his last World Cup. He had travelled to England under Feola four years earlier, although only made the one appearance after the coach had changed his entire defence for the crucial game against Portugal.

Alongside him was Piazza who had played most of his career as a holding midfield player. Ahead of the tournament, playing for Cruzeiro, he had filled in as an emergency cover when his team were down to ten men, and it was a similar event that led to him playing alongside Brito at the heart of the *Seleção* back line. With a Cruzeiro team-mate apparently ahead of him in the pecking order for a place in midfield, Piazza's chances of featuring in the World Cup were hardly spectacularly bright, but that changed one day in training ahead of the game against Austria when two defenders were unable to take part and Zagallo pushed erstwhile midfielder deeper to cover. To commit himself to a new role was undoubtedly a risk, but also an opportunity.

When the defenders regained fitness they would be fighting to get their places back but, with Piazza convinced that he was unlikely to play in his established role, it offered a pathway into the team, and he grasped the opportunity with both hands, convincing Zagallo to start him against the Austrians and all three Mexican clubs. Having the footballing skills of Piazza in his defence, despite his lack of experience as a centre-back, was a compelling opportunity for Zagallo. Piazza would accompany Brito in the opening two group games against Czechoslovakia and England, before slotting back into midfield for the final rubber against Romania, and then returning to defence for the remaining games.

The left side of the back four was the real surprise. First choice was Everaldo who, as mentioned above, had forced his way into Zagallo's thinking at the 59th minute of the 11th hour, and would start every game in the tournament except for the quarter-final against Peru. An injury in the final group match had forced him from the field to be replaced by Marco Antônio on the hour. The Fluminense defender would also start the game against Peru, but Everaldo was back for the semi-final. Of the block of regular starters, all were numbered one to 11, save for Everaldo. Sporting the number 16 on his back suggests how late he was to the party.

The remaining six positions were fairly fluid throughout the tournament, each assuming legendary status as the World Cup progressed. But, with Brazil in possession, there was a 4-2-4 formation. Gérson and Clodoaldo provided the middle of midfield, with Clodoaldo the least celebrated and lauded of the pair. The Santos player was certainly more defensively minded of the two, allowing Gérson to push forward, create and score, but he still exhibited exorbitant skills. Jairzinho would be on the right flank, and would score in every game in Mexico. Rivellino took up position on the left, at least until Brazil lost possession, with Pelé and Tostão nominally in the middle.

There's already been plenty said about Pelé, and rightly so, for he was the totemic talisman of the team. Tostão, however, is worthy of similar acclaim but, for many outside of South America at least, he remains the least lauded member of the forward quartet; being more remembered for his tortuous journey to the finals than his accomplishments on the pitch. That should not be the case, and certainly isn't in Brazil, as Andrew Downie would confirm, 'Tostão is not a lesser celebrated member of the squad in Brazil. In Brazil everyone recognises he was one of the great performers in that tournament. Tostão and Pelé played in similar positions for their clubs and he knew he wasn't going to unseat Pelé so he decided to change his role to fit in, and it only came good days before the tournament. But Tostão was a key player.' Downie makes the point well, but it should be added that not only did Tostão excel, he did so by sacrificing some of his own natural abilities, by occupying opposition defenders and creating more space for Pelé, for the greater good of the team.

Of the squad selected, those 11 players provided the core of the team that would carry Brazil to World Cup glory. Five others would make appearances, some of them fleeting. The Cruzeiro defender Fontana played in his seventh, and last, international for the *Seleção* in the final group game against Romania, as Piazza moved forward into a temporary midfield role, replacing the injured Rivellino, who had been moved into a central midfield position to replace the injured Gérson in the previous game.

Paulo Cézar was called on as a substitute to replace Gérson against Czechoslovakia after 62 minutes. With the game won, Zagallo opted against risking more damage to the injury that the midfielder had been carrying into the tournament. Paulo Cézar then retained his place in the team, against both England and Romania, with Gérson not recovering in time to reclaim his starting berth until the quarter-finals.

Wearing number six, Marco Antônio was the only player with a numbered shirt between one and 11 not to be part of the regular starting 11, losing out to Everaldo. He would make two cameo appearances. First, he replaced his nemesis on the hour against Romania, and then was sent on as Jairzinho was substituted against Peru with ten minutes to play, and Zagallo looking to see the game out with his side 4-2 ahead. The young Santos forward Edu had made the squad despite falling down the pecking order under Zagallo, after being a regular starter under Saldanha. His only time on the pitch in Mexico was as a late substitute for Clodoaldo with quarter of an hour to play against Romania.

At one stage during the preparations for the tournament it had seemed likely that it would be Roberto Miranda rather than Tostão leading the attack alongside Pelé. With the Cruzeiro forward returning to fitness and considered the better option by the coach, however, Roberto Miranda fell out of favour. He made the trip as part of the squad but only managed two brief substitute appearances. Twenty-two minutes against England after replacing Tostão and a further ten, after coming on for Jairzinho in the quarter-final against Peru, completed his World Cup active service.

The other forward who had been considered as an option, had Tostão not been given the green light by the medical staff and Zagallo, was Dário, the Atlético Mineiro man and rumoured President Médici favourite. Had Zagallo not delivered the trophy, the fact that Dário never got on the pitch in Mexico may have required some explanation to the junta's top man. Taking the World Cup home, however, negated any such requirement. Aside from the two goalkeepers mentioned above, fate would also deny any playing time to three defenders selected in the squad: Zé

Maria of Portuguesa, Santos's Joel Camargo and Baldocchi of Palmeiras. With the studious preparations complete and the squad confirmed, all was now set.

On Friday, 29 May, ahead of the opening ceremony that would take place two days later, writing in *The Times*, Geoffrey Green cited the words that Sir Stanley Rous, president of FIFA, would use to invite the Mexican president to officially declare the tournament open, 'All is ready for a memorable feast of top-level football and it gives me the greatest pleasure to ask you, Mr President, to declare open the championship.'[30] Green then went on to comment in the same article that, 'In three weeks' time we shall hope to look back and find that it all was memorable and a feast.'[31] Twenty-one days later, neither Green nor any observer with the ideal of beautiful football in their soul would be disappointed. It would indeed be a most memorable feast. Probably the greatest team in the history of the World Cup would outshine even the dazzling light of the Mexican summer sun, and enthral the watching millions across the world, as they were invited to join Brazil's 1970 World Cup Samba Party.

* * *

The Group Stages – Getting the Ball Rolling

To many people, the 1970 World Cup was the first of the modern era. The ninth edition of the tournament was the first to be played outside of either Europe or South America, and with the advancement in satellite technology it was the first to broadcast games around the globe in colour,

---

30 'Temperature divides contenders', *The Times*, 29 May 1970
31 'Temperature divides contenders', *The Times*, 29 May 1970

attracting a record television audience and delighting FIFA as sponsorship revenue from such organisations as Esso, Philips and Martini reflected the worldwide coverage of their names on hoardings surrounding the pitches.

Another first for the tournament was the link to global television satellite technology. The Adidas Telstar ball made its first appearance at a World Cup, taking its title from the satellite of the same name due to its black-and-white-panelled appearance apparently echoing the dotted solar panels on the celestial communications device beaming images around the world. The ball's revolutionary design had originally been created to aid visibility in monochrome television broadcasts but, from this time forward, it would forever be associated with the 1970 World Cup. *GQ* magazine summed the instantly totemic status of the new ball nicely, 'Funkier and almost instantly iconic, the Telstar heralded a new, looser decade, in the process asking the footballing nations to undo their top buttons. The Brazilians were only too willing to comply.'[32] And didn't they just.

Ahead of the tournament, there were concerns about how the heat of a Mexican summer, coupled with the high-altitude locations for some of the stadiums, would impact matches, causing cautious tactics as teams played slow and defensively to conserve energy. As things transpired, despite both of those factors being apparent, the 1970 finals produced an abundance of attacking football and a record average of goals per game in postwar tournaments that remains unsurpassed up to the time of writing. The fervour of the Mexican supporters, the shimmering heat, the accompanying crackling commentary sounding as if

---

32 https://www.gq-magazine.co.uk/sport/article/mexico-1970-world-cup

it was coming from the moon, and the vivid colours on television screens all conspired to deliver a unique World Cup experience. All that was needed now was a team to claim the starring role and define it as their own. The world would not have to wait long for their identity to be revealed.

Outside of Brazil, and even outside of South America generally, the *Seleção* were not widely regarded as one of the favourites. Even inside the country, despite the obviously required optimism of the players, hopes were not high, as Andrew Downie suggests, '[The players] still believed they were the best in the world and wanted to prove it again and show that 1966 was an aberration. I don't think anyone goes into a World Cup thinking they want to provide the best World Cup team of all time. Brazil went to the 1970 World Cup under a cloud. No one in Brazil thought they were going to win.' Even allowing for a measure of necessary audience-empathy, Geoffrey Green's assessment in *The Times* ahead of the tournament that England, West Germany, Russia and Uruguay were more favoured to prevail was pretty much in line with mainstream opinion. Green did offer some measure of support for Brazil, but commented, '[Brazil] for all their mastery with the ball, and Italy, for all their technical flair, are both suspect when the tide runs against them.'[33]

Predicting the outcome of a single game of football, let alone an entire World Cup with three group matches and then the same number of knockout rounds, is a perilous occupation at the best of times but, if solely informed by outdated evidence, then the task is made all the more difficult. It's perhaps safe to say that Green's assessment

---

33 'Temperature divides contenders', *The Times*, 29 May 1970

of Brazil's prospects was based more on their performance in England four years earlier than the form running up to the start of this World Cup, where they had won all six of their qualifying games, scoring 23 times and conceding just twice.

Further confounding the thoughts of the illustrious scribe, on the occasions when 'the tide runs against' Brazil, they proved themselves to be far from 'suspect', refusing to allow it to wash away their aspirations. They fell behind in their opening game against Czechoslovakia, and also in the semi-final against Uruguay. Plus, in the final, they were pegged back when Roberto Boninsegna equalised following a defensive error, after Pelé had opened the scoring. In each game they turned back the tide and won. Such resilience was highlighted to the author by Andrew Downie, 'Brazil scored 12 of their 19 goals in the second half [of games]. That tells its own story. FIFA even made a mention of it in their official report.'

As part of Brazil's charm offensive ahead of the tournament's start, Pelé had donated a pair of well-worn football boots to the Industrial History Museum in León in what was reported as being a 'respectful tribute to Mexican soccer'.[34] The Brazilians would also hold 'open' training sessions where the players would hand out flowers and souvenirs to the groups of young Mexican fans watching. Courting local opinion is always a wise move, and it brought huge dividends to the *Seleção*, cementing an already pre-existing passion among the Mexican fans, second only to their adoration of *El Tri*. That approach can be seen in stark contrast to the attitude adopted by Sir Alf Ramsey's England

---

34 'Temperature divides contenders', *The Times*, 29 May 1970

team, who were kept distant from the local press and hadn't even appointed a Spanish-speaking press officer. While the Brazil squad were cheered and lauded whenever seen, the England training sessions were interrupted by Mexican fans chanting 'Mexico', or, just as importantly, 'Brazil'.

Away from training, the England players were mainly contained in their Paro de Princes hotel. While boasting many internal comforts, the impression from outside was fortress-like in outlook, boasting more than 30 uniformed Mexican police officers and an unknown number of Secret Service agents. Stone-faced and unsmiling, Ramsey was keeping the portcullis down and the drawbridge up. Conversely, at the entrance to Brazil's headquarters, Samba music was playing loudly.

The difference was not lost on the locals. Mexico were fancied to qualify from their group but perhaps not to go too much further. With *El Tri* eliminated, there was little doubt as to who the home support would swing in favour of, and this was even before a ball had been kicked and the *Seleção*'s entrancing football had won the hearts of so many neutrals across the world. The welcoming Samba Party atmosphere of the Brazilians only emphasised the cussed aloofness adopted by Ramsey, and imposed on the England party. All of this was despite reported threats of kidnapping Pelé having been received by the CBD, and the star forward apparently sleeping in different rooms each night to foil any such attempt.

As is traditional, the opening game of the tournament featured the hosts as Mexico entertained the Soviet Union in front of 107,000 people at the Estadio Azteca. Sadly, as spectacles go, the match was largely disappointing. Neither team seemed overly committed to win if it increased the possibility of losing and a consequent uphill fight from there to qualify. The game ended in a goalless draw and referee Kurt Tschenscher, who had adopted a *laissez-faire* attitude four years earlier when Bulgaria launched assault after assault on Pelé, this time delivered a far stricter performance in booking five players. The guidelines for officials at the tournament, as had also been the case in 1966, were targeted to protect skilful players and punish overly aggressive challenges. In 1966 Tschenscher had been criticised for being too lax. This time, the charges levied against him were for being too harsh, with claims of dire consequences to follow if other officials followed the German's lead. João Saldanha, who had returned to his 'day job' of journalism after being ousted by Havelange, and the Médici military junta, in favour of Zagallo, was reporting on the World Cup for TV Globo, and forecasted three weeks of 'defensive, slow, stop-go football with the tightest of official control'.[35]

Journalists are often criticised for having a chameleon-like view of things, but it seemed a strange stance for Saldanha to take given his past comments. The previous year, while in charge of the *Seleção*, Saldanha had visited Europe to watch some qualifying games. On his return he expressed alarm at the physicality he had witnessed, 'If the Mexicans, Uruguayans, Peruvians or ourselves are kicked this way there will be trouble.'[36] Now, he seemed to be criticising a referee for seeking to eliminate the more robust approaches to the game he had condemned, claiming it would lead to dull football. Whatever the sincerity of his words, he need not have worried. The team he had coached

---

35 'England must unravel blanket cover', *The Times*, 1 June 1970
36 'Rules problem in World Cup', *The Times*, December 1969

to a six-and-zero record of wins in qualification, before Zagallo replaced him, would prove his assessment to be very much wide of the mark.

Ahead of Brazil's opening fixture against Czechoslovakia, the view in the British press was that the team, and Zagallo, still had plenty to prove, as was suggested by Green's comments. Not only were observers unsure that the new man had restored a harmony and that 'balance' alluded to by Downie, but also that the players were ready to perform. This, from an article in *The Times*, summed up the issues to be addressed, 'Zagallo has only held his position for three months after taking over from Joao Saldanha. [He] had been fortunate in inheriting a wealth of talent and concentrated on building up the team's morale following the internal struggles which threatened to wreck Brazil's chances. A lot will depend on how Pelé and Tostão operate.'[37] It did, but perhaps not how that particular scribe imagined it.

Brazil opened their World Cup campaign on 3 June and, even before kick-off, as the teams lined up for the national anthems, there was an unintended suggestion as to what may follow. The Czechs wore an all-white strip with their goalkeeper dressed in black. If they were the aged and monochrome manifestation of football, albeit entirely worthy, workmanlike and well drilled, Brazil were the technicolour equivalent with their *Canarinho* shirt edged in green trim, and blue shorts, and the verdant green pitch as their canvas. Colour television had come to the World Cup and Brazil would paint some entrancing pictures with the new palette available to them.

---

37 'Brazil put pride at stake', *The Times*, 2 June 1970

After arriving in Mexico, the Czechs had struggled with the heat and endured acclimatisation difficulties. A week or so ahead of the opening game their team doctor Neadikaen Kahini explained that training had involved the players only working at half pace and 'a long way from being acclimatised', adding 'The heat is also giving them a lot of trouble.'[38] That may well have been true. A lot of European teams, especially those from the north of the continent, experienced similar issues. The outcome of this game had less to do with Czechoslovakia wilting in the heat of the Mexican sun though. Instead, they would be burned by the searingly *Canarinho* yellow heat of the Brazilians' play as they scorched the pitch with their magical football.

As the anthems ended and the teams broke away, doves were released into an unusually cloudy Mexican sky. Brazil's football would soon take flight too, lighting up the game, regardless of the sun being reluctant to peer out from behind the clouds. It meant that the celestial star missed the opening overture of the earth-bound ones, dressed in the same colour.

Less than four minutes had been played when a driven low cross from the left caused havoc in the Czechoslovakia defence as the ball arrived at Pelé's feet a few yards out and in front of a gaping net. Leaning back, however, the star could only place the ball high over the bar. Minutes later a deceptive dummy by the same player, allowing the ball to run under his feet, opened up space for Tostão to gather possession and advance into the area, but his shot was scuffed and easily gathered by Ivo Viktor in the Czechoslovakia goal.

---

38 'Heat trouble for Czechs', *The Times,* 26 May 1970

It had been a busy and purposeful opening by Brazil, but the next opportunity came at the other end. Ladislav Petráš collected a pass and muscled his way past Piazza before cutting back and evading a diving challenge by Clodoaldo. As with Pelé's chance, the moment got the better of him and he blazed wildly high and wide with just Félix to beat. He sank to his knees, head in hands. Four minutes later he would fare much better with his second opportunity and adopt a similar, if this time more celebratory, pose.

Pelé had pushed and probed at the Czechoslovakia defence without any tangible reward as Brazil began to assume control of the game, but things swung sharply in favour of the Europeans as a defensive error saw the ball gifted to Petráš just outside the Brazil box. Advancing, the Inter Bratislava forward ran on, evaded Carlos Alberto's challenge, and fired high into the net as Félix advanced to meet him. Awash with emotion, Petráš ran towards the touchline before falling to his knees and crossing himself in thanks to the celestial powers above him. That tide was now turning against Brazil. How would they respond? Andrew Downie described the prevalent attitude, 'Brazil always felt – and this was a really clear feeling at Santos – that no matter how many goals they conceded they could always score more. That carried on to the national side. Their array of talent was unbeatable.' If Petráš's prayers had included a supplication for his team to go on and win the game, it would fall on deaf ears. The tide would soon turn back in Brazil's favour.

The first chance of redemption fell to Tostão not even 60 seconds after the *Seleção* had fallen behind. A shot from distance by Gérson was half blocked, and the ball ran free to the striker. His shot beat Viktor but found the outside of the side-netting. Conceding a goal had hardly put a stumble into Brazil's stride and they continued to press forward, displaying the confidence in their ability to outscore their opponents that Downie had cited. A powerful shot from Rivellino was blocked, and then gathered by Viktor. Pelé's extravagant fall in the area brought no response from Uruguayan referee Ramón Barreto, but a worrying lack of concentration apparent in the back line nearly cost Brazil a further goal. Advancing from defence, Carlos Alberto played a casual pass inside but the captain's intention had been telegraphed. Karol Jokl stepped forward to intercept and deflect the ball to František Veselý but, at the key moment, a lack of composure betrayed the Slavia Prague forward. The shot was high and the chance was gone. Within a minute, the full cost of that miss would be apparent.

The Mexican crowd, who had been firmly behind Brazil from the start of the game, began to roar on their encouragement as Gérson and Clodoaldo exchanged passes before finding Pelé as he advanced once more. Moving the ball quickly on to Tostão opened up a gap on the edge of the box but, before he could collect the return pass and inflict any damage, Pelé was brought to the floor by a clumsy challenge from opposing captain, Alexander Horváth. The ball was placed a foot or so outside the area as both Gérson and Pelé stood over it, surveying opportunities while Viktor organised his defensive wall. The goalkeeper set the line of defenders to cover one half of the goal, positioning himself in the other half. Jairzinho had joined the end of the wall though, intent on opening up a gap.

As both Pelé and Gérson stepped back from the ball, taking a long run Rivellino thundered forward and struck powerfully with his left foot as Jairzinho pushed at the white-shirted wall. The goalkeeper was probably unsighted as the shot flew past the edge of the trimmed wall and towards the far corner of the net. Viktor's dive was more of a gesture than a genuine attempt to deny Rivellino and, despite a glancing touch on the ball, it ripped into the net for the equaliser. Brazil were now level and, given the flow of the game, very few observers would now be expecting anything but a win for the South Americans, as the *Canarinho* shirts piled up on top of the goalscorer. Firecrackers exploded across the crowd from the Brazilian fans, echoing Rivellino's own explosive pyrotechnics.

Much as conceding a goal had hardly affected Brazil's play, scoring one had a similarly irrelevant outcome. Confident in their ability to score, the *Seleção* continued to control the game with their increasingly dominant football. Control, dribbles, flicks and dummies tested the Czechoslovakian resolve to the limit, relentlessly draining their reserves of energy and belief as they forlornly chased possession that always seemed to just elude them.

A second goal nearly followed quickly. A delicate floated pass by Gérson had Jairzinho galloping towards goal with Viktor out to challenge. The forward just got to the ball first, clipping it forward, as the goalkeeper and a covering defender collided in a heap with the Brazilian winger. The ball drifted agonisingly wide and, to make matters worse, what surely should have been a free kick to Brazil for Jairzinho being clattered after playing the ball by both goalkeeper and defender was deemed to be merely a goal kick; shades of Harald Schumacher and Patrick Battiston a dozen years later, albeit with far less violent intent.

That additional goal before the break still looked inevitable. Viktor leapt to tip a Tostão shot over the bar, but a moment of unrivalled magic from Pelé came even closer with five minutes to play. The sanctuary of the half-time break and coolness of the dressing room were in sight for the Czechs when a Clodoaldo tackle broke up a rare attack from the Europeans. There seemed little immediate danger as the ball ran to Pelé inside his own half of the pitch. Advancing into the centre circle with the ball at his feet, he looked up and saw Viktor well advanced from his line. Striking with his right foot from a position still behind the halfway line, Pelé sent an arcing shot high towards goal. Realising the peril, Viktor feverishly back-pedalled but the height and power of the shot forbade any intervention. It would have been a goal of immense skill and daring, but the ball drifted just wide, and Viktor breathed a sigh of relief as he patted the goalpost in gratitude on the way to collect the ball. Later, Pelé would claim that he had noticed Viktor's tendency to roam away from his line when there seemed no danger, in order to cover the space behind his back line. The goalkeeper may have reviewed that habit following Pelé's attempt. Throughout this World Cup, the *Seleção* in general and Pelé in particular would produce some moments of true footballing magic. This was the first of two exquisite examples of the maestro's talent. As with Cruyff's 'turn' 24 years later, neither of Pelé's moments would lead to a goal, but are no less worthy of celebration for that.

Czechoslovakia held on until the break and headed back to the dressing room to rest and recover. As with a boxer sitting on his stool having taken a bit of a battering in the first round, there was the dread realisation that the respite would be all too brief and the resumption of hostilities was likely to bring far more punishment. Before the restart, Czechoslovakia coach Jozef Marko sought to inject some new life into his team, sending on the vastly experienced Andrej Kvašňák, to replace the weary Ivan Hrdlička in midfield. The change meant that, as he took to the field, Kvašňák was the only player, on either side, to have played in the 1962 World Cup Final between the two nations. With Brazil's overture now delivered and the full glory of their Samba football about to be released in the second half, it's questionable whether 11 substitutes would have been sufficient.

Mere seconds after the restart, the pattern of the first half was nearly repeated when a cross into the Brazil goalmouth and a scramble saw Félix's point-blank save maintaining the equilibrium of the scoreline. It may have been a wake up and smell the coffee – Brazilian coffee, of course – moment for the *Seleção*, as just seconds later a Gérson shot, hit with the outside of his left foot, struck the post with Viktor an impotent spectator. Less than a minute later it was Rivellino shooting narrowly wide from distance. Normal service had resumed.

For the following dozen minutes or so, the play became increasingly concentrated in the Czechoslovakia half as Brazil pressed, with their opponents compelled to defend, and looking increasingly forlorn in their attempts to compete. The second goal was only a matter of time. Pelé had shots on goal, as did Gérson and Rivellino, and minutes in Jairzinho tempted and teased as he cut in from the right before playing a neat one-two pass with Pelé. It took the winger into the area but, with the ball stuck under his feet, the chance was compromised and the shot was screwed wide. But in two minutes either side of the hour the game would be definitively settled.

With fatigue gnawing at their muscles and waves of lactic acid washing away their energy, the Czechoslovakia midfielders, anxious and determined to limit time and space on the ball for Brazil's creative forwards, were becoming increasingly absent from their posts. The benefit of the meticulous Brazilian preparation ahead of the tournament was becoming evident for all to see. The situation gave Gérson all the opportunity he needed, and the São Paulo player put his opponents to the sword with two precise passes in as many minutes. Firstly, a lofted ball over the Czechoslovakia back line met up perfectly with Pelé's run. Exquisite chest control and a rifled finish completed the move. Brazilian flags and banners exploded around the stadium, creating a virtual sea of green, yellow and blue. On the field, Czechoslovakia were about to be just as submerged by a *Canarinho* tide as the *Seleção* ruthlessly killed off the game. The Samba beat echoed around the stadium and Brazil danced to its rhythm.

After the second goal, Czechoslovakia weren't quite beaten, not yet anyway, but they needed a quick riposte. In a clearly practised move, a corner from the right was swept low towards the edge of the penalty area where Hagara met up with it, and clipped the ball low across goal. Advancing, the wise old head of Kvašňák had taken him into the perfect position to score. Connecting with the ball on the six-yard line, it was a tap-in as easy as Pelé's had been early in the first half. Much as had happened with the Brazilian, however, composure deserted the veteran. The ball flew over the bar and away. Seconds later, all lingering Czech hopes of an unlikely comeback had followed suit. Veselý's squandered opportunity in the first period had quickly proven to be costly and the same would apply now, as Kvašňák rued his miss.

Again, Gérson was allowed a scandalous amount of time and space in the centre circle in which to look up and pick his pass. The wand of a left foot weaved its magic again and the ball flew forward unerringly towards an offside-breaking run by Jairzinho. In the first period, an attempt by the same player to lift the ball over an advancing Viktor and into the net had drifted wide. There would be no mistake this time. Carefully flicking the ball above the reach of the goalkeeper, Jairzinho advanced, controlled and smashed his shot into the unguarded net. Czechoslovakian appeals for offside were as hopeful – and hopeless – as they were belligerent, but tired legs and even tireder minds had betrayed them with the winger's run being timed so well. Ironically, the linesman who had ruled Jairzinho onside was none other than Arturo Yamasaki, the then Peruvian, now naturalised Mexican, official who had put Garrincha's World Cup Final appearance in peril eight years earlier.

Soon afterwards, Zagallo removed Gérson, who had been carrying an injury that would see him miss the next two games, and introduced Botafogo's Paulo Cézar. A fortnight before the tournament started, the prematurely balding São Paulo playmaker had damaged a hamstring and his presence in Mexico had briefly even been under threat. Fortunately the injury wasn't as serious as first thought and, such was the high importance that Zagallo placed on winning the first group game, he had decided to gamble on the midfielder's fitness. He reaped the dividend of a stellar performance. So well had Gérson performed that even the linesman, Abraham Klein, patted him in congratulation as he passed on the way to the bench. The price would be, however, that Gérson would now miss the next two matches. The change meant that Rivellino could now move from his left-wing 'false 11' position and drop back into his more accustomed orthodox midfield role, replacing the now departed Gérson, with Paulo Cézar taking over on the left.

For much of the remainder of the game, Brazil were content to keep their opponents at arm's length while always on the lookout for a fourth goal to embellish their now assured win. At the same time, the Czechs dropped back into deep defence keen to avoid shipping any more punishment. That unagreed stalemate would prevail until seven minutes from time. Jairzinho had already given warning of his desire to drive at the left flank of the Czech defence when his run was eventually halted at the expense of a corner. His second such sally would be more productive when Pelé swept a ball out wide to him. With little support, the winger turned and powered past a first defender, then a second, and finally a third, before firing low across Viktor and inside the far post from a tight angle. The goal brought a measure of accuracy to the scoreline in reflecting the flow of the game. Brazil had delivered a loud and clear statement of intent to the rest of the teams in Mexico.

The cat was now out of the bag and at full time any doubts about Brazil, and whether Zagallo could pick up on Saldanha's work to turn a group of extravagantly talented individuals into a scintillating team, were cast to the four winds. After England's stodgy 1-0 victory over Romania the previous day, the *Seleção* had illustrated just how big a task it would be for Ramsey's men to retain the Jules Rimet Trophy. Brazil had declared their intention not only to reclaim their crown, but to do so in a style that would ensure the most honoured of shrines in the pantheon of the greatest teams ever to play in a World Cup.

In typical poetic fashion, writing in *The Times* the following day, Geoffrey Green eulogised about the performance, 'It is difficult to find words to describe my feelings for Brazil's game. [I might] as well try and put a colour to the wind. Here was a different dimension of football: a different kind of magic. These Brazilians live by pure skill alone.'[39] Green was clearly enamoured, as were so many others who had witnessed their performance, and in the next day's issue of *The Times*, he continued to wax lyrical about Zagallo's team. 'We were,' he enthused, 'led into another world, a lifetime away from all the modern scientific and practical defensive football.' He went on to explain, 'Even if Brazil are unable, or not allowed to produce balletic entertainment again, that performance alone will have made the trip [to Mexico] worthwhile.'[40] But there was so much more still to come. Félix would later recall, 'After that first game, we really took off.'[41] The Samba Party had begun. Next up would be England in a game between the country that invented football and the one that had now delivered it as an art form.

It's difficult to conceive of a greater contrast in affection and respect than that displayed by the Mexican fans about Brazil and England. There's little doubt that the opening group games had revealed, even if there had been much to debate beforehand, the colossal gap in entertainment that would be on display from the two teams. England had been artisan and broadly efficient in their 1-0 win over Romania, while the *Seleção* had been artistic and ebullient in netting four goals against Czechoslovakia. But the reasons for affection on one hand and antipathy on the other ran much deeper.

---

39 'Brazilians serve a warning to England', *The Times*, 3 June 1970

40 'Brazil open up a new football world', *The Times*, 4 June 1970

41 Downie, Andrew, *The Greatest Show on Earth* (London: Arena Sports, 2021)

Nineteen days after Brazil faced England in Guadalajara, they would play Italy in the World Cup Final, and Andrew Downie offered his explanation as to why all the local support was strongly behind the South Americans to lift their third Jules Rimet Trophy, 'It was partly because Brazilian teams had played tours in Mexico. The fans knew them and liked them because they played great football. They were also Latin American and two-times world champions. And they beat England, whom everyone despised because they hated Sir Alf Ramsey.'

As holders of the World Cup, England's situation in Mexico could have been handled so much better. In fact it's difficult to imagine how it could possibly have been done less well. While the entire Brazil entourage enthusiastically courted public favour in a country where, once the hosts had been eliminated, a nation's passionate support would be looking for a surrogate, England – and especially their taciturn and uncommunicative manager – adopted a broadly isolationist policy, presenting an unsmiling, borderline arrogance that understandably prompted resentment. Each approach brought its own consequences. Brazilian smiles and openness, with Samba music playing and even, on occasions, players appearing at the entrance of their hotel to briefly dance to the intoxicating rhythm with the fans there, ensured that so many Mexicans took the *Seleção* to their hearts. England's insularity and refusal to integrate into Mexico – they had even brought their own water, food and team bus with them – unsurprisingly brought no such benefit. There was nothing but celebration when England were eliminated by West Germany. As much as passion requires something to love, it also needs the opposite to complete the circle; a god and a devil, a local hero and a public enemy, an angel and a demon. Once those identities have been established, the task for the passionate is to do all that they can to favour those on the side of good, and denigrate those perceived as promoting malevolence. In such actions, the often-blurred line separating what is acceptable and what goes beyond that boundary is barely visible at all.

On the night before the game against Brazil, that antipathy towards England would present itself in a volatile, visible and noisy manner. The hotel where Ramsey's team were staying was surrounded by many hundreds of Mexicans, supplemented by some Brazil fans, swelling the numbers. They were clearly intent on denying England players any sleep. Car horns, incessant drumming and chants of 'Brazil! Brazil! Brazil!' filled the night air with rumbustious vigour. Some reports even suggest that a small number of the besiegers may have penetrated the protective ring of security thrown around the hotel, and run around the 12th floor where the England players were housed, banging on doors before being apprehended and ejected.

As midnight passed into the early hours of the day of the game, some of the England players were moved to rooms at the rear of the hotel, where there was at least some minor diminution of the cacophony. Given they occupied the entire 12th floor, it may well have been naivety on the part of Ramsey not to expect such riotous behaviour and have placed his players in those rooms to begin with, thus avoiding a problem rather than seeking to mitigate its effects. Such behaviour is hardly that unusual ahead of big games in South American football, and indeed in Europe at times, and is taken largely as merely part of the experience of travelling to away games. This wasn't the case for England though and, to some extent, it may even have been counterproductive, building up a cussed motivation to ensure that, despite lack of sleep, the England team's commitment to win and defy their barrackers was given increased impetus.

In contrast to the hearts and minds – and indeed actions – of so many Mexicans, there was a clear and deep respect between the two teams. England's late defeat to Brazil in Rio, almost precisely 12 months before their clash in Mexico, had suggested to many that Ramsey had a blueprint in his mind for defeating the South Americans. Given more resolute defending, with legs and minds tired, plus a smile from the fates, those two late goals may not have occurred and denied his players an important, and confidence-boosting, victory. Now the teams faced each other again.

For both Brazil and England, the encounter was seen as achingly important and yet still somehow hardly definitive. The likelihood was that whoever lost would still have a very good chance of qualifying by beating whichever eastern European team they faced in the final round of games. And yet, that likelihood of both teams winning their final matches and qualifying for the quarter-finals, regardless of the result of this meeting, still carried an extra significance. Whoever won would surely end up topping the group, remain at the relatively low altitude of Guadalajara, and play the runners-up from Group 4.

If the widely held assumption that West Germany would win that group came to pass, the possible contenders for second spot would be Peru, Bulgaria and Morocco. The South Americans appeared almost certain to achieve that, having already defeated Bulgaria in their opening game, and Morocco on the day before Brazil faced England.

Conversely, the losers would then have to travel to the higher altitude of León and probably face the Germans, with the greater potential for elimination that such a game would carry. Additionally, given it was a contest between the two teams who had held the World Cup for the previous dozen years between them, the status was clear, as was the importance of the result.

It was also a match of huge contrasts, as Sam Kunti aptly related in his book on the 1970 World Cup, describing, 'A clash of cultures and different schools of football. England were a precision-engineered machine with a wellspring of energy and a rich seam of resolve, yet without flair in attack. Brazil, on the other hand, were the masters of the beautiful game, albeit with a bumbling back line.'[42] Kunti's analysis had many supporters.

In a reflective piece dating from 2002, writing in *The Guardian*, Will Buckley suggested, 'Few games have been more highly anticipated than the 1970 match. It pitched the team with the finest defence against the team with the finest attack. The best team in Europe against the best team in the world. An England team who were considerably stronger than the one that had won the trophy against a team who are still considered the greatest to have ever won the trophy. A top-of-the-range confrontation and also a struggle between two differing philosophies of the game. Sir Alf Ramsey's England against Mário Zagallo's Brazil; northern Europe v Latin America.'[43]

---

42 Kunti, Sam, *Brazil 1970: How the Greatest Team of All Time Won the World Cup* (Worthing, England: Pitch Publishing Ltd, 2022)

43 https://www.theguardian.com/football/2002/jun/16/worldcupfootball2002.sport3

Buckley also quoted an earlier article from the fluidly lyrical pen of Hugh McIlvanney, who considered, 'Yet at its highest levels the game can acquire something akin to the concentrated drama of the prize ring. Players go into some matches with the certain knowledge that the result will stay with them, however submerged, for the rest of their lives. Defeat will deposit a small, ineradicable sediment, just as victory will leave a few tiny bubbles of pleasure that can never quite disappear. Brazil v England was that kind of match.'[44] It's wonderfully evocative writing. Andrew Downie emphasised the importance of the game from the Brazilian perspective, 'The Brazilian players called it the final before the final. They knew it was a key match and that if they won that it would give them a boost.'

Due to the powerful demands of worldwide television for such an important game, kick-off was scheduled for noon back at the Estadio Jalisco, where both teams had triumphed in their opening games. The searing heat of the midday sun would surely sap the strengths of the players, but England were considered likely to suffer the most. Rumours of fitness concerns about Everton full-back Keith Newton following his substitution after 52 minutes of the opening game proved to be valid, with club-mate Tommy Wright stepping into the breach, as he had done against the Romanians.

Aside from that change, the other ten players who started the first game were retained. Gordon Banks was in goal, behind Wright, Brian Labone, Bobby Moore and Terry Cooper. The midfield quartet comprised Alan Ball on the right, with Alan Mullery offering the defensive reassurance

---

44 https://www.theguardian.com/football/2002/jun/16/
    worldcupfootball2002.sport3

alongside Bobby Charlton in the middle and Martin Peters on the left. The front two were Geoff Hurst and Francis Lee. Reports suggested that Mullery had been given the unenviable task of subduing the threat from Pelé. Do it effectively and, taking those two players out of the equation, leaving a 'ten v ten' contest would surely be to England's advantage. Mullery was encouraged to be as robust as he thought he could get away with in pursuit of his project, but with little success. Subduing Pelé in his prime was a task akin to catching sunlight and trapping it in a closed box.

Zagallo was also compelled to make a change from the team that had started against Czechoslovakia, but his loss was far more significant than Ramsey's. Before being substituted in the second half of that game, Gérson had been an outstanding creative force, even casting the performances of Pelé into the shadows. His two intricate and precisely delivered passes had been the catalysts for Pelé's strike and the first of Jairzinho's two goals. Despite intensive treatment in the intervening days his hamstring injury had hardly been helped by playing against the Czechs, and recovering fitness in time to face England had never been a genuinely realistic option. Much as Newton's replacement had been selected to start this game, so was the case with the man who came on for Gérson against the Czechs.

Félix was in goal, with Carlos Alberto, Piazza, Brito and Everaldo providing the defensive unit. In midfield, Clodoaldo was joined by Rivellino, who was moved inside to compensate for the loss of Gérson. Paulo Cézar replaced Rivellino on the left, with Jairzinho on the right. Pelé and Tostão in the middle completed the forward line. With Rivellino now already ensconced alongside Clodoaldo, and Paulo Cézar hardly best suited to the role, it fell to Pelé and

Tostão to undertake the 'Zagallo-esque' responsibility and reinforce the Brazilian midfield when required. Especially against England, the coach was concerned that his team should not be overrun in the middle of the field. Very few expected Brazil to be able to carve swathes through the England defence, as they had done against Czechoslovakia, particularly in the second half. To win this time would take a far more studied and patient approach. And yet the opening goal so nearly came with just ten minutes played.

For the second successive game, Brazil were facing a team wearing all white, but England would prove to be far more formidable opponents than Czechoslovakia, as Andrew Downie confirmed, 'In truth, [Brazil] were a bit lucky. Félix had his best match and England came close on several occasions.' With the teams breaking from their line-ups as the anthems were completed, a huge roar erupted from the crowd of more than 66,000 – comfortably the highest attendance in Group 3 – it was abundantly clear that the contingent of England fans were massively outnumbered by the overwhelming support for Brazil, be it from fans of that country, or Mexico, who wanted to see the *Seleção* triumph almost as much as they wanted to see Ramsey's England beaten.

When the first real chance arrived, they nearly saw their wish delivered. Peters had already seen a shot from distance smothered by Félix, and Mullery had introduced himself to Pelé in the most impolite of manners when Carlos Alberto fed a long, low pass down the right flank, allowing Jairzinho to out-sprint Terry Cooper. The game had started relatively sedately with both teams seeking to feel each other out and establish a foothold. By now though, the pace had picked up and the first piece of drama was about to unfold. Reaching the byline before the ball ran away, Jairzinho skipped past Cooper and crossed towards the far post. Jumping clear of his marker, Pelé rose and headed the ball firmly towards the bottom corner of the net. Legend has it that, so convinced was he that he had scored, Pelé shouted 'Golo!' as the ball homed in on its target. But it wasn't to be.

After arriving in Mexico, Gordon Banks had been impressed by the large gloves with raised contours on them, similar to the dimpled surface of a table tennis bat, as worn by many South American goalkeepers. He had bought a couple of pairs and was wearing one of them for this game. As the ball bounced a couple of metres from goal, Banks had flung himself across his line to intercept but, had the firm surface of the pitch caused a higher bounce of the ball, he may well have been beaten. As the ball bounced up, Banks's only option was to help it on its way and try to push it high over the bar. Aided by the size and surface of his gloves, not to mention his supreme athleticism and outstanding ability, to the amazement of players, crowd and the watching millions on television, that is precisely what he achieved.

All around him, as he climbed to his feet, players held their hands in the air, shaking their heads at what they had witnessed. Many years later in the run-up to the 2018 World Cup, the author was guesting on a talkSPORT radio programme with Paul Coyte and Alvin Martin discussing previous tournaments, and including telephone interviews with past players. One of these was Mullery and, when the conversation turned to that save from Banks, the former Spurs player was keen to mention that as the goalkeeper climbed to his feet, Mullery had quipped, 'You should have caught that, Banksy!' Fortunately, he then declined to say what Banks's reply had been. It was a 'game on' moment.

Brazil had shown they could compromise England's defence, but Ramsey's team had refused to concede. Strangely, both teams felt encouraged by what had happened.

Brazil's approach was in contrast to the almost devil-may-care attitude displayed against Czechoslovakia. The absence of Gérson's creativity was surely a factor, but Zagallo had clearly requested a more cautious approach to the game, with solidity in defence a higher priority than was the case in the opening game. This allowed England a more than fair share of possession, and for the remaining time of the first period they offered as much threat as Brazil, as both defences remained resolute.

The best chance of the remaining time of the opening 45 minutes fell to England just past the half-hour mark. A pass down the right from Mullery drove Wright to chase the ball as it seemed destined to run out of play. Sprinting to save possession, however, he hooked over a cross that found an unmarked Lee delivering a powerful diving header on goal from six yards. Félix parried instinctively but the ball ran loose and, as Lee sought to bundle the rebound home and the goalkeeper dived to recover, the forward appeared to kick him. Lee instantly apologised but, given the tension of the game, a few angry confrontations were inevitable before Israeli referee Abraham Klein cooled the heated exchanges. It was of little surprise though that, just minutes later, a robust challenge on Lee by Carlos Alberto with scant regard to the location of the ball would be delivered accompanied by a heavy hint of retribution.

After treatment Félix was fit to resume but much as Pelé's header had been denied by Banks so too had Lee been thwarted by the reactions of the Brazil goalkeeper. Although the earlier save is the most celebrated, Félix's double stop is probably worthy of equal merit and stands as an illustration of Downie's earlier comment concerning his performance in the game. Lee's opportunity, unmarked, nearer to goal, and with pace already on the ball, was probably a better chance than Pelé's, but the underrated Félix had denied him.

At the break the scoreline remained goalless as both teams left the field for the cool and dark of their dressing room. Brazil's disciplined play had served to keep the game locked at 0-0, with a restricted emphasis on attack blunting their goalscoring potential somewhat, and the consequent greater commitment to defence having the same effect on the England threat. The vast majority of the crowd had arrived hoping for, and expecting, Brazil to swat away the reigning champions with an extravagant swagger, but their subdued response to the action on the field illustrated that simply hadn't been the case.

Had Zagallo made the calculation that a draw would favour his team more than England? With their goal difference standing at plus three, compared to England's plus one, the consequence of each team taking a point was that if they both then went on to win their final matches, England would need to comfortably outscore Brazil to gain top spot in the group. Given the *Seleção*'s destruction of the Czechs and England's narrow single-goal win against Romania, that event hardly seemed likely. Playing with such a restrained outlook was hardly part of the Brazilian DNA, however, and when the game resumed they would be the team more committed to seeking victory, as England grew increasingly weary in the relentless heat of the Mexican sun.

When the game restarted, the opening minutes hardly suggested that would be the case as England assumed the ascendancy and pressed forward as if intent on notching an early goal. When that failed to materialise, the play briefly assumed its earlier ebb and flow with possession largely equal and defences dominating, before Brazil began to assert themselves. Seven minutes in, the first sign that this may lead to some tangible reward arrived. A long through ball from Pelé set Jairzinho running clear of the England back line but Banks dashed from his area to hoof the ball clear. However, when there's magic in your feet and rhythm in your soul it's difficult for someone else to quell the music for too long.

Pelé went on a run from the right, evading two, three, then four challenges before Mullery hacked the ball away. Then Rivellino cut in and fired off a signature thunderbolt shot that Banks parried away. The temperature of the game was rising, and not only because of the sun. Brazil had picked up the pace and England were struggling to keep up as the pressure increased. Just ahead of the hour mark, what had looked increasingly likely to happen occurred as Brazil went ahead.

Twisting and turning on the left of the England area, Tostão neatly nutmegged Moore before clipping a pass to Pelé in space by the penalty spot. Controlling the ball, he stopped, drawing three defenders towards him like moths hypnotised by a doomed, irresistible and magnetic attraction to a flame. With supreme timing he then burned them as he rolled a short pass out to the right and into the path of the rapidly arriving Jairzinho. One touch to control, one to fire past Banks and England were undone.

Green, yellow and blue erupted in the crowd like an explosion in a paint factory that had a very limited stock of colours. Literally jumping for joy, the goalscorer set off on a wild cavorting celebration. Two steps and a jump. Two more and a jump. Now three, and another jump. It wasn't Samba, but it was a dance of unbridled ecstasy. The dam had been breached and the flood of Brazilian joy was clear for all to see. On the England bench, alongside Ramsey, coach Don Howe put his head into his hands. It felt like a symbolic acceptance of a fate that now seemed to be laid out before England.

Instinctively, Ramsey's team tried to fight back. They were still world champions and were hardly likely to cave in without a fight. Charlton fired wide after a determined run but the scales were now tipped in the *Seleção*'s favour. Momentum had donned a *Canarinho* shirt. It was a situation confirmed by the delighted chants of 'Brazil! Brazil! Brazil!' echoing from the crowd in all corners of the Estadio Jalisco. Ramsey played his final cards. Charlton and Lee were removed, with Colin Bell and Jeff Astle taking their places. With Hurst now joined by West Bromwich Albion frontman Astle, the tactic was clear. An aerial assault was on the cards and England sought to deliver high crosses into the box whenever the opportunity presented itself. The problem was that, with England now committed to attack, the back door was offering tantalising openings to Brazil.

In one such break, with a two-v-two situation, Jairzinho raced forward and chanced his arm against Moore on the edge of the England box. With impeccable timing the England captain jabbed out a foot, won the ball and carried it forward before finding Bell. The moment of skill by Moore so nearly turned the game on its head. Another deep cross into the Brazilian box saw Brito and Everaldo tangle with each other and the ball rebounded off the latter to fall invitingly to Astle close to the penalty spot. It was the best chance of the game by a country mile.

In a ten-year career with the Hawthorns club, Astle would score 137 league goals, earning a reputation as a reliable goalscorer of the highest order, and he had finished the previous season as the First Division's top striker after netting 25 times. In this moment, so early after his introduction into the game, nerves and the pressure snatched away his composure, and he scuffed wide of an open goal with just Félix to beat. In the following years, many fans of opposing clubs would take delight in reminding Astle that he had cost England the World Cup. It was a malevolent chant built on folly. Even had he scored, and England scrambled a draw, their inferior goal difference at the end of the group would still have placed them in second spot. At that moment, however, such calculations would have been the coldest of comforts on this hottest of days.

Soon afterwards, Zagallo decided to refresh his own forward line by removing Tostão and sending on Roberto Miranda. Tostão was elegant and intelligent, but the newcomer was more the natural frontman and the coach needed someone to provide a focal point to help his team move upfield more easily. There was a little over 20 minutes to play and, despite the effect of the heat sapping their strength and eroding their resolve, England pushed forward in search of an elusive equaliser. There was plenty of effort, but tired legs and tireder minds are hardly the best allies when seeking salvation on a football pitch. Maybe it was the adrenalin rush of going ahead, because they were more accustomed to the heat, or more likely the benefits of that altitude training were beginning to play out, but as England visibly tired, Brazilian legs looked fresher. The preparation invested across the previous weeks and months was now paying dividends.

Astle and Hurst were the archetypal frontmen of English football but, as time ran away, the bludgeoning edge of England's broadsword attack was largely blunted, enveloped by the suffocating yellow blanket of the Brazil defence. England were relying on a blood-and-thunder approach, but it turned out to be more thud and blunder compared to the rapier-like, razor-sharp thrusts of the *Seleção*. A shot from Ball, profiting from a poor headed clearance, clipped the top of Félix's bar but that was as close as Ramsey's men were to come. England had only beaten Brazil once in the history of their encounters. This game hardly ever looked likely to double that total. Keeping the ball when they had it, jealously hoarding possession like a child refusing to share his bag of sweets, Brazil ticked off the seconds on their way to victory, keeping England's attack at arm's length. At the full-time whistle, Zagallo's plan to temporarily rein in the attacking flair of his team to secure victory over the reigning world champions had been fully vindicated.

Across the six games they played in the 1970 World Cup, the *Seleção* would score no fewer than 18 goals. The game against England was the only time they had failed to score at least three times. The change of tactics was a clear sign of respect to England, and recognition that this was likely to be their most difficult match of the tournament. And so it proved to be. The image of Bobby Moore and Pelé standing together after exchanging shirts became a symbol both of the occasion and the respect between the reigning champions and the team that would take their crown. Moore would later say that, in that moment, he suggested to Pelé that the teams would meet again in the final, and the Brazilian agreed. Pelé would make that date but Moore and his England team-mates would be absent.

The game had been billed as the encounter between the best two teams in the world, and perhaps that was so, but it was like meeting someone on a pair of escalators. Brazil were very much moving up to a higher level. In contrast, although it wasn't clear at this point, England were traveling in the opposite direction. When Brazil travelled to West Germany to defend their title four years later, England hadn't even qualified for the finals. Mexico in 1970 would be the last time that the Three Lions appeared at a World Cup for a dozen years. The fall from being world champions to missing out on successive qualifications was catastrophic. England, as expected, defeated Czechoslovakia in their final group game to take second place. They then travelled to León to face West Germany in the quarter-final, losing out 3-2 after being two goals clear with a little over 20 minutes to play.

Had there been any doubt about who the Mexican fans had adopted as their favourites, aside from *El Tri*, this was dispelled by the reception the Brazilian contingent received when arriving back at their hotel after the game. A jubilant cocktail of Brazilian and Mexican supporters hailed the team as their coach drew up. Chants, car horns, drums and other assorted musical instruments serenaded the *Seleção* for the following hours as afternoon passed into evening. It was probably as well that the game had been a midday kick-off. With the raucous celebrations showing little sign of diminishing for quite a while, any attempt at sleep would have been impossible. Brazil had started the party. Now, everyone seemed intent on joining in.

With two wins safely ensconced, Brazil would only need a draw in their final group game, against Romania, to guarantee top spot. On the day before Brazil met England, the Romanians had prevailed in the all-eastern European game against Czechoslovakia, winning 2-1 despite falling behind to another early goal from Petráš with just five minutes played. It meant that there was still an outside chance for Angelo Niculescu's team to qualify ahead of England. All they needed to do was overcome the *Seleção* and hope that their eastern European neighbours took at least a point from Ramsey's team. Neither of those unlikely scenarios came to pass.

There had been some speculation, particularly in the English press, that Brazil may field a weakened team against the Romanians, calculating that even a 1-0 defeat would still see them top the group but also require England to defeat Czechoslovakia by at least a two-goal margin, or miss out on a quarter-final place. Whether it was mere wishful thinking on the part of the English journalists, or driven by an overly inflated perception that maybe Zagallo's team were afraid of playing England again, was unclear, but chauvinism had clearly made its way across the Atlantic along with some journalists' pencils, notebooks and toothbrushes. When the Brazil coach named his team, such conjecture was dispelled. It was the same 11 that had started against England, except for Rivellino who was not fully fit after taking a knock. Gérson was still short of a full recovery from his injury and, with Rivellino now also unavailable, Zagallo pushed Piazza further forward into a midfield slot alongside Clodoaldo, who would assume the more forward-focused role in the centre of the pitch, while Paulo Cézar was retained on the left flank. Fontana replaced Piazza to form the centre of the Brazil defence next to Brito.

Hubris was not confined to English minds. It had also infected parts of the Brazilian squad as well, with Pelé later admitting that, ahead of the final group game, the team had 'suffered from overconfidence' and consequently delivered their 'worst performance'.[45] The Romanians had nothing to lose and a potential massive advantage to gain. It was a situation likely to make them difficult opponents, irrespective of any overconfidence.

More than 66,000 fans had watched Brazil defeat England on 7 June. Three days later in the same Estadio Jalisco, as the *Seleção* lined up to face Romania, that number was less than 51,000 but they would be treated to an enthralling encounter, with the eastern Europeans playing their full part in an entertaining game. Both teams' first colours were yellow shirts and blue shorts, so a change of strip was required. Brazil won the draw to play in their traditional colours and Romania changed to a light-blue shirt, white shorts and red socks. Romanian skipper Mircea Lucescu later revealed that the team didn't have any suitable change strip with them, so he visited a local market and purchased a set of light-blue shirts to which the national badges and numbers were then attached – shades of Brazil ahead of the 1958 final. Although, for the Romanians, the outcome of the game was less favourable than when the *Seleção* faced Sweden in newly purchased shirts, also blue, albeit of a different hue.

Despite kicking off four hours later than the game between Brazil and England, the mercury in thermometers was still rising in the blistering sunshine. Even in the shade of the main stand, it suggested temperatures of 86 to 88 degrees Fahrenheit. In the main part of the pitch, where

---

45   do Nascimento, Edson Arantes, *Pelé – The Autobiography* (London: Simon & Schuster UK Ltd, 2006)

it escaped the stand's shadow, the unbridled effect of the sun pushed the number comfortably into the 90s. With the Brazilian right flank, and the Romanian left, bathed in the relatively cooling shadow of the stand, it was of little surprise when both teams began the game concentrating on those particular routes for attack.

Conversely though, the first shot of the game came from the Brazilian left when Paulo Cézar cut in and fired in a powerful effort. In goal for Romania, Stere Adamache parried and then collected the ball as Tostão closed to pounce. Any potential danger was negated, however, as a linesman's flag indicated that the forward had been offside when the shot was struck. Brazil had begun at a leisurely pace, perhaps betraying that overconfidence suggested by Pelé, but still looked the more dangerous of the two sides as the game passed through the early minutes. The thing about potentially being overconfident is that it's evidence you have something to be confident about.

Inside 60 seconds later it was Clodoaldo trying his luck from distance, but the ball cleared the crossbar with Adamache unworried. The Santos midfielder was a talented player but his record of just 13 goals across 510 league games for the club suggested that, as potential replacements for Gérson and Rivellino go, he was more make-do-and-mend than ideal and, with just a point needed to guarantee top spot in the group, there was sound logic to Zagallo's chosen formation. That didn't stop Clodoaldo pushing forward though, and another run through the centre of the field, with the ball at his feet, looked likely to produce a shot on goal until a tug on his arm by Radu Nunweiller brought him crashing to the floor just outside the area. With Rivellino absent, free-kick duty was assumed by Pelé. Striking the ball with the outside of his right foot, he failed to impart the desired swerve on the shot and it flew well wide of the post.

Romania were offering little going forward, seemingly content to keep a tight rein on defence and look for a chance to break, but their plan was nearly scuppered with eight minutes played. Out on the left flank, the pacy Paulo Cézar played a ball past Lajos Sătmăreanu and scampered after it, leaving the defender struggling to catch him. Reaching the the ball before it ran out of play the Botafogo winger declined the opportunity to cut a pass back towards a supporting player, and crashed it towards goal instead. Surprised by the audacity of the attempt from such an acute angle, the ball flew past Adamache, striking the underside of the crossbar and bouncing out towards the touchline on the opposite flank. Some may venture to suggest that it was a mishit cross, but the fact that the ball was struck with such venom gives the lie to that theory, and the young wideman so nearly notched one of the goals of the tournament just six days ahead of his 21st birthday.

Brazil were now beginning to exert a little more pressure on the Romanian back line and, out on the left, in the dazzling sunshine, Paulo Cézar was looking like the brightest option to create an opening. Another run forward dragged defenders out of position before the ball was laid off to Tostão, dropping deep to utilise the space created by the Romanians' attention being drawn to the threatening winger. Advancing towards the penalty area, he slipped the ball past Nicolae Lupescu, but his dart to re-collect was brought to a shuddering halt by a bodycheck from the experienced Rapid Bucureşti defender.

Austrian referee Ferdinand Marschall stood over the ball with his left arm raised indicating that the offence only warranted an indirect free kick. Pelé tapped the ball short to an onrushing Paulo Cézar, but the Romanian wall charged out to thwart the plan. The ball ran loose to Everaldo who hammered in a shot from around 30 yards out which arrowed towards the far corner of the net, but Adamache threw himself across goal to turn the effort away. Still inside the first ten minutes, Brazil were turning up the heat.

Romania sought to relieve the pressure by retaining possession, even if it offered little threat. Keeping the ball away from their opponents proved difficult, however, with Clodoaldo and Piazza a combative midfield combination, harrying and snapping into tackles. Inevitably possession was often lost. In contrast, Brazilian control of the ball was comfortable and played at an easy pace, with often only token challenges until they advanced into the final third of the field, where the Romanians were largely camped.

Romania battled manfully and at times strung some passes together that offered hope of progress, but there was little penetration to their efforts and Félix had little to do other than calmly collect tame efforts on goal and restart the game after back passes. The contrast at the other end of the pitch was clear. Despite failing to turn their dominance into any kind of tangible reward, Brazil's ability to carve holes in the Romanian defence was illustrated time and again. Just past the quarter-hour mark, Clodoaldo advanced, skipping past one laboured challenge and then another one before feeding the ball out to the right. The cross from Jairzinho eluded defenders as it arrowed towards the six-yard line, but was just too far ahead of the run from Paulo Cézar charging in from the opposite flank. A goal looked to be inevitable, and it was.

In the space of 60 seconds, Clodoaldo twice struck powerfully at goal. The first effort was deflected for a corner; the second flew high and wide. Despite his record of only scoring once in his international career, the midfielder was clearly looking to exploit the extra forward options now available to him, with the reassuring presence of Piazza playing alongside him in midfield. When the goal arrived, however, it was from a much more likely source.

Clodoaldo played for Santos, and it was his celebrated team-mate from the *Alvinegro* who showed him the way to find the back of the net. A clumsy challenge on Pelé gave Brazil a free kick on the edge of the penalty area. Tostão's quickly taken clip flew just over the bar, but Marschall ordered a retake, as he had not pushed the defensive wall back the requisite distance and signalled for the restart. Finally happy, as the Austrian stepped back, two Brazilian players joined the end of the wall attempting to block the goalkeeper's view of the kick being taken, before peeling away at the critical moment. On the second attempt Tostão was a dummy runner, stepping over the ball as Pelé ran in to fire home through a gap in the less than solidly built wall, leaving Adamache well beaten and berating his defenders.

It hadn't been difficult to discern that the Romanian plan had been to defend in depth and strike on the break to steal a one-goal win. With Brazil now ahead, that ploy was consigned to the rubbish bin and the already slim Romanian hopes of progress into the knockout rounds were now looking more like emaciated. On the bench, coach Niculescu blew out his cheeks and looked at the ground in front of him. His team now had a mountain to climb, but worse was to follow just a few minutes later.

The early passages had seen Paulo Cézar offer the major threat to Romania, operating from the sunlit left flank. As the game progressed, however, the muscular pace of Jairzinho became more and more of a factor as he emerged from the shadows – in more ways than one. With the Romanian attack starved of possession, and chances at the highest of premiums, Carlos Alberto was increasingly involved in Brazil's forward play down the right, allowing Jairzinho the opportunity to move further inside. It was on one of those such occasions that the erstwhile flank player had drifted into the middle of the attack. He played a pass off to Paulo Cézar, inviting the left-winger to skip past his marker and scamper towards the byline. Jairzinho then paced his run perfectly to connect with the cross that found him just a couple of yards from the goal line. A simple side-footed finish doubled Brazil's lead and surely confirmed the eastern Europeans' fate.

There was fleeting hope of the unlikeliest of revivals when a seemingly harmless cross into the box was somehow completely missed by Brito, a lapse in concentration perhaps, and Florea Dumitrache found himself clear with just Félix to beat, albeit from a tight angle. The Dinamo Bucureşti striker was a consummate goalscorer, notching 115 league goals for his club in just a shade more than 200 games and scoring 15 goals in 31 appearances for the national team. Perhaps it was the surprise, but his undoubted technique failed him as his attempt to lift the ball over the goalkeeper was woefully over-hit and the rarest of chances was gone.

A few minutes later, Niculescu had even more reason to accept that this perhaps wasn't his day. Two goals down, his most trusted marksman squandering the only opportunity in the game and with his team being thoroughly outplayed, the gods of football twisted the knife a little further as Adamache was forced to leave the action, to be replaced by Necula Răducanu. It was the first time in the history of the World Cup that a goalkeeper had been substituted. The change hardly weakened the team, however. The tall and muscular Rapid București stopper – his physique would become significant later in the game – had arrived in Brazil as the first choice and indeed had been given the number one shirt, but a reported incident of ill-discipline ahead of the tournament (some suggestions were that he pushed someone into the hotel swimming pool) had caused Niculescu to promote Adamache instead, and he had played every minute of every game up to that point.

Much to Niculescu's chagrin, Răducanu wasn't the only first-choice player to be left out of the Romania team for ill-discipline. Nicolae Dobrin had been Romanian Footballer of the Year in 1966 and 1967 – and would be again in 1971. Despite making the trip to Mexico and surely a shoo-in for the line-up, a fondness for bars and dislike for training in the heat meant that he never played a minute in the tournament. Just when the night appears to be at its darkest, however, a shaft of light can be the herald of a breaking dawn.

Perhaps Brazil eased up a little; a two-goal lead looked comfortable enough. Or, with little to lose now, maybe Romania decided to push forward more but, quickly after the change of goalkeeper, a run by Emerich Dembrovschi took him past two tepid challenges and to the edge of the penalty area where he slipped a pass to Alexandru Neagu, whose low shot was smothered by Félix. That it was two midfield players pushing forwards to cause danger was perhaps significant, and on the bench Niculescu applauded his team's enterprise, while Zagallo sat stone-faced in comparison, perhaps fearing what his players' easing down may lead to.

Encouraged by the shot on goal, Romania dominated the ball for the next few minutes, ending with a flighted pass into the box from Ion Dumitru that found Neagu in space around eight yards out but his attempt to shoot on the volley was badly mistimed and the ball was hacked clear. The referee's decision to award Brazil a free kick for some indiscretion in the box negated any potential danger anyway, but hardly disguised how the Romanians' newfound attacking zeal had exposed defensive frailties in the *Seleção* back line. On another day, Brazil's two-goal advantage could have disappeared in as many minutes. They had escaped, but the respite would be brief.

Ten minutes ahead of the break, with the eastern Europeans now having gained at least parity in terms of the flow of game, the goal came. Once again a simple ball into the Brazil penalty area from Dumitru caused more problems than should surely have been the case. The pass found Dumitrache, with his back to goal, but with both Brito and Fontana in close attendance there was still plenty to do. Turning adroitly, he found space outside of his marker and, with Carlos Alberto vainly seeking to close him down, the forward stretched out a foot to prod the ball into the net. For the third time the central defensive partnership of Brito and Fontana had been cruelly exposed by a simple lofted pass towards a single forward in the penalty area. Zagallo would not utilise the pairing again. For the next game, Piazza would be back alongside Brito. Fontana would never play for the *Seleção* again. That was for the future though; with Romanian hopes now experiencing a Lazarus-like resurrection, there was plenty for Brazil to concentrate their minds on.

Lifted by the goal, and driven on by the demands of their coach, Romania pushed forward and for a few minutes Brazil were akin to a boxer floored by an unexpected haymaker from a desperate opponent who had been outfought for all of the contest. They needed to clear their heads and get back into their pattern of play, but Romania were still swinging those punches. Dembrovschi advanced into the Brazil half, exchanging neat return passes with Dumitrache, before laying the ball off to Lucescu, as he was closed down on the edge of the penalty area. The Romanian captain fired off a shot but Brito plunged to block and the ball was cleared. The momentum was with Romania, and the last thing they needed as half-time approached was a prolonged break in play, but that's what happened after Ráducanu collided with Jairzinho as the Brazilian chased a long ball. A slight touch by the goalkeeper was sufficient to negate any claims for a penalty, but the inevitable impact of the muscular frame of Ráducanu into the winger's groin caused the referee to halt the game moments later to allow treatment to be ministered.

The minute or so of the game being halted was sufficient for Brazilian composure to be largely restored, and at least a few holes in the previously sieve-like defence to be blocked up. As the action restarted, Brazil began to do what they did best. They attacked, forcing the Romanians on to the back foot as they had been for much of the play. Tostão fired a shot wide, then a surging run by Pelé was only halted by the most cynical of trips from behind by Dumitru. Marschall brandishing the yellow card to the apologetic midfielder was inevitable. The *Seleção* had dampened the brief flame of Romania's fightback and they reached the break with a measure of comfort.

While things were relatively calm in the Brazil dressing room with control of the game now re-established, things were very different for the Romanians. Niculescu had seen his team launch an unexpected fightback after Dumitrache's goal and expose deficiencies in the Brazil back line. The break for the injury to Jairzinho and then the half-time whistle had worked against his team, but the coach urged his players to take a front-foot stance from the restart and attack. As the second half began, the shadow of the main stand had now crept more than halfway across the pitch, offering the players more relief from the hot sun, but with their coach's urgent demands ringing in their ears the Romanians were loath to offer any other kind of comfort to Brazil.

Despite the Romanian players' attempts to turn Niculescu's promptings into tangible action, the hesitancy that seemed to engulf the *Seleção* after conceding the goal had now largely been vanquished. Zagallo too had been at work with his players during the break. Piazza and Clodoaldo were once again a wall in midfield and, as the early minutes ticked by, a fairly tame header from Neagu that drifted wide with Félix unworried was all they had to show for their early endeavours. In fact, it was the Brazilians carrying the greater threat. Six minutes in, Pelé controlled the ball on the edge of the box but was tumbled to the ground before he could get his shot away. A short pass to the same player from the free kick, and a flighted shot, required a diving save from Răducanu to prevent Brazil restoring their two-goal advantage.

A dozen minutes after the restart, Brazil's defence was briefly disrupted as Everaldo was forced from the field after taking a knock while blocking out a cross for a corner. Despite receiving attention for a few minutes, he was unable to continue and Fluminense's 19-year-old defender Marco Antônio was called from the bench to replace him. The change did little to affect the established flow of the game, with the early Romanian ardour now largely subsided, and Félix yet to be called into any meaningful action since the restart. Four minutes later the result looked to be settled as Pelé, chasing a lofted through pass, muscled his way past the last defender and stroked the ball past Răducanu, but the goal was chalked off by the referee for a push in the back on Cornel Dinu. The lack of celebration at the goal, surprise or dissent about the decision from the Brazilian star suggested it was probably the correct decision. The next time Pelé had the ball in the back of the net, however, the outcome would be different.

Approaching the midway point of the second half, an overlapping charge down the right by Carlos Alberto earned Brazil a corner after Lupescu blocked the attempted cross. The ball was then played short to Jairzinho who crossed towards the near post, where Tostão acrobatically flicked on. It dropped perfectly for Pelé as he ran forward into space and stretched out a leg to divert home, defeating Răducanu's forlorn dive across goal. This time the celebrations were instant and unrestrained, with nothing to rule out the strike.

Although limited, Romania had been worthy opponents and stretched Zagallo's team, especially towards the end of the initial 45 minutes, requiring them to effectively 'win' the game twice after taking their foot off the pedal when two goals ahead in the first half. Now, with just the final quarter to play, Brazil in the ascendancy, and two goals clear again, the possibility of another comeback looked even more remote than in the first period. The shadow from the main stand was now almost completely covering the pitch, and the bright hopes that Romania had cherished late in the first half had also fallen into darkness.

With 18 minutes to go Niculescu played his final card, replacing the weary Dumitrache with Gheorghe Tătaru. Two minutes later, Zagallo responded in kind as the young Santos winger Edu replaced Clodoaldo. Entering the final 15 minutes it was the Romanian substitute who called Félix into action in any meaningful way for the first time since the restart as he leapt to guide what was surely a mishit cross over the crossbar. The corner was played short and Romania worked a bit of space for Tătaru in a strikingly similar place from where he had troubled Félix seconds earlier. This time there was no doubt that he hit a shot on goal, but it flew comfortably wide and Félix's dive towards the ball as it arced further and further away from goal was the sort of unnecessary extravagance often termed as being 'one for the cameras'. In fairness it was at least a chance for the goalkeeper to take an active part in the game – and he took it. At the other end of the pitch, moments later, Răducanu's dive was far less frivolous as he plunged to stop a viciously hit free kick from Carlos Alberto, and was then required to repeat the feat as the Brazilian skipper raced on to a quickly taken restart before firing in another ferocious shot.

If another goal was coming then it would surely be for Brazil, but football is nothing if not contrary. With half a dozen minutes to play, a seemingly harmless cross from full-back Lajos Sătmăreanu somehow enticed Félix into a major error as he committed himself to punch the ball clear, but failed to make any contact and Dembrovschi nodded into the unguarded net.

Time was running out and the chances of an equaliser were about as slim as the final sliver of sunlight escaping the shadow of the stand, now almost completely covering the entire playing surface, but it was undeniably there. Score again, get a draw and then hope for a bit of eastern European solidarity from Czechoslovakia when they faced England the following day was now a surprisingly realistic target, should they be able to apply some pressure, and Brazilian composure melt away again.

It seemed a fanciful target as Brazil edged home, restricting Romania to hopeful shots from distance but, when another over-hit cross from Tătaru had Félix scrambling back to touch the ball over the crossbar, the impossible loomed into merely being the improbable. With Romania pushing forward, the danger of conceding on the break was always there and, when Jairzinho played Pelé into a wide position and his cross found Tostão around the six-yard box, a goal looked inevitable until Răducanu threw himself forward to block the shot with his huge frame. It was the closest either team came to scoring as the unforgiving sands of time ran through Romanian fingers. Many years later, Pelé conceded that, despite falling two goals down, Brazil 'were very nearly punished by a courageous and committed Romanian side'.[46]

Compliments, ifs, buts and could-have-beens were scant consolations. Romania were out and Brazil had survived a couple of scares to march into the knockout stage of the 1970 World Cup. Their three group games had each been different, and yet there was also a consistent thread. The

---

46 do Nascimento, Edson Arantes, *Pelé – The Autobiography* (London: Simon & Schuster UK Ltd, 2006)

sauntering, ebullient display against Czechoslovakia had been followed by the uncharacteristic restrained discipline when overcoming England. Then they exhibited the composure to withstand two fightbacks against Romania, when defensive uncertainties had threatened to derail the whole project.

In each match, however, the belief that no matter how many goals Brazil conceded they would always score more shone through. Scoring eight times across the group fixtures, including a game against the reigning world champions, was impressive, and a record only bettered by West Germany, who scored ten in what was a less competitive set of games. Progress may not have been perfectly serene but it was hugely entertaining. The perfect recipe for a party, and their next task would see that continue as the *Seleção* met up with an old friend.

* * *

The Quarter-Final – Friends Reunited

Brazil's quarter-final opponents would be Peru, who had qualified for the tournament at the expense of Argentina thanks to a draw in Buenos Aires on the last day of August 1969. It was the final qualifying group fixture, and only a win for the home team would have seen them progress. There was more than a sense of moral justice at play when *La Albiceleste* fell short on that day.

Alongside Peru and Argentina, Group 1 of the CONMEBOL qualifying programme was completed by Bolivia, who had dealt a serious blow to Argentine aspirations by defeating them 3-1 in the rarefied heights of La Paz in the group's opening game on 27 July. A week later Peru pushed the erstwhile group favourites on to the precipice of elimination when a single strike by Pedro León brought Peruvian delight and victory in Lima. Peering over the edge of the cliff, and compelled to contemplate an outcome that would mean Argentina failing to qualify for a World Cup for the first time in the history of the tournament, urgent action was deemed necessary. Reports suggest that a deliberation was made in assuming that the Peruvians presented the main danger to any Argentine renaissance and that representatives from, linked with or under instructions of the Argentine FA then took a hand in trying to swing things back into favour of *La Albiceleste*.

A week after Didi's team had defeated Argentina, Bolivia hosted Peru in what had now assumed the status of a key contest in deciding who would progress from the group and qualify for Mexico. It was surrounded by the sulphurous whiff of scandal as the deliberations of Venezuelan referee Sergio Chechelev seemed to consistently favour the home team – a scenario highlighted when he ruled out what appeared to be a perfectly valid goal by Peru for an indiscretion unseen by anyone other than the official himself. Bolivia went on to win 2-1. Chechelev would later claim that he had been paid by agents clandestinely working for Argentina to ensure them a favourable result. As the fates would conspire, however, any money invested brought little return.

A week later, Peru took revenge by comfortably defeating the Bolivians – who were apparently blameless, and unaware of the Argentine shenanigans – 3-0 in the return. It left two matches to play, with Argentina hosting Bolivia on 24 August and Peru the following week. A brace of wins for the home team would have seen those two early defeats overturned, and a tainted reward gained for their clandestine investment. A second-half penalty by Rafael Albrecht was sufficient to secure the first of those two victories, meaning that if Argentina could overcome Peru the following week then they would qualify, with any other result seeing Didi guide his team to Mexico.

It wasn't to be. In an inevitably tight and tense encounter staged at Boca Juniors' theatrically steeped bear pit *La Bombonera* (translated as the Chocolate Box; the ground's actual name is the Alberto José Armando Stadium), it was an appropriately tasty encounter, without much regard for soft centres, that remained goalless until 20 minutes from time when Oswaldo Ramírez put Peru ahead. Albrecht equalised with ten minutes to play, but hopes of late Argentine glory were quickly dashed when Ramírez restored the lead 60 seconds later. An Alberto Rendo goal in the dying embers to bring the scores level was far too little, and far too late. The draw had rendered the underhand tactics redundant. Argentina stayed at home. Peru went on to Mexico to compete in their first World Cup since the inaugural tournament back in 1930, where they had been invited to take part rather than earned their place through any qualification process.

In the tournament, the South Americans were drawn in Group 4, based in León, alongside West Germany, Bulgaria and Morocco. The Africans appeared to be the makeweights but applying similar status to Bulgaria may have been dangerously presumptuous. The eastern Europeans had qualified for the last three World Cups and, giving the lie to the widely held belief that Soviet bloc countries were poor travellers, especially to different continents, had won the silver medal in the Olympics two years earlier – also held in Mexico. They had topped their opening group and then defeated Spain 2-0, and the hosts 3-2, before losing out 4-1 in the final to a powerful Hungary side fresh from their stirring displays in the 1966 World Cup in England two years earlier where they had defeated Brazil. They had also faced Peru in a couple of warm-up games ahead of the tournament getting under way, winning the first 3-1, before falling to a 5-3 defeat a few days later.

Just days before Didi's team faced Bulgaria in their opening group game on 2 June, back in Peru a devastating earthquake had struck with calamitous effect, claiming the lives of thousands of people and destroying much of the country's fragile infrastructure. A decision was made to keep news of the events back home away from the players for as long as possible. On reflection, it may feel callously calculated and single-minded by the authorities in Mexico when family and friends were suffering back home, but there was a measure of logic to it. There was probably little of any real effect that a group of footballers in Mexico could do to alleviate the situation, and any success that the team could achieve may at least serve as some balm for the battered souls at home. Better to let them continue with their preparations without the dread, fear and concern about loved ones hanging over them. Logic and intent can go so far, but maintaining an effective embargo on news that was inevitably spreading rapidly across South America, and indeed the wider world, may have been like that Dutch boy trying to plug leaks in a dam with an insufficient number of fingers.

When the game against Bulgaria got under way, the form of the eastern Europeans appeared to be franked as they led 2-0 minutes into the second half. A free kick from Botev Plovdiv's Dinko Dermendzhiev opened the scoring after a dozen minutes and, when goalkeeper Luis Rubiños allowed a long-range effort from Hristo Bonev to squirm away from him and into the net just after the restart, the impression that the Peru players' thoughts were elsewhere was entirely understandable. An impressive fightback by Didi's team, however, thanks to goals by Alberto Gallardo, skipper Hector Chumpitaz and Teófilo Cubillas, turned the game on its head. It may have been of minor significance when ranged against the disaster unfolding back home, but the players were doing what they could to help, as Cubillas would later recall, 'Knowing that we'd brought a little bit of happiness to the country was a feeling that is impossible to put into words.'[47]

Peru took the points and, with the game against Morocco to follow, were well on track to achieve qualification regardless of the result against the Germans in their final group match. Conversely, Bulgaria's bright start fell away badly. They were comprehensively beaten 5-2 by West Germany and then only salvaged a fig leaf of pride by avoiding the 'wooden spoon' after drawing 1-1 with Morocco. The tournament was a largely disappointing affair for teams from the east of Europe. Despite four of the nine European qualifiers coming from the Soviet bloc, only the Soviet Union themselves progressed from the group stages, before defeat to Uruguay in the quarter-finals summarily ended their run.

Four days after the comeback win over Bulgaria, Peru completed a much less dramatic victory over Morocco with Cubillas netting another brace. Roberto Challe scored the

---

47   Downie, Andrew, *The Greatest Show on Earth* (London: Arena Sports, 2021)

other goal to complete the 3-0 success. West Germany had also defeated both Morocco and Bulgaria, the former with two second-half goals after surprisingly falling behind to a first-half strike by Houmane Jarir. The game against Bulgaria was much more straightforward despite again conceding the first goal. A strike on 12 minutes from Asparuh Nikodimov had given the Bulgarians hope but, by the time Todor Kolev added their second in the final minute, the Germans had already found the back of the net five times.

With qualification now assured for both Peru and West Germany, the final group game looked to be something of an anti-climax despite top spot in the group still to be decided and consequently who each team would face in the quarter-finals. The runners-up from four years earlier had added some youthful talent to the seasoned campaigners now looking to go one better than in 1966, and still had the wily coach Helmut Schön at the helm. They illustrated the point powerfully against Didi's team. A *blitzkrieg* of a 20-minute first-half hat-trick by Gerd Müller had decided the game before yet another Cubillas goal brought a measure of respectability to the scoreline. The Germans secured top spot and the prospect of staying in León to face England. For Peru, the task was for Didi to see if he could inspire his young, energetic group, fired by the goals of Cubillas, to bring down his former team.

Despite the defeat against the Germans, Peru still retained plenty of optimism for the clash against Brazil. Their two narrow losses to the *Seleção* in the friendlies of April 1969, both by a single goal, had suggested that they could at least be competitive and, with the confidence of two wins and some tournament experience behind them, plus a coach who knew the opposition so well, perhaps it was Peru's best opportunity to upset the established order of South American football. Pelé and Zagallo, who had featured alongside the Brazilian coach now in charge of Peru during his playing career, would have nothing but respect for him, but that wasn't limited to his former team-mates. Gérson would later describe Didi as 'one of Brazil's greatest midfielders' and 'one of our heroes'.[48] A competitive performance was expected from Didi's team. The outcome of the game would not disappoint.

Ahead of the tournament, Didi had declared, 'Peru will attack at every opportunity. Because this is what we do best. It is what brings us our victories.'[49] The six goals garnered in the 3-2 win against Bulgaria and the 3-0 victory against Morocco suggested that the coach's words were anything but unsubstantiated bluster and the free-scoring Cubillas's award as the FIFA Young Player of the Tournament underscored the fact. The total of seven goals they scored across their group fixtures was only one fewer than Zagallo's team had achieved. They had conceded five in return, but even the *Seleção* had seen their defence breached on four occasions, with only England failing to find a way past Félix.

If Didi was bent on shaping his Peru team from the template of the Brazil he knew so well, perhaps the way the game transpired suggests that, at this stage, they were still more akin to 'Brazil-Lite' than the finished article. Both teams had strong attacks but Brazil's was stronger. Both teams had vulnerable defences but Peru's was more vulnerable. Both teams played to entertain, but for all

---

48 Donald, Michael, *Goal!* (London: Hamlyn, 2017)
49 'Heat – England's only worry', *The Times*, 28 May 1970

Peru's attacking ambition this was Brazil's party. For both teams it was their first experience of playing another South American opponent in the tournament. 'It was a joy to play in,' Pelé remembered. 'Both teams, being South American, refused to play the defensive game preferred by the European teams, and it was attack followed by attack from both sides.'[50] Attack was certainly the strongest suit of both teams, but in an open game, despite Peru inevitably having some moments of joy, the boisterous ability of Zagallo's front line was always likely to prevail, especially if it was at anything resembling its full strength.

Fortunately, the four-day gap between the game against Romania and the last-eight encounter with the *Seleção*'s South American neighbours was sufficient to allow Zagallo to welcome some of his injured players back into consideration for selection. He took full advantage. Gérson, now fully recovered, returned to his midfield berth alongside Clodoaldo, allowing Piazza to drop back alongside Brito, replacing the discarded Fontana. Given his performance against Romania, Paulo Cézar was surely unfortunate to lose his place (although he would appear as a second-half substitute) but the option of restoring Rivellino to the left flank of Brazil's attack was irresistible. The one enforced change, with Everaldo unavailable following his injury against Romania, saw Marco Antônio, who had replaced the Grêmio defender when he had been forced from the field in the final group game, positioned on the left of Brazil's defence.

---

50 Downie, Andrew, *The Greatest Show on Earth* (London: Arena Sports, 2021)

Didi's starting 11 also showed several changes from their final group game. Rubiños had played every minute of every match to that point and would continue to do so against Brazil. Interestingly, despite their perceived frailties in defence, much the same was true for the players comprising the remainder of the Peruvian defensive unit and midfield. Central defender and skipper Chumpitaz and left-back Nicolás Fuentes were also ever-present, as was the central midfield pairing of Ramón Mifflin and Challe. Sporting Cristal's Eloy Campos had started the tournament as right-back against Bulgaria, but an injury saw him replaced by Pedro González inside the first half an hour of the opening game. With Campos unfit, the Universitario de Desportes defender had then been selected for the games against Morocco and West Germany. Didi may well have been relieved that Campos was fit and available for selection against Brazil for more than the obvious reason of being able to restore a first-choice player to the starting 11. González had been dismissed, along with Gérson, in the game back in April 1969, when Brazil overcame Peru 3-2 at the Maracanã. Didi's decision to restore Campos to his defence against Brazil was an easy one, and González returned to the bench.

The other defensive change would also have echoes of that previous encounter, but be far more controversial than merely restoring a first-choice player back to the starting 11 after injury, and would lead to friction in the squad. Campos's Sporting Cristal team-mate, Orlando de la Torre, had been Chumpitaz's partner in the centre of defence for all of the group games, but Didi decided to replace him for the Brazil encounter. Back in that controversial match in April of the previous year, an overly robust challenge by Gérson on

De la Torre had led to both the Brazilian midfielder being dismissed and the Peruvian leaving with what looked like a serious injury. De la Torre had a fiery temperament and the siren calls for some kind of retribution against Gérson may well have been a burning demand too hot to deny. At least, that was Didi's worry. Losing a player to a red card, driven by a red mist, was not a palatable option, and the coach considered that trusting De la Torre would keep a cool head was too much of a gamble. Instead he opted for the safer option of deploying Universitario's José Fernández, who had also replaced De la Torre when he was substituted back in that tempestuous encounter of the previous year, alongside his captain. Fortunately for Didi, Fernández was an able deputy; the widely respected 31-year-old had been playing for his country for 11 years and had just captained his club to the Peruvian league title.

Inevitably the decision did not go down well with the player who was now fated to miss what was probably the biggest game in Peru's footballing history. 'I went mad when I heard I wasn't going to play. I was spitting fire,' he recalled.[51] Later, rumours circulated that the frustrated defender had to be restrained from attacking the coach. Didi's caution about playing De la Torre was perhaps understandable but, having played in the three group games alongside Chumpitaz, the pair had built up an understanding. Throwing the widely experienced Fernández into such an important game may have felt like the sensible option but, without him having experienced a single minute of time on the pitch in the tournament to date, it was also a gamble in so many other

---

51 Downie, Andrew, *The Greatest Show on Earth* (London: Arena Sports, 2021)

ways. The only other change was the return of Alianza Lima's Julio Baylón in place of the young Hugo Sotil in attack. It was far less contentious.

Just before midday on 14 June at the Estadio Jalisco, the two teams lined up either side of the halfway line as the preliminaries began. As if they were exotically coloured birds of paradise, the bright sunshine picked out the vivid and iconic plumages of both teams. Brazil, later described by James Sharp in the *Daily Mail*, were the more familiar: 'That shirt, thick and yellow, bright as the summer sun, those circles of green cotton around the neck and biceps, on top of tight blue shorts. As soon as the image forms, all memories of the most beautiful team in World Cup history crash back into your mind in a rolling flood.'[52] I'll let *GQ* speak of Peru, while also offering acknowledgement to Brazil's famous colours. 'Yes,' the magazine's online article conceded. 'There's no doubt that the gold and light blue of Brazil are the colours that most immediately evoke Mexico '70. But the presence of Peru that summer … opened the world's eyes to these alternative South American style icons. Their kit – all white but with a wide, bright-red diagonal slash from shoulder to waist – was an instant classic.'[53] Throw in the bright colours of flags, banners and shirts of the crowd and the stage was set. The innovation of colour television allowed the world to share, along with the 54,000 fans in the Estadio Jalisco, the iridescent imagery in all its glory. The question now was, once the gilded cage of the preliminaries were completed, whether these exotic birds

---

52 https://www.dailymail.co.uk/sport/football/article-8444069/Im-not-dead-Pele-inspired-Brazil-redemption-1970-World-Cup-Mexico.html

53 https://www.gq-magazine.co.uk/sport/article/mexico-1970-world-cup

could fly in a manner that would do justice to the picture that had been painted.

Of all the anthems played for each of the 16 teams in Mexico, it's difficult to imagine that there was one that demanded the rigid attention of its countrymen for longer than the 'Himno Nacional del Perú' as its six verses and repeated choruses were dutifully sung out by the team. Each player stood with his right hand on his heart and a bouquet of flowers held in his left, hanging down by his side. If nothing else, the stoic commitment to last out the full stanzas without wavering in tone or intensity suggested that Didi's team were well prepared and would not lack in application.

As the final notes drifted away and the players shook their arms and legs, now freed from the rigid stance required by the anthem, the cheer arising from the crowd was also significant. A flock of doves were released into the air as the teams prepared for kick-off. The doves had soon flown clear of the stadium, leaving the stage clear for those birds of paradise, brightly plumed in yellow and blue, red and white, to take flight for a game that would be widely regarded as the most entertaining of the entire tournament.

All of Brazil's previous three matches had been against European opposition, with two of the three against Soviet bloc sides. There had been a reasonably large contingent of England supporters for the game against England but, even then, they were vastly outnumbered and drowned out by the Mexicans and Brazilians supporting the *Seleção*. This game would be somewhat different. Even though the green and yellow flags, banners and garb of those supporting Brazil remained in the majority, there was also an undeniably sizeable contingent waving the red and white flags of Peru, more than willing to voice their support. Minutes later, as the final strains of 'Hino Nacional Brasileiro' drifted away, the raucous cheer that erupted suggested that the competition between the teams, anticipated to be both competitive and colourful, would have echoes from the crowd.

The sun had briefly hidden behind one of the scattered clouds as the game got under way, but the eager ambitions of both teams to attack as soon as they gained possession was bright enough with plenty of promise of goals to come. Less than four minutes had been played when a perfectly flighted through ball from Gérson met up with Pelé's diagonal run from the right to the edge of the penalty area. Adroitly positioning himself inside of Nicolás Fuentes, who had tried to track the forward's run, Pelé muscled himself clear, controlled the ball with his chest and fired low past Rubiños's left hand. The game looked set for an early goal but the ball struck the post and jagged back across the box. Pelé chased but it had run past the far post by the time he reached it. Unable to chance an effort on goal from the angle, he opted to backheel the ball towards the penalty spot. Chasing in with intent, Tostão's attempt to capitalise on the opening was thwarted as two defenders closed him down and his effort ballooned high and wide, but the blue touchpaper had been lit.

Peru tried to respond in kind, maintaining possession for a couple of minutes, but the Brazil back line was calm and composed. Brazil pushed forward again and a Jairzinho pass allowed Pelé to deliver a neat flick aimed at Tostão as he darted through the narrowest of gaps in the Peru defence before being tumbled to the ground on the edge of the area. A brains trust briefly formed over the ball, in deep discussion as to how best to exploit the position, before each drifted away, leaving just Pelé and Gérson to close out the decision. The latter placed the ball meticulously as Belgian referee Vital Loraux laboured to drive the Peru wall back to something resembling the desired ten yards. In goal, Rubiños had required his defenders to split into two small walls, leaving a gap between them so that he could see the ball being struck. The passageway to goal was a tempting target.

At Loraux's whistle, Pelé swept forward but ran over the ball, hoping that the deception would open up a gap for his team-mate following behind. The man advancing to take the kick, however, wasn't Gérson, who had placed the ball. With all eyes on the two Brazilians standing over the ball as the wall was persuaded to retreat, Rivellino had quietly moved to a position from where he was now tearing forward to hammer a shot with his fearsome left foot. The ball arrowed towards the gap between the two defensive ramparts with just enough curve imparted to take it away from the goalkeeper. At the last moment though, a knee jabbed out from the edge of the ball provided sufficient contact to deflect the shot wide. Peru had escaped twice inside the first six minutes. One wondered how much longer their luck would hold if Brazil kept pressing with such impressive insistence.

Attack being the best form of defence was a credo adhered to by both teams and Peru sought to keep the pressure away from their goal by threatening at the other end. Cubillas dipped and weaved past a couple of challenges as he cut in from the right before laying the ball off. A lofted pass was then aimed towards Julio Baylón dashing into the Brazil box, but the returning Alianza Lima forward had made his run too early and was flagged for a clear offside infringement. Despite falling foul of the linesman, the move had at least concentrated play at the other end of the pitch for a while – but not for long.

Minutes later, Jairzinho's powerful run took him past Fuentes to reach the byline and cut a pass back towards Pelé, but his flick only found a welcoming Peruvian foot that unceremoniously hacked the ball clear. The resultant throw-in led to a Rivellino shot from distance but, unusually, it lacked power and Rubiños collected with relieved comfort. Peru had shown plenty of ambition and drive to fulfil their coach's avowed aspirations to attack. While their efforts broke down on the edge of the Brazil box, the *Seleção*'s thrusts were much more incisive with players allowed time and possession inside the penalty area on repeated occasions. There would be a price to pay for such generosity.

With 11 minutes played, a casual cross from Pelé evaded Tostão, the only Brazilian in the penalty area. Control and clearance should have been a straightforward matter. It wasn't. Attempting to bring the ball down with his chest, the returning Campos allowed it to run too far in front of him and then slipped as he sought to regain control. Closing in from the left, Rivellino struck the ball with the outside of his left foot with the precision of a guided missile. It skimmed along the ground, bypassing the dive of a despairing Rubiños and found the back of the net after clipping the far post. Brazil were ahead. As the saying goes, 'it had been coming.' Rivellino swung his arms in rapid rotation before being hoisted into the air by Gérson as Tostão raced past the fallen goalkeeper to crash the ball into the net again, just to make sure everyone had noticed, before joining the growing huddle of *Canarinho*-shirted celebration.

A blanket is cold comfort for a dejected Pelé as he limps out of the 1966 World Cup in Brazil's last group game against Portugal. Disgusted by his brutal treatment, he vowed never to play in a World Cup again.

Wearing an unfamiliar blue shirt – as Sweden wore yellow and blue – Mario Zagallo scores in the 1958 World Cup Final. He would also feature in the 1962 triumph, and later coach Brazil in the 1970 tournament.

Felix – Brazil's often maligned goalkeeper who played every minute of every game in the 1970 World Cup.

The Adidas 'Telstar' ball used in the 1970 World Cup.

The wall provides little protection against a swerving Rivellino free kick, as Brazil equalise against Czechoslovakia.

West Germany captain Uwe Seeler shakes hands with Peru counterpart Héctor Chumpitaz ahead of their decisive Group 4 encounter. The Germans would prevail 3-1, sending Peru to face Brazil in the quarter-final.

Jairzinho puts Brazil ahead against England.

Plenty of mutual respect as Pelé and Bobby Moore embrace after Brazil beat England.

Gordon Banks leaps high to deny Pelé. The goalkeeper's brilliance – including "that save" from Pelé – kept Zagallo's free-scoring team at bay, for almost an hour, until Jairzinho struck

The Ghost of World Cups Past? Uruguay's Luis Cubilla puts his team ahead in the semi-final. Was Brazil's party over?

Brazil fell behind to Uruguay in the semi-final in Guadalajara's Estadio Jalisco, but rallied to score three times and reach the final.

Karl-Heinz Schnellinger scores his one and only goal for West Germany. His late strike sent the semi-final against Italy into a titanic extra-time battle.

Brazil and Italy line up in the Estadio Azteca before the 1970 World Cup Final.

Pelé turns in triumph after heading Brazil ahead in the World Cup Final.

Italy goalkeeper Enrico Albertosi is beaten by the ferocity of Gérson's shot as Brazil retake the lead in the final.

Jairzinho scored in every Brazil game in the 1970 World Cup. Here, he celebrates Brazil's third goal against Italy in the final.

The coup de grâce. Carlos Alberto drills Brazil's fourth goal home to complete a wonderful flowing team move.

The emotions break free for team physical fitness trainer Admildo Chirol as Brazil win the World Cup.

It's coming home! Captain Carlos Alberto holds the Jules Rimet Trophy aloft. It now belongs to Brazil in perpetuity.

Pelé celebrating as Brazil win the World Cup.

Peru were clearly rattled and Brazil pressed quickly in search of a second strike. Tostão and Pelé developed their own game of keep ball, passing back and forth between themselves on the edge of the penalty area between helpless defenders, before the latter was hacked down. Inside the area or outside was the immediate question, swiftly and accurately answered by Loraux as being outside. Again, Rubiños split his defensive wall to allow him a sight of the ball. It was a high-stakes gamble but Gérson's shot failed to find the gap and the ball was scrambled clear. Another goal looked imminent though and when Tostão drifted to the left to collect a pass from Pelé it allowed Rivellino to move into the gap in the middle that the forward had vacated. Seeing the move, Tostão crossed low towards the penalty spot but Rivellino was just beaten to the ball by Chumpitaz, who cleared for a corner.

The corner was played short by Tostão to Rivellino, who then returned the pass as the Cruzeiro forward scampered towards goal along the byline. With the area crowded from expecting a cross from the corner, there was precious little space or time for Tostão to assess his options as two defenders closed on him. Eschewing the obvious lofted pass into the danger area, instead Tostão opted to shoot from the tightest of angles and whipped the ball inside the near post with Rubiños slightly out of position expecting a cross. It was a strike of impudent opportunism, and the sort of thing you only see once in a game. Well, perhaps twice on the rarest of occasions.

Just 15 minutes had been played and, for both teams, the situation had an eerie familiarity about it. Brazil had been two goals clear against Romania before conceding, and then looked decidedly nervous for a while. Peru had trailed Bulgaria by two goals before fighting back for victory. In both those games, the teams winning 2-0 had conceded the next goal before enduring a difficult period. With Brazil seemingly in imperious form, here that looked unlikely. Football has a way of turning the unlikely on its head though and, in more ways than one, history would repeat itself.

For all Peru's commitment to attacking, it was clear that, for at least the next few minutes, they had to be watertight in defence. To concede a third goal would surely be a death knell. For many, that bell rang just two minutes after Tostão had doubled the *Seleção*'s lead, as Brazil had the ball in the net for a third time. A bouncing ball was contested by Clodoaldo and Pedro Pablo León, around midway in the Peruvian half of the field. With both players keen to gain possession, raised feet clashed and a free kick was inevitable. Initially it appeared that the award was in Peru's favour, but when Rivellino claimed the ball it was clear that Loraux's decision had gone Brazil's way. The ball was placed around 30 yards from goal. Despite the distance, as Rivellino backed away ten, then 15, then 20 yards, his intent was clear. Charging forward, he smashed the ball left-footed and it arrowed into the net with Rubiños stationary as it flew past him. The Brazilian contingent in the crowd roared in celebration, but the emotion wasn't echoed on the field. Standing on the edge of the box as Rivellino addressed the ball, Loraux had his arm raised indicating that the free kick was indirect. Joy quickly turned to disappointment among those supporting Brazil, as the reason for Rubiños's lack of interest in the thunderbolt shot was illustrated. Whether Rivellino hadn't realised that the free kick was indirect or had fired the shot in hoping for a deflection on the way wasn't clear. If it was the latter, however, it would have taken a measure of courage to get in the way of the ferociously struck shot.

Could the event be described as another escape for Peru? Perhaps not. The absence of a defensive wall and the goalkeeper's lack of interest suggested that the referee's assessment of the offence had been noted, and they knew a direct shot on goal would only bring a goal kick to restart. The emotional impact of Rivellino's strike, however, only served to raise Brazilian confidence further as they continued to press in the sure expectation that another goal was coming.

Peru were now walking that most perilous of tightropes. They needed to balance their natural tendency to attack in pursuit of a way back into the game with maintaining a solid back line. Whenever they pushed forward, the Brazil defence that had looked less than convincing against Romania and Czechoslovakia had now acquired a resolution and organisation lacking in those games. Tackles, interceptions and blocks, plus the intervention of the linesman's flag for offside, thwarted Peruvian attacks time and again, with Félix having little to do other than collect over-hit passes and make himself available to receive the ball from his defence. Each occasion meant a loss of possession and the onset of another Brazil attack.

It all looked a little too easy as the *Seleção* dropped into a comfortable pattern of play, with Gérson and Clodoaldo controlling the midfield at a stroll, keeping their opponents at arm's length and passing the ball between them. Perhaps it felt too comfortable. A warning was delivered when Cubillas and Mifflin combined to open a gap for the latter. The return pass had drifted too far across Cubillas as he ran into the area. A left-foot shot was required but, not trusting his weaker foot, the forward stretched across to shoot with his right, compromising the power he could deploy. Félix, called into rare action, showed his concentration hadn't wavered and charged forward to block the shot before collecting and taking a blow from the Peruvian as he tried to capitalise on the temporarily loose ball. As the Brazil medical team came on to give the ubiquitous cold water and sponge treatment to the fallen goalkeeper, Peru's players were left to reflect that what had certainly been their best and, arguably, only genuine chance of the game so far had been squandered. Would they get another opportunity before Brazil struck again? Five minutes later that question would be answered.

Just as Rivellino's disallowed goal had encouraged Brazil, despite offering no tangible reward, Cubillas's chance also lifted both Peruvian spirits and confidence. Eager in the challenge and with renewed vigour moving forwards, they began asking more searching questions of the *Seleção* defence. Cubillas had a goalbound shot blocked and then Campos's enthusiastic run was thwarted on the edge of the box. Brazil still enjoyed plenty of possession but their attacks lacked the determination and urgency of the first quarter of an hour or so. Approaching the half-hour mark, that wasn't the case at the other end of the pitch.

There seemed little danger when Chumpitaz advanced towards the halfway line before lofting a pass wide to the left flank looking for Alberto Gallardo. The long-legged forward, back at Sporting Cristal after spells with AC Milan and Cagliari in Italy plus a stay with Palmeiras in Brazil, collected and ambled towards the left of the penalty area where he was confronted by Carlos Alberto. Gallardo's gangly run looked unnaturally awkward but his unusual gait could put defenders off balance and, as he jinked once, then twice, in front of the Brazilian captain, he was about to exploit that characteristic once more. Pushing the ball towards the byline, rather than try to dribble round his opponent, utilising the limited space the move had created, he struck the ball hard and low towards goal. Twenty-three minutes earlier, Rubiños had committed the cardinal goalkeeping sin of leaving enough space on his near post to be beaten there.

Such a mistake rarely happened in games at the highest level, so for there to be two instances in the same 90 minutes was surely unique but, as Gallardo's shot headed towards goal, Félix joined the Peruvian goalkeeper on the 'naughty step' reserved for players whose *faux pas* passes all expectation. The ball whistled past a shocked Félix and into the net. Neither Rubiños nor Félix would ever be counted among the top echelon of international goalkeepers, and their errors in each conceding from an impossible angle demonstrated why that was the case. Goalkeepers are often considered to be the weak point of great teams and, usually, unfairly so. This occurs as they are called on to do so little and, when brought into the game, even rare errors are magnified. For Brian Glanville, however, there were plenty of flaws in Félix's game. 'Indeed,' he posited accusingly in *The Times*, 'the goalkeeper was probably the worst ever to receive a World Cup winner's medal. Content to watch the high crosses fly by as though he was an aeroplane spotter.'[54] All that mattered little to Peru and their supporters. They were back in the game and as Félix contemplated his misdemeanour, at the other end of the pitch any empathy

---

54 'Abysmal Brazil explode the myth of Zagallo', *The Times*, 13 July 1998

Rubiños may have been feeling for his fellow custodian was probably submerged under a wave of relief.

Was the game now assuming the role of some kind of storied repeat? Two similar goalkeeping errors. Brazil had been two goals up against Romania and then conceded. Peru had been two goals down against Bulgaria before scoring. Now there was a further addition to the series of echoes from past games. The goal that fired Peru's comeback against the eastern Europeans had been scored by no other than Gallardo, also converted from a tight angle. The fervent hope of the Peru team was that the set of repetitions would now be completed by them scoring twice more and defeating Brazil, as they had done with Bulgaria. Unfortunately for such fanciful aspirations, this *Seleção* was an entirely different proposition to Bulgaria.

Brazil had been pegged back and, from the restart, Pelé sought to remedy the situation immediately. Receiving the tapped centre-spot restart, he hit the ball long and high towards the Peru goal, reprising his effort in the group game against Czechoslovakia. It was extravagant in the extreme but, as was demonstrated by his attempt to confound Viktor, it was something comfortably within his capabilities. Whereas the shot against the Czechs had only narrowly missed its target, this effort sailed well over Rubiños's crossbar.

Feeling the momentum was now with his team, the goalkeeper was quick to get the game under way again and, justifying his thoughts, just seconds later Campos drove between two Brazilians on the right flank but his cross towards Cubillas was over-hit and drifted away. There were now 15 minutes left before half-time and if either side could score again before the break, the game would surely swing in their favour – and both seemed to realise that.

Jairzinho began to menace down the right again, giving Fuentes plenty of work to do. One cross was only narrowly wide of Tostão. At the other end, intricate interplay nearly opened a gap for Cubillas before he was denied by a converging posse of yellow shirts. Clodoaldo fired a shot in from distance but it lacked direction. The Brazil fans picked up the chant of 'Brazil! Brazil! Brazil!' as Baylón stumbled forward with the ball before laying it off to León. From there it was moved on to Cubillas, whose return to León drew a foul a few yards outside of the penalty area. Chumpitaz played the ball square to Campos, who feinted to shoot before skipping past Marco António, but his shot was woefully mishit and easily cleared. The game was now wonderfully open with both teams pressing to score and leaving gaps at the back as a consequence. It was enthralling fare.

The next chance was manufactured by Tostão, running at the Peru back line, beating one man, then another. Each time he seemed to have pushed the ball too far ahead of him but managed to get a toe to it just in time to retain possession. Then he was into the area, but his attempted shot under pressure trickled wide, deflected by a Peru foot. At the other end, León chased a through ball from Mifflin but Félix charged forward to dive on the ball. Surely a goal was coming, and it so nearly did thanks to another error from Rubiños.

Jairzinho strode forward on the right before clipping a pass inside to Pelé. Around 25 yards out, his shot was speculative rather than convincing as it arrowed towards the goalkeeper's waiting arms. It may have been that Pelé's use of the outside of his left foot imparted some late movement on the ball, or maybe the goalkeeper simply misjudged the flight. Instead of thudding into his midriff, with arms then wrapped gratefully around it, the ball clipped Rubiños's right arm and spun towards goal before striking the far upright and bouncing on the line, as the goalkeeper gratefully plunged on top of it. It was the second time that Pelé had seen his efforts thwarted by the post.

With around five minutes to play, Peru supporters tried to rally their team to a late effort chanting 'Peru! Peru! Peru!' as Gallardo chased a through pass, shadowed by Brito. The defender hesitated, expecting his goalkeeper to come and collect the ball, but Félix was frozen by that same hesitation. Pouncing, Gallardo charged into the gap and only a block by Brito prevented him reaching the ball. Penalty? It was certainly an offence and all of Peru screamed for the spot kick as Félix collected the ball and hurled it downfield while Brito gave the most unconvincing display of innocence.

The speed of the break had left Loraux stranded upfield, a long way from the incident and, as he raced towards the location of the challenge, there was time enough to consider whether he was going to point to the spot. Entering the area though, he stopped suddenly, standing rigidly still with his right arm raised, indicating an indirect free kick for obstruction. Despite Brito complaining vociferously about the decision, there was no hiding his relief at the awarding of the much lesser sanction. Replays suggest that the defender may well have been fortunate.

In the game against Bulgaria, after Gallardo had struck the first goal for Peru, it was Chumpitaz who added the equaliser following a Peru free kick. Now the captain was poised over a similar situation. Another repeat? Surely not. Indeed not! It was a repeat of a different kind. Much as Rivellino had lashed an indirect free kick directly at goal earlier, this time it was Cubillas with a similarly confusing approach. Unlike the Brazilian's effort, the Peru forward's clipped shot cleared the crossbar but, had it found the back of the net, it would have counted for nought.

The final drama arrived as the clock ticked towards 45 minutes and the sun dipped behind the cloud for the first time since kick-off. Out on the left, Rivellino dropped a shoulder and, jinking inside Campos, fired a shot towards the far post. It was hardly struck with the power often imparted by the winger's left foot, but its accuracy demanded action from the goalkeeper. Rubiños dived to his left and palmed the ball away from goal. Running in from his full-back position to cover, Fuentes was helpless as the ball then cannoned against him and back towards goal. Fortunately Rubiños managed to dive and collect the ball as it passed him, avoiding another calamitous error.

Moments later, as Pelé hit a shot from distance high over the bar, the referee blew to end the first period. It had been 45 minutes of scintillating entertainment. Two teams both conscious of their defensive vulnerabilities had served up a delicious feast of football, leaving the crowd in the stadium and the watching millions around the world hungry for more. Brazil had been at their party best for so much of the half but Peru had only been second best by a relatively small margin.

After Gallardo's goal, the old maxim of the next goal being vital had been evidently true, and that remained the case as the players walked from the field and the crowd applauded and lauded their efforts. What was valid then was probably even more the case now. If Brazil scored the next goal, it may well be sufficient for them to drop back into their comfort zone and close out the game. If Peru struck next though, all bets were off. As the teams headed towards the different stairways that would take them down towards their dressing rooms, Didi stood at the top of the stairs greeting each of his players in turn, with pats on the back, arms around shoulders and quiet words of encouragement. The Peru coach clearly thought there was plenty left in the game for his team in the second period. The final 15 minutes of the first half had shown that both teams were capable of grabbing that vital strike. If there was plenty to debate about who would take that advantage, one thing was certain: another enthralling 45 minutes of football was on the menu.

The buzz of half-time conversation and debate hushed slowly as the Peruvians re-emerged from their underground sanctuary. Not in any orderly line, at a trot, but walking in twos and threes, or singularly, joining with others and then drifting apart again. There was something unconsciously significant that order and organisation was not guiding their return to the pitch. It was their natural freedom. It had served them well in the first 45 minutes and would be their mantra when the game restarted. Brazil emerged moments later, and in very much the same order. As the teams crossed and mingled to take up their starting positions, brief conversations rose and passed. Peruvian Spanish and Brazilian Portuguese were different languages, but their approach to football was the *lingua franca* understood by all. When Loraux signalled for Cubillas to restart the game, the crowd that had been briefly subdued when the players reappeared picked up the noise levels. They too were participants in this party.

There was plenty of reason for each side to be cautious in the opening few minutes of the second half. Brazil had a lead to protect and Peru would have feared conceding again, leaving them with a mountain to climb. Such thoughts, however, seemed distant from the players on the pitch. Inside the first 60 seconds, out on the right flank, Tostão drew Fuentes towards him before skipping past with a wonderful sleight of foot. The move came to nothing but it suggested that the half-time break had done little to dim the positive enterprise of the *Seleção*. Peru sought to respond in kind but two searching passes, first intended for Cubillas and then the second towards Gallardo, were comfortably dealt with by the Brazilian back line.

A free kick to Brazil, awarded for a clumsy challenge on Pelé by Fernández just outside the Peru penalty area, offered the first real sight of goal since the restart. Rivellino drove hard and low but the ball flew straight into the waiting arms of Rubiños, and he collected gratefully. Brazil had certainly started as if keen to hit that vital third goal. A minute or so later, Rivellino comfortably evaded a lunging tackle by Campos out on the left and drifted a cross into the box. Only half-challenged by Tostão, Rubiños threw up a despairing hand but only achieved minimal contact on the ball. It fell invitingly towards Jairzinho standing near the penalty spot. Eyeing up the far post, the winger cut across the ball with his right foot, ensuring its passage would evade the goalkeeper. It did so but there was just insufficient curl on the ball to bring it back inside the post and it drifted wide. Another passage of Brazilian possession, wonderfully manipulated by Gérson, ended with Pelé rolling a pass out towards the right of the penalty area for Carlos Alberto to run on to and shoot. Seven days later, an almost mirror image of that ploy would produce one of the World Cup's most iconic goals. On the day, however, the scrambling blocks of Fuentes and Chumpitaz denied the Brazilian skipper a foretaste of what was to follow, and a relieved Rubiños threw himself on to the loose ball to nullify the danger. The Brazilian threat was growing and half a dozen minutes into the half, they struck.

Rivellino clipped a casual 30-yard pass to Pelé, in unforgivably copious amounts of space in the centre circle. He controlled with casual ease before moving the ball on to Jairzinho. The winger trotted inside as Pelé jagged to the right in front of him, accelerating between Fuentes and Fernández. Neither tracked his run, as if they were transfixed by Jairzinho's gentle jog towards them. It was a fatal error. A simple pass between the defenders was all that was necessary to set Pelé clear on goal. Jairzinho delivered it to perfection. Rubiños advanced as Pelé hit the ball across him towards the far post. Given the great man's ability to curl the ball, it's difficult to discern with any certainty that the shot was heading wide of the far post, but it appeared to be as the goalkeeper flung out a right hand to try and save. He may well have done so, but before it reached him the ball struck the leg of a recovering defender and ballooned over his flailing arm, bouncing gently just a few yards from goal. Following in, Tostão joyfully crashed it into the roof of the net and Brazil had their third goal.

Peru had looked to threaten since the restart, but their advances had been largely blunted by misplaced passes or calm Brazilian defending. In contrast, the *Seleção*'s attacks had carried menace and the goal was hardly a surprise. The mountain that Peru had feared was now looming large on their horizon. Didi quickly accepted that such a climb was unlikely to be achieved with the 11 players who had struggled to contain Brazil since half-time, let alone find a way back into the game, and he removed the fairly ineffective Baylón for the more energetic dynamism of 21-year-old Deportivo Municipal forward Hugo Sotil, seeking to add momentum to a team that was now looking to be very much on the back foot. It was the same move that Didi had made just after Gallardo's goal had cut Bulgaria's lead in half. Twenty minutes later, Peru had turned the game on its head. Could a repeat happen here? Three years on, Sotil would earn fame when he moved to Barcelona and formed an attacking partnership with Johan Cruyff. In his first season at the Camp Nou he would win the club's first La Liga title for 14 seasons. Didi needed such skills immediately though, not three years down the road, if Peru were to get back into the game.

But the main action continued to be at the other end. Spotting a Jairzinho dart from deep, Rivellino rifled a long ball into the space ahead of the winger's run with Fuentes in hot pursuit. The powerful Jairzinho was too strong, and muscled his way ahead, chesting the ball down as he entered the area. With the defender running back to try and cover the line, Rubiños charged forward to confront Jairzinho forcing him wide with a desperate dive. It was all he could do, and at least the angle was now acute as Jairzinho collected the ball by the byline, once more to be confronted by a now recovered goalkeeper. The speed of the break had left Jairzinho bereft of any support and, standing almost on the edge of the pitch, faced by a goalkeeper and no less than three defenders now covering the goal line, the sensible thing may well have been to keep possession of the ball, and await team-mates to arrive. This was Brazil, however, and such a thought may not have entered Jairzinho's head. Striking the ball with the outside of his right foot, he attempted the most extravagant of efforts on goal. The shot flew past Rubiños, but one of the covering defenders hurled himself forwards into a diving header and the ball flew back into the goalkeeper's arms.

Peru needed to react, but the nearest they came to striking back came from a Gallardo free kick after he had been felled by Gérson. His shot from 20 yards was bent around the wall but, after failing to catch the ball cleanly, Félix collected at the second attempt. Brazil were now in confident mode – playing the ball around with calm assuredness and rotating positions among the forwards as Tostão drifted wide, inviting Jairzinho and Rivellino to utilise the space created inside, with Pelé a constant threat with the ball at his feet and Gérson pulling the strings from midfield and Clodoaldo his energetic sidekick. The introduction of Sotil had hardly made any difference to the flow of the game and, as it had been since the restart, it was Brazil looking more likely to score the next goal. As the hour mark approached, a run and cross from Jairzinho fell slightly behind Tostão as the forward entered the penalty area, but it seemed to matter little in the context of the match. Brazilian chances were now arriving like those London buses, with another one expected to come along shortly.

A minute later, Didi made another change. Much as had been the case with Baylón since the break, León had struggled to get into the game and may have been struggling with fitness. The only option left to the coach was to send on the Juan Aurich defender Eladio Reyes, making his debut for the national team. It hardly felt like the change that would bolster Peru's attacking threat, and yet inside nine minutes they could have scored. All that seemed far away as the debutant trotted on to the field with Brazil seemingly in total control and keeping the Peru threat at arm's length with some measure of comfort. Perhaps an extra defender wasn't such a bad thing after all.

Reyes's first contribution to the game was to bring Rivellino to the floor as he jinked past wide on the left flank. In what was surely a rehearsed move, the winger fired the free kick towards the near post, tying up with a late run of Gérson. The midfielder got contact on the ball, but the effort was quickly smothered by an alert Rubiños, bravely diving at the Brazilian's feet, with the loose ball then hacked clear. The goalkeeper paid the price for his save by receiving a rap on the wrist from Gérson's follow through, but was quickly on his feet and ready to continue after medical attention.

Three quarters of the way through the game, Zagallo repeated his decision from the group match against Czechoslovakia. With his side leading 3-1 and in apparent total command, Gérson was withdrawn and Paulo Cézar joined the action, dropping into his usual left flank role with Rivellino shifting into the middle to partner Clodoaldo. Gérson was 29 years of age and offering him a rest with the game won looked to be a sensible move. Against the Czechs, removing the *Seleção*'s midfield puppet master had hardly caused any disruption as his team added a fourth goal afterwards. If Zagallo was thinking along similar lines here, Peru were to prove that perhaps there would be a cost to pay for the change. Dropping on to the Brazil bench, Gérson readily accepted the offer of a drink of water from one of the coaching staff before turning to offer a thumbs up and a weary, if contented, smile, acknowledging a shout from behind. Out on the pitch, things were about to turn against his team.

All seemed fine when Jairzinho menaced Fuentes again down the right before cutting the ball across the edge of the penalty area for Pelé to hit in a shot that was blocked when looking bound for the back of the net. Rivellino's corner was scuffed badly and cleared by Campos towards substitute Reyes, who allowed it to run on to Mifflin. The ball was worked forward via Cubillas, then Mifflin again, to find Reyes now on the edge of the Brazil penalty area before being brought down by a clumsy challenge as he controlled the ball. The opportunity was squandered as Gallardo's tame curling shot was comfortably collected by Félix. The next challenge posed to the goalkeeper would be much more testing.

As a Brazil sortie was broken down, Peru advanced with the ball. Sotil played a forward pass and then collected the quick return. Charging into the area, he was upended as Marco Antônio dived in to challenge. A penalty? It mattered little. The loose ball struck the defender on the back, ballooning into the air before dropping to Cubillas who hammered a left-footed volley past Félix, with the goalkeeper beaten by the sheer ferocity of the shot. Despite being in almost total control of the game since the restart, scoring and creating numerous other opportunities, Brazil had been pegged back to 3-2 with 20 minutes still to play. Had Zagallo's decision to take off Gérson contributed to the goal? It's true that the attack came straight through the middle of the field, where the withdrawn player would have been stationed, but it was the heart of the *Seleção* defence that was surely the most culpable. The line that had looked unusually consistent and confident up to that point melted into disarray as Sotil charged at them. It was not the first time in this World Cup that Brazil would be asked to win a game for the second time, having already seemingly done so once. Their reaction would be swift. Peru had a grasp of the momentum but their time to exploit it would be brief, lasting no longer than five minutes.

Urged on by their supporters' chants, Peru were understandably energetic from the restart, chasing forward with the ball eagerly, and harassing any Brazilian in possession, but the unforgiving heat, plus the fatigue from already playing for 70 minutes of such a competitive game when the ball seemed to be constantly in play, served to cool their ardour. Unmistakably, there was a new confidence about the Peru play, now just trailing by a single goal. When possession was gained they interchanged passes with rapid repetition, searching for another opening, as players poured forwards to support the front line, but a packed Brazil defence denied them a clear sight of Félix's goal.

Such adventure was understandable but was always likely to be exposed. As attacks broke down, Brazil were quick to funnel the ball forward, especially to the flanks where Jairzinho on the right and Paulo Cézar on the left were granted extra time and space as Campos and Fuentes scuttled urgently back into position. One such sortie forward had Jairzinho driving forward before playing the ball across the pitch to the newly introduced Botafogo winger, who was keen to get involved. Having only joined the fray a few minutes earlier, his energy levels were as much a threat to the Peru back line as his dribbling skills. Controlling the ball, he jinked inside of a weary Campos towards the edge of the penalty area before being clipped by the defender diligently chasing him. The contact was insufficiently robust to send him to the ground, but enough for Loraux to consider a free kick justified.

Rivellino looked the prime candidate but instead it was Pelé placing the ball on the spot indicated by the referee with studied precision. In the end it was neither of those two firing in the shot. At the whistle, Rivellino ran forward with Paulo Cézar alongside him, and it was the latter whose effort cleared the wall, requiring Rubiños to scamper across his line and tip the ball over the bar. The goalkeeper flapped at the resulting corner, allowing the ball to drop dangerously in the area, but the situation was rescued by the referee's whistle for a Brazilian offence.

The game was now entering the last quarter of an hour and Peru's search for the equaliser was intensified by the unforgivingly nagging fingers of the clock marking off the last minutes. Urgency and precision are seldom good friends, and Peru's imperative would be their downfall. Sotil had been a big positive for Peru since his arrival on to the pitch after an hour. Not only had his direct running with the ball caused the havoc that led to Cubillas's goal, but a desire to take players on and draw defenders out of position had been a growing thorn in the side of the Brazil back line. It was the precise impact that Didi would have been imploring the celestial powers to grant him, but requests granted often carry a disguised price tag. As Oscar Wilde wrote, 'Quando dio vuole castigarci, ci manda quello che desideriamo' (When the gods wish to punish us, they answer our prayers).[55]

On 75 minutes, another mazy run by Sotil was halted as Pelé stole the ball away from him and fed it forward to Tostão. Peruvian legs were now angrily denying the demands of the brain as insistent fatigue all but drowned out the

---

55 Wilde, Oscar, *An Ideal Husband*, 1895

urgent promptings to funnel back when possession was lost. It meant that, as the forward trotted into the Peru half of the field, Tostão had taken the ball for 20 to 30 yards before being challenged. In such circumstances Brazil's dazzling ability was always likely to prevail. Tostão laid the ball off to Jairzinho who had drifted into the middle of the field. Responding to a call from Rivellino, now occupying the Gérson role, the winger laid the ball back, before turning and running powerfully towards the Peru penalty area.

Not only had Rivellino assumed Gérson's position in midfield, the pass he struck to meet up with Jairzinho's run could not have been bettered by Gérson himself. Lofting the ball left-footed over the Peru back line, it dropped perfectly in front of Jairzinho. Playing it past the onrushing Rubiños, the ball ran a little wide to the left of goal, but there was never a hint of doubt in the winger's mind. Coolly controlling with the outside of his right foot, the option of squaring a pass to Tostão, running into the area in support, was never considered. Instead, as Chumpitaz sprinted back to form a barrier between ball and goal, the man who had scored in every game so far revelled in his confidence, feinting to draw the defender into a desperate dive to block a shot that didn't come before calmly clipping the ball over the prostrate Peru captain and into the far corner of the net. A wonderful piece of forward play. It kept his goal-per-game record going, and effectively killed off the stubborn resistance of Peru.

The theatrical and joyous waving of Brazil flags and banners in the crowd underscored that was the case. Five minutes earlier Peru had looked like a team energised. Now that adrenalin rush had been spent and, despite pushing forward, with faint hope more than expectation, it was driven by obligation more than belief, with leaden legs, and minds damned to accept the inevitable. That the challenge was done also seeped into Brazil's play. They had answered the question when it had been posed, and now were content to play out time, as other challenges awaited.

With ten minutes remaining on the clock, Zagallo removed Jairzinho to give Roberto Miranda his second taste of World Cup action following his substitute appearance against England in the group game. It was a late invite to the party, but better late than never and there was still time for the Botafogo forward to enjoy his 11th, and penultimate, appearance for the *Seleção*. His final outing would come in October in a 5-1 friendly victory against Chile. He would score in his swansong but would surely have been more than happy to swap that goal for a strike against Peru, even though it would have had little impact on the outcome of the game. A goal would be denied him, but after a neat piece of interplay from a corner with eight minutes to play his astute cut-back to find Tostão free in the penalty area should have set his team-mate up for his hat-trick goal. In his desire to make sure, a couple of feints compromised the forward's chance, and the ball was smuggled away.

By the final whistle, Brazil had played out the remaining minutes following Jairzinho's goal with relatively little discomfort. A game which for so long had been competitive had eventually drifted to its conclusion. Peru had come up short but not by a large margin. Didi's men had more than done themselves justice in Peru's first World Cup quarter-final, and to finish second best to this Brazil team could hardly be deemed as a disappointing failure. It had to be considered as a success for Peru's coach and, after the World Cup, Didi went on to coach major clubs in Argentina, Brazil, Peru, Europe and the Middle East, but never had an opportunity to take control of the *Seleção*. Why? It may not be too simplistic to say that there were very few black coaches in Brazil football, and that rarity was even more pronounced with regard to the national team.

For supporters of *La Blanquirroja* it was a rare opportunity to celebrate their team's achievements as Peruvian sports and Latino culture writer Luis Miguel Echegaray illustrated when writing about his country's football team in 2015: '[My father] helped me understand the complexity of what it means to root for *La Blanquirroja*. Understand that this is not the same as being a Brazilian, or an Argentinian, or dare I say it, a Chilean. We don't hold the luxury of success, or at least the confidence of knowing that at least we'll be there to compete. For Peruvians, the only assurance that we have in life is that we make the best *ceviche* in the world and that we won't qualify for the World Cup. We are not even Cinderella – at least she made it to the ball.'[56]

In truth, Didi's team had been constructed with the 1958 World Cup triumph as its template. In the intervening dozen years since, football had moved on tactically, and Zagallo ensured that the *Seleção* were up to the pace. It was an important factor in deciding the outcome of the game. Didi's approach had taken Peru far, but against Zagallo they had come up short.

As Echegaray suggests, the perspective from a Brazilian viewpoint is quite different, and certainly was so after the match as far as their coach was concerned. Zagallo's team had been superior in all aspects of the game. He later suggested that the margin of victory could, perhaps should,

---

56 https://www.theguardian.com/football/blog/2015/nov/16/welcome-to-the-choke-the-ballad-of-a-peru-fan

have been larger, 'I admit we could have made it five or six on several occasions but we didn't have much luck with finishing.'[57]

It may not have been an overstatement. The Brazil defence, although reminding the world of their suspect vulnerability at times, had largely kept Peru's forwards at bay, while Didi's rejigged back line had struggled to contain the ebullient attacking play of Pelé, Tostão, Rivellino and Jairzinho, who carried far more threat than Peru's front line. It was perhaps in midfield, however, where the game was won. Gérson, and latterly Rivellino, alongside the often-underrated Clodoaldo maintained control over the efforts of Mifflin and Challe. Even when comparing goalkeepers Brazil came out on top, despite Félix's error to allow Gallardo's goal. At the other end of the pitch, the mistakes of Rubiños were both more plentiful and more costly. That said, later Chumpitaz would seek to minimise the extent of blame for the defeat that was dropped into the goalkeeper's gloves. 'Rubiños made some mistakes,' he conceded, before adding, 'But the goals came because of the quality of players Brazil had.'[58] That the *Seleção* had quality players was plain for all to see, and the prospect of that third World Cup triumph now looked to be increasingly within their reach.

The other quarter-finals were all played at the same time across the country. Despite leading 2-0 with a shade over 20 minutes to play, England failed to repel a West Germany comeback and eventually fell 3-2 after extra time. In the semi-final, Helmut Schön's team would face

57 Downie, Andrew, *The Greatest Show on Earth* (London: Arena Sports, 2021)

58 Downie, Andrew, *The Greatest Show on Earth* (London: Arena Sports, 2021)

Ferruccio Valcareggi's Italy. European champions two years earlier, the *Azzurri* were fancied alongside England and West Germany to offer the strongest European challenge to the expected hegemony of South American teams playing in their own hemisphere.

Ahead of the tournament, there had been much heated debate among the *tifosi* as to which of two midfield stars of the San Siro should be the pivot around which the coach built his team. In the red corner was AC Milan's Gianni Rivera, winner of the Ballon d'Or in 1969 and star of the club's European Cup success in the same year, dubbed as the country's 'Golden Boy'. Sharing the stadium with Rivera and competing for the role as the *Azzurri*'s midfield key was Inter Milan's Sandro Mazzola in the blue or, more correctly, the *Nerazzurri* corner. Rivera was considered to be the more creative, but Mazzola the more consistent. Inter had finished as runners-up in the 1969/70 Serie A table, with Milan two places below them, so there were strong arguments voiced on behalf of both players. Perhaps betraying a characteristic born of years coaching in Serie A football, Valcareggi went with the more reliable option and Mazzola started all of the group games.

The Italians had endured a turgid group stage. A single-goal victory over Sweden and a goalless draw against Uruguay took them into the last match against Israel and needing at least a point to reach the last eight, amid a deafening clamour from home for the flair of Rivera to be included and revive Italian hopes of success. Valcareggi then hit on the idea of deploying the *staffetta* – akin to a baton in a relay race. In 1969, with qualification for the World Cup assured, the coach arranged for the squad to travel to Mexico and play a couple of friendlies against *El Tri* in the Estadio

Azteca. A 3-2 win and 1-1 draw were useful confidence boosters for the team, but the experience of playing in the stifling heat of a Mexico summer also had a significant impact on how Valcareggi would look to deploy his forces the following year. The idea of the *staffetta* was born.

Mazzola would play the first half and then Rivera would replace him for the second period, playing against a tiring team when his attacking flair could be deployed most effectively. It sounded logical but, despite a goalless draw against the Israelis being sufficient for progress, it hardly suggested that the ploy was the answer to Italy's problems. Brazil had scored eight goals in their three group matches. The *Azzurri* had netted just once. Writing in *The Times*, Roger MacDonald described the Italians' performance in the group stages as being 'less of a team than a savings bank'.[59] They had certainly displayed a frugality worthy of the most cautious of financial institutions.

The goal drought would have been even more frustrating as Italy's squad included probably Europe's most in-form forward in Luigi Riva, famously christened by Italian journalist Gianni Brera as *'Rombo di Tuono'* (Roar of Thunder). Riva was fresh from leading his Cagliari side to their first Scudetto, rattling in 21 goals in 28 Serie A games. He would surely be the prime source of goals if Italy were to prosper. Three group games had seen the marksman draw a blank, and the introduction of Rivera against Israel, although surely offering the best opportunity for Riva to open his account, brought another frustrating goalless return.

---

59 'Seeler: Half a team', *The Times*, 18 June 1970

If the *staffetta* failed to deliver against Israel however, in the quarter-final against Mexico that would change. At the break, the scores were level at 1-1 but, following Rivera's arrival, Italy scored three more times to head into the final four with Riva now settling into his stride after netting a brace against the hosts. The semi-final against the Germans in the throbbing and unforgiving heat of the Estadio Azteca would deliver one of the most dramatic and brutally exhausting contests of this, or any other, World Cup. Outside of the stadium a plaque commemorates that tie, hailing as *Partido deal Siglo* (Game of the Century), but more of that later.

While the Italians and Germans would be battling it out to see which of Europe's big guns would contest the World Cup Final in Mexico City, Brazil would remain in Guadalajara, awaiting the arrival of Uruguay to decide on South America's contender for the biggest game on the planet. After the final four teams had finally secured their semi-final berths though, even the location of Brazil's meeting with their neighbours was far from sealed.

* * *

The Semi-Final – Neighbours, Rivals and Spectres

Geographically, Uruguay is one of South America's smallest countries. Its surface area of just under 70,000 square miles and population of some 3.5 million is dwarfed when compared to Brazil's 3.3 million square miles and population in excess of 217 million. And yet, in football terms, as the two countries approached the 1970 World Cup semi-final, there was very little to choose between them. There's an argument to be made that Uruguay's record on the international stage was superior at that time.

Hosting the first tournament in 1930, Uruguay had claimed the Jules Rimet Trophy to add to the three South American Championship titles they had won and Olympic gold medals secured in both 1924 and 1928. They had then boycotted the next two World Cups, held in Italy and France – a result, some reports suggest, of a reprisal against the European teams that failed to travel to South America in 1930. They returned to the fold in the first postwar tournament in 1950 and, as hauntingly bitter Brazilian memories recall, defeated the *Seleção* in the infamous *Maracanazo* to reclaim the trophy that, they may consider, had merely been loaned to Italy in 1934 and 1938.

They would go on to remain unbeaten in any World Cup until losing to the Magical Magyars team of Puskás, Hidegkuti, Kocsis, Czibor, *et al.* after extra time in the 1954 semi-final. A run of 24 years without defeat is noteworthy enough, even if it only includes three tournaments. In 1970, Uruguay were also the reigning South American champions having won the trophy in 1967, although both Brazil and Peru were absent. It was their sixth title. Brazil only had three to their name, and hadn't been continental champions since 1949. The country may be small, with a population roughly equivalent to that of Wales, but Uruguay's footballing pedigree was sufficiently impressive to demand respect on the international arena.

La Celeste had qualified for the 1970 World Cup from a group including Chile and Ecuador, winning three of their four games and drawing the away fixture in Santiago without conceding a goal. It was the sort of form they took forward to Mexico as they were placed into Italy's group, and only in the last minute of the final group game was their defence breached. Following a 2-0 win over Israel and a goalless draw against Italy, qualification was all but secured barring a defensive capitulation against Sweden. That unexpected event never looked on the cards despite late substitute Ove Grahn blotting the defensive copybook with a winning goal in the last minute, and Uruguay advanced into the quarter-final against the USSR. Much of their success had been built on that solid defence and the ability of Peñarol goalkeeper Ladislao Mazurkiewicz, whose displays in Mexico would be recognised when he was elected as the tournament's best goalkeeper, and it was of little surprise that their defence was the key component that saw them through to the semi-final against Brazil.

For the first two group games, coach Juan Hohberg – a former Uruguay international, although born in Argentina – had sent his team out with an unabashed approach of playing to their strengths in a 4-5-1 formation, before introducing a nominal second forward in the final group encounter against Sweden, and it was this arguably more progressive formation that he deployed against the Soviet Union. Any suggestion that a more positive front-foot approach would apply though was far from the mark. Reporting in *The Times* the following day, Frank Keating was scathing about Hohberg's tactics in both this game and their group encounters. 'Uruguay have been nothing these past weeks but dowdy, workaday cabbage whites,' he wrote, going on to add, 'For as long as they could contain things just in front of the high wall they had constructed 18 yards from goal, Uruguay were quite content to potter around the middle of their garden.'[60]

---

60 'Well-timed winner', *The Times*, 14 June 1970

Unsurprisingly, given Hohberg's penchant for defensive solidarity over enterprise and the excellence of Mazurkiewicz, the 90 minutes of the quarter-final were played out without any score and extra time was required to settle the issue. Of that additional 30 minutes, just three were left when the deadlock was finally broken. The Soviet Union had actually found a way past Mazurkiewicz just after the start of extra time, but Anatoliy Byshovets's strike was ruled out by Dutch referee Laurens van Ravens. Suitably, when the goal did come, it was very much in fitting with the game to that point. Anything more elegant would surely have been out of place. Midway inside the Soviet Union half, a Uruguay free kick was touched short to captain Luis Ubiña, who hoisted a hopeful long ball towards the far post. Albert Shesternyov jumped to head clear, challenged by *La Celeste* defender Atilio Ancheta, who had been sent forward. Neither made clear contact and the ball ran free towards the byline before being collected by Luis Cubilla, surrounded by three red-shirted defenders. Profiting from a bagatelle of ball against feet, he eventually broke clear as defenders' arms were raised claiming the ball had run over the line and out of play. He clipped a cross towards the near post where substitute Víctor Espárrago nodded past a helpless Anzor Kavazashvili to secure the win. Protests from the Soviet Union players as they surrounded Van Ravens were brushed away, although replays of the incident suggest that they may well have had a legitimate case.

Espárrago had been the lone man leading the line against Israel and Italy, but the forward from Montevideo's Club Nacional de Football had lost his place against Sweden and was relegated to the substitutes' bench for the quarter-final that had spared FIFA the unedifying spectacle of the game, and a place in the semi-finals of a World Cup, being decided by the toss of a coin.

Brazil had left the field after overcoming Peru still not knowing who their opponents would be in the semi-final. With all four quarter-finals being played out concurrently and the game in the Estadio Azteca deadlocked going into extra time, there was plenty of time for the *Seleção* and their contingent to be showered, changed and crowded around a radio to hear the final minutes. With time almost up, as Cubilla wriggled free from the posse of defenders to take the ball perilously close to the byline – or arguably over it – and cross for Espárrago to score, it set up an all-South American semi-final. In his autobiography, Pelé recalled the moment of the final whistle, 'So, it would be Uruguay. I remembered instantly my promise to my father back in 1950, after that terrible defeat against Uruguay in the Maracanã. I had sworn that Brazil would not have lost had I been there, and now I had my chance for some kind of revenge.'[61]

Two of the next three games hosted by the Estadio Azteca – the third/fourth play-off in any tournament is inevitably a flat, atmosphere-less affair – would live long in the memory of all who were privileged to watch them, and those who have seen replays of them since. The largely turgid play-off was best soon forgotten. Only 26,000 people were in the cavernous stadium to see it. It's questionable if any, outside of those supporting either of the two teams playing, didn't regret their decision to go, but perhaps they should have taken heed of recent matches. Juan Mujica had scored Uruguay's second goal against Israel five minutes

---

61   do Nascimento, Edson Arantes, *Pelé – The Autobiography* (London: Simon & Schuster UK Ltd, 2006)

after half-time in their opening group clash. Since that time, Hohberg's team had played 337 minutes of football without finding the back of the net again, until Espárrago's late intervention. If Brazil were the World Cup's party people – and in the opinion of Geoffrey Green of *The Times* they surely were when he wrote, 'They are the ones who live off the cuff, and give the other person a chance. Their attitude is – you score four and we will score five. That is how football should be played. That is entertainment, and that is what the world loves – goals and entertainment' – then Uruguay were surely the tournament's wet blankets.[62] Both Peru and Uruguay were neighbours of Brazil. In the quarter-final, Didi's team had looked to be the type of neighbour keen to join in with Brazil's Samba Party. In contrast, Uruguay's record across qualifying and in the tournament to date suggested they were the kind of neighbours who would bang on the door of the party and insist that the noise was kept down or they would call the police.

Zagallo's team were almost everyone's favourites to overcome their neighbours at the Estadio Jalisco on the afternoon of 17 June and take their place in the final. And yet there was a lurking danger for them in the way that both they and Uruguay had progressed to this stage. Brazil had conceded goals in all but one of their games so far – the 1-0 win over England being the exception – and had even fallen behind in their opener against Czechoslovakia before cantering to victory. Experience the same fate as Uruguay, however, a team that had now only conceded a single goal in the tournament to date – and that in the very last minute of their group game with progression surely already assured

---

62 'Four best teams in semi-finals', *The Times*, 15 June 1970

– across six qualifying matches, plus now an additional four after arriving in Mexico, and getting back on terms may well be the *Seleção*'s sternest test so far. And, of course, with this being the case and bearing in mind Green's description of their ethos, conceding the first goal was precisely what Brazil did. Before the tie even got under way, however, there was plenty of controversy to set a simmering heat to the fixture.

The original schedule for the tournament had both semi-finals slated to be played on consecutive days at the Estadio Azteca. Inevitably this would mean that, going into the biggest game on the planet, one team would be benefitting from an extra 24 hours of rest and preparation time that came their way while their opponents would still be battling to reach the final. Four years earlier, West Germany had beaten the Soviet Union at Goodison Park to reach the final 24 hours before England had overcome Portugal at Wembley, but in both 1958 and 1962 the semi-finals had been played in different stadia at the same time. Such an argument may well have strengthened the hand of the CBD when they met with FIFA officials to lobby for a change of venue, and concurrent match times.

Whatever persuasive means had been deployed, the CBD negotiators achieved their target. The all-European semi between Italy and West Germany would be played in the capital city on 17 June with a 5pm kick-off. At precisely the same time, Brazil would face Uruguay in Guadalajara's Estadio Jalisco. There were immediate complaints from the Uruguayan contingent about the apparent back-door diplomacy that had led to the change. Brazilian representations had been heard, and the decision made, without anyone from the Uruguayan side in attendance. It had all the hallmarks of a stitch up and to the Uruguayans that's how it felt. Midfielder Ildo Maneiro, who started every game for Uruguay in the tournament, spoke for many of his compatriots when he later asserted that FIFA 'had done the dirty on us'.[63] Had they, though?

An injustice was clearly felt and at one stage Uruguay informed FIFA that, should the decision stand, they would consider withdrawing from the tournament. Sir Stanley Rous was the most powerful man in world football and knew that such a threat was wildly unlikely to be carried through. Had they done so, the consequences for Uruguayan football, both domestically and on the international stage, could have been catastrophic with FIFA-imposed sanctions almost inevitable. Rous held all the cards. He knew it, and he knew that the Uruguayans knew it too. To emphasise his iron-clad resolve not to be swayed from the decision, Rous publicly requested that the Soviet Union party should delay their planned flight back to Europe and be prepared to face Brazil, replacing Uruguay, should the South Americans head for home early. It was more than sufficient. Uruguay had threatened to walk out of the door. Rous had responded by threatening to open it for them to do so. The door remained closed, and Uruguay were compelled to accept the unavoidable truth that they had been outwitted by Brazilian enterprise. Inevitably, it left a sour taste in their mouths, and any existing animosity between the teams had now been turned up a notch or three. The Uruguayan tactics would have relied on their hunger for success, fierce determination

---

63   Downie, Andrew, *The Greatest Show on Earth* (London: Arena Sports, 2021)

and robust approach to the game anyway. That hunger now had something extra to feed on.

On the surface it's easy to feel sympathy for the Uruguay case, but were the Brazilians simply being proactive in convincing FIFA of the merits of their position, regardless of it happening while the Uruguayan players and staff were still awash with elation and celebrating their victory over the Soviet Union? At 11pm on 14 June the news had filtered through to the Uruguay camp that the venue had been moved. It may well have deflated the ongoing celebrations.

Was the change such a big deal? Regardless of the 'fair play' merits of scheduling the games simultaneously, there's no doubt that moving the tie to Guadalajara was a boon to Brazilian aspirations. Uruguay had been based at Puebla and played all of their group games in the Estadio Cuauhtémoc in the city. Puebla was just 100km from Mexico City and, alongside the neighbouring Estadio Luis Dosal in Toluca, had a similar height above sea level to the capital. It meant that, while the Guadalajara altitude was the lowest of any of the stadiums used, the summer weather there was always very hot and humid compared to the still hot but fresher climate at the higher-altitude stadiums. There were other issues as well. Instead of taking a two-hour bus ride from their base to Mexico City, the change meant that, while Brazil awaited them, still ensconced in their established *concentração*, the Uruguayans now faced a much longer trip. Instead of the bus journey being the maximum extent of their journey to the game, on 16 June it was merely the first leg of Uruguay's 350-mile trek to Guadalajara ready for action the following day.

They left their camp at 5am, after only having a cold breakfast due to a lack of forward planning. It set the stage for a strength-sapping odyssey that included a bus journey to the airport, a flight from Mexico City, and then another coach journey to their hotel in Guadalajara. Forty-eight hours after leaving the field following their quarter-final victory, the last thing that a weary Uruguay team needed was to discover that the air conditioning was not working, and their hotel was in the middle of a fiesta, with another one following later in the evening, accompanied by loud music and fireworks. For at least a couple of weeks the overwhelming population of Guadalajara had been seconded to become part of the extended *Seleção Canarinho*. To all intents and purposes, it was a Brazilian city.

If events ahead of the game seemed to all fall in favour of Brazil, there was one spectre haunting the hopes and dreams of all *Seleção* supporters. The *Maracanazo* was an open wound that refused to heal as it gnawed mercilessly at the soul of Brazil, feeding on hope and turning it into dread despair. The decisive game of the 1950 tournament was now two decades distant and for many of the squad that had travelled to Mexico it was something they had been told about, rather than experienced. The young soldier on duty at the Estadio do Maracanã back in Rio de Janeiro on that fateful June day in 1950, who was now coaching the squad in Mexico, was an exception, and for others there were laments etched into memory.

At 29 years old, Pelé was one. Gérson was of a similar age but his memories were only vague. He could only recall having watched a single game during the 1950 World Cup, when Brazil had scored six times against Spain. As for the final match, he knew the outcome, but had no memory of it. Piazza was two years younger but his recollections were even more shadowy. He was just seven years old at the time and, where he lived, his family had no electricity or transistor radio. The story of the World Cup only reached him later, and at that tender age it had meant very little. Much the same was true of many of the younger players. Clodoaldo was 20, as were Edu and Leão. Marco Antônio was only 19 and, along with Edu and Leão, had been born after the game. The problem was that, despite only a few members of the group carrying the heavy weight of an unwanted memory, newspapers have perfect recall and, for them, with Uruguay awaiting in the first World Cup encounter between the teams since 1950, the *Maracanazo* was front and centre of their attention.

For the four days between the quarter-finals and semi-finals, Brazilian newspapers and press had little else on their minds, and whenever speaking with members of the squad or coaching staff that became painfully clear. The openness of the Brazilian camp had served them well early in the tournament, helping to foster an affinity with Mexican fans. Now, however, that accessibility was becoming far less advantageous, as the constant press attention about the game 20 years earlier seeped into the public consciousness. Pelé would later recall how, on the eve of the semi-final, anyone arriving at the team's hotel was insisting on how important it was to defeat Uruguay regardless of what happened afterwards. Exorcising the ghost of the *Maracanazo* was not the most important thing, it was the *only* thing. Losing to Uruguay again, missing out on glory again, having dreams destroyed by *La Celeste* again, it would be too much to bear.

Despite all attempts to deal only with the future rather than invoke the past, as skipper Carlos Alberto recalled, when talk of a subject is constant, passionate and seemingly everywhere, even the most determined of barriers are found to have holes, 'And as people were talking about 1950 it's going to get into your head. Into everybody's head. Right? And I think that's what happened.'[64] Over in the Uruguay camp there was an awareness of the significance of the fixture, but it was far less prominent.

Despite Carlos Alberto's assertion and Zagallo's own memory of the *Maracanazo*, it was the latter's recollection of a far more recent game that drove his tactical thinking ahead of the semi-final. Uruguay's sky-blue shirts were similar to those worn by England in the group encounter when Brazil had compromised their normal flair to see off the reigning world champions. Caution had proven effective on that occasion. Against Uruguay, however, perhaps aided and abetted by the constant reminders of 1950 that got 'into everybody's head', Brazil's opening phase of the game was subdued to the point that, as Zagallo commented, 'Our team was unrecognisable.'[65]

Before kick-off there had been a boost for the *Seleção*. Injury had deprived the coach of the services of Everaldo against Peru. Marco Antônio had provided more than sufficient cover on the left of the defence but, with the Grêmio defender now recovered, Zagallo was happy to welcome him back into the starting 11. With Félix in goal, behind a back line of Carlos Alberto, Piazza, Brito and Everaldo, Clodoaldo and Gérson occupied the middle of the field. Further forward, Jairzinho had the right flank and Rivellino the left, leaving Pelé and Tostão up front. This was Zagallo's team of choice. Two games away from

---

64 Downie, Andrew, *The Greatest Show on Earth* (London: Arena Sports, 2021)

65 Downie, Andrew, *The Greatest Show on Earth* (London: Arena Sports, 2021)

glory, and his favoured players were all available to him. The same 11 would play out the remainder of Brazil's World Cup campaign, but with around 30 minutes played that campaign was looking likely to be curtailed.

As the teams lined up for the anthems, the mood of the 65,000 fans inside the stadium was self-evident 'with their Samba bands and drums throbbing and their green and yellow flags beating the air' as Geoffrey Green described for *The Times*.[66] A fiesta was required, but would it happen? Would the flair of Brazil triumph over the doughty resilience and fierce national pride of the Uruguayans? Could the team wearing dancing shoes overcome the opponents in hob-nailed boots? 'Who breaks a butterfly upon a wheel?'[67] The script was written but, as the game started, Brazil began to fluff their lines.

Uruguay's opening to the game was every bit as robust as many expected it to be. As far as Hohberg's team were concerned the doves released into the air ahead of kick-off signified anything but a peaceful start. Just five minutes had passed, with both teams offering cautious openings, when Carlos Alberto rolled a pass out towards Jairzinho on the right-hand touchline. The winger had just played the ball back towards his skipper when Juan Mujica clattered into him from behind. It was one of those incidents often politically described as a 'bad challenge'. In reality it was no challenge of any kind at all. Any relationship to the location of the ball and Mujica's target of contact was purely coincidental. Spanish referee José María Ortiz de Mendibil flourished the yellow card at the uncompromising Nacional

---

66 'Brazil in World Cup final again', *The Times*, 17 June 1970
67 Pope, Alexander, 'Epistle to Dr Arbuthnot', January 1735

defender, as Jairzinho painfully hauled himself to his feet. It wouldn't be the last time that Ortiz de Mendibil would have cause to sanction such behaviour.

It would be easy to blame the *Seleção*'s early mistakes on the physical approach of their opponents. Easy, but also incorrect. Facing such attention was nothing new to these players. There were other factors at play, as Pelé recalled, 'There were a lot [of] nerves ... it was as though all of us had been there on that July day 20 years ago, and were now making the same mistakes. Bad passes, weak defence, and we couldn't get through our opponents at all.'[68] To make matters worse for Brazil, Uruguay seemed to sense the hesitancy, with an unusual lack of conviction in their opponents' play, and sought to take advantage of the opportunity it presented.

Still inside the first ten minutes, receiving possession from a throw-in and under no pressure at all, Clodoaldo scuffed an intended forward pass from the edge of his own area, gifting the ball to a surprised Ildo Maneiro. Recovering composure and control, he played the ball to Julio Morales before looping round outside to receive a return pass. Striking a shot from 20 yards, the ball flew straight towards Félix who collected safely after a brief bout of juggling. Anywhere wide of the goalkeeper would surely have caused him problems. It was the first genuine threat on goal. More would follow in the coming minutes and, unexpectedly, mostly from those wearing blue shirts. This was the period when Zagallo described his team as being 'unrecognisable'.

---

68   do Nascimento, Edson Arantes, *Pelé – The Autobiography* (London: Simon & Schuster UK Ltd, 2006)

Morales drove down the left before crossing into the box. The ball was half cleared by an Everaldo header towards Dagoberto Fontes, but his shot from distance lacked genuine menace and Félix dropped on it to smother. Uruguay were undoubtedly in the ascendancy, with the *Seleção* nervous, error-strewn, and unconvincing. If Brazil were forgetting their script, the same wasn't true of Uruguay. Despite showing more enterprise than in their earlier games, they remained true to type when required. Everaldo advanced to try and support the attack but, when he turned as if to lay off a pass before flicking the ball forward, Fontes felled him with as much power as he wished he had put into his shot a few moments earlier. With a gesture surely destined to be as forlorn as any, he held both arms in the air, looking towards the referee. It was less of a *mea culpa* and more of a 'Soz, my bad. Oops!' but it failed to get him off the hook. Ortiz de Mendibil merely tapped the pocket where his cards were housed, removed the yellow one and noted the offender's name.

That was after 18 minutes; 60 seconds later the first goal arrived, with an inability for the guilty party to get off the hook becoming the theme of the moment. Defending on the right of Brazil's defence, Carlos Alberto played a casual ball inside to Brito. The bearded centre-back looked calm as, in turn, he played a simple pass to the player in front of him. Unfortunately that player was wearing sky blue rather than *Canarinho*. This error would cost.

Morales advanced unchallenged towards the penalty area arc before clipping a flighted pass inside of Piazza towards the run of Cubilla. Controlling the ball with his thigh, the forward – who had returned to Uruguay with Nacional after periods of globetrotting with Peñarol, Spain with Barcelona, and then Argentina with River Plate – drifted wide, creating a tight angle for any direct attempt on goal.

Félix stood on his near post and Piazza charged back to get in a challenge as Cubilla got off his shot. Struck with his ankle or shin, rather than foot, the effort lacked power and looped along with a bounce as the goalkeeper seemed hypnotised by its flight. Félix took half a step then stopped, then started again. It was too late. The ball drifted past him and found the far corner of the net. As Green poetically described in the same article, 'It went past Félix like a weary sob.'[69] To many, it looked like a catastrophic error by Félix, to be beaten by a mishit shot from such a tight angle, but was there more to it than that?

Félix later argued that at least a portion of the blame should be apportioned to the coach. After the Peru game, Zagallo had apparently berated Félix for conceding the goal scored by Gallardo, struck from an even more acute angle. He insisted that Félix had been badly positioned, consequently offering the Peruvian a sight of goal at the near post that simply shouldn't have existed. Félix stood his ground and said that wasn't the case, but Zagallo was adamant. In any similar circumstance in the future, he should be much closer to the post and, Félix insisted that the coach assured him, if that caused a problem, he would take the blame. There's no reason to suggest that conceding the goal was in any way an attempt by the goalkeeper to prove a point to Zagallo. Félix was far too professional and dedicated for such childish one-upmanship. The goal had been a catalogue of errors, and yet it would be difficult to

---

69 'Brazil in World Cup final again', *The Times*, 17 June 1970

say that Uruguay hadn't earned their lead. The spectre of the *Maracanazo* roared with laughter at the misfortune of his victims once again, grinning with macabre satisfaction.

As the Uruguayans celebrated uproariously, Brazilian heads were bowed and shaken in disbelief. It couldn't happen again, could it? Pitched against a team with the tournament's outstanding goalkeeper, that had only conceded a single goal – and that a virtually meaningless strike – across their last ten games, Brazil looked to be out of form, out of luck and on their way out of the World Cup. The *Seleção* needed to pick themselves up from the floor. Concede again and their dreams would be shattered.

A Uruguay corner from the left was headed out but the ball ran to Maneiro, lining up a shot. Enthusiasm got the better of the midfielder, though, and the ball was blazed extravagantly over the bar. Brazil needed a calming voice and it came from Pelé. Uruguay's Roberto Matosas recalled that he was encouraging his team-mates when they were losing 1-0, his team had lost their way, and Pelé was the only one who was calm. Without him, the Uruguayan mused, any comeback may not have happened.

Gradually, as Uruguay failed to add to their lead, the reassuring words of their talisman began to take effect and Brazil eased themselves into the game. Zagallo trusted his players to adjust their tactics on the field as the situation demanded, and that latitude was key in their renaissance. In the early minutes Hohberg's approach to stifle the creativity of Gérson, with an overload in midfield, had prevented the *Seleção* from developing any momentum moving forwards. As the match progressed, and accepting that he was having little effect on matters, Gérson told Clodoaldo to take up a more advanced position while he dropped deeper to cover.

The effect was for Gérson to drag his marker out of position and allow Clodoaldo to exploit the space that was created. With Rivellino also going deep at times and Tostão's intelligent response of drifting left into the new space, Clodoaldo pushing forward would create new problems for Uruguay. A passage of play ending with a long-range shot from the young midfielder that flew narrowly wide of Mazurkiewicz's goal suggested that the ploy held promise of success.

The change in approach from Brazil required a response from Uruguay and, while adjustments were taking place, Gérson took the opportunity to drift forward. His cross to Pelé opened up a rare gap in the Uruguay back line but the header floated wide. With growing confidence, Brazil were now happy to illustrate that they could fight fire with fire if required to do so. The foul committed by Carlos Alberto on the troublesome Morales could have come straight out of *La Celeste*'s playbook, nullifying an attack before it had a chance to develop. Levelling up the physical challenge was one thing, but they needed the tangible reward of a goal to do the same to the scoreline.

Following a short corner on the right, Pelé's attempt to jink his way between two defenders on the edge of the area was foiled by a foul from Mujica. Rivellino lined up to take the free kick but, for once, he eschewed the potent power of his sledgehammer left foot. Instead he attempted a delicate curling shot that cleared the five-man wall and headed towards the near top corner of the net, but Mazurkiewicz was in the perfect position to flick it over the bar. It was the left-winger again causing problems minutes later when his quick feet allowed him to cleverly skip past Julio César Cortés's lunging challenge, but the recovering Peñarol midfielder felled him. This time it was Pelé hitting in the free kick. Again, the defensive wall erected by the goalkeeper was successfully bypassed. Once again, Mazurkiewicz was perfectly placed to receive the ball into his midriff, wrapping his arms safely around it. Finding gaps in such a well-drilled defensive barrier was challenging enough, even for a team so extravagantly talented as the *Seleção* now pressing with increased frequency. Once that seemingly impenetrable block was breached, however, the imposing figure of Mazurkiewicz, dressed all in black, remained defiant.

Moving towards the break, chances were appearing more frequently as the Uruguayans eyed the sanctuary of the dressing room and half-time. Jairzinho drifted in from the right, feeding a pass towards Tostão, but the forward's shot was dragged well wide of the near post. There were a mere 60 seconds separating Uruguay and the reassurance of having their lead intact at the half-time whistle when Brazil finally cracked the code.

Rivellino advanced with the ball at his feet across the halfway line, sliding a pass to his left and the supporting Everaldo. In the middle of the field, with Gérson hanging back in the centre circle, Clodoaldo sprinted forward into space ahead of the Uruguayan back line. Receiving the ball, he switched quickly wide to Tostão who had drifted to the left flank. Gérson's holding position had opened up space in midfield for Clodoaldo, and Tostão's move out wide had performed the same service for the midfielder further forward. Touching off the pass first time, Clodoaldo drove forward into the box with Atilio Ancheta turning to try and track his run but trailing by a crucial couple of strides. Out on the left, Tostão gave credence to that old adage of forwards being the ideal players to cross balls into the box as they know precisely where they should be delivered in order to give team-mates best chances of converting them. It was a perfect pass. Clodoaldo strode forward to meet up with it and fired an unstoppable shot past the erstwhile unbeatable, unflappable Mazurkiewicz.

It was the 20-year-old's first goal in an official international for the *Seleção* and, in a career that saw him appear 38 times for them, it would be the only time he found the back of the net. As in all things, context is everything, and there could hardly have been a better time to score your only international goal. The game was level and the man who had no recollection of the 1950 World Cup – being less than a year old at the time – had laid to rest the ghost of the *Maracanazo*.

Mere seconds later, José María Ortiz de Mendibil brought the first half to a close. The body language of Hohberg's team as they headed towards the dressing room was telling. Uruguay walked off slowly, deflated by seeing their lead snatched away right at the death and now fearing a resurgent Brazil in the second period. The 120 minutes against the Soviet Union, the hours of travelling from Puebla, the change from playing temperatures rarely rising above 20 degrees to now a stadium where twice that value was normal, and the rest denied them at the hotel, thanks to the raucous activities of those supporting Brazil, now weighed down on them like concrete overcoats.

The momentum had swung in Brazil's favour, but as the *Canarinho* shirts left the pitch the heads popping through the top of them were hardly wreathed in smiles. In the dressing room, Zagallo launched into his players with a venom that had been brewing across the previous 45 minutes as he watched his players labour fitfully. It was not a classic 'hairdryer' fuselage, full of invective, but more to show that he believed, he knew, his team was far superior to the opponents they had struggled against. He wanted more. He expected more. He demanded more. Brazil's preparation consistently gave them the edge against opponents after the break. 'Physically, Brazil was flying,' Rivellino recalled. 'Brazil's second half … the second half was always better than the first.'[70] In the second half the coach's team would deliver for him.

For Brazil, the second half was full of opportunities. The past was where it belonged. They had taken the best – and physically, the worst – that Uruguay had to offer and had come through it. As time moved on, the aggression that had been effectively destructive in the first period assumed more of a desperate rationale. Brazil hadn't always scored the first goal up to this point; Czechoslovakia and now Uruguay had both taken the lead against them. They had, however, consistently scored the last goal, and would continue to do so. The preparation and physical conditioning undertaken was the ace up the sleeve to complete their Royal Flush. They had the perfect ten-out-of-ten performances of Jairzinho, scoring in every game, the jack-in-the-box power of Rivellino, Gérson's midfield majesty and the regal presence of *O Rei*, Pelé. There was no way they would lose the game from here.

The second half began as if Brazil were expecting to score and Uruguay were hoping not to concede. The *Seleção* pressed forward and Uruguay retreated to man the ramparts of their defence. Early intent was illustrated by Jairzinho's

---

70 *CHAMP10NS*, Netflix

run down the right. Evading two defenders, he reached the byline but his cut-back was smothered by Mazurkiewicz. If Hohberg's team were to have any chance of revival, it would surely come in the early minutes of the half, before fatigue had eaten too much of their resolve and reserves of energy away.

Mujica had a shot from long range but it was never a threat to Félix. Such enterprise, albeit of a limited nature, carries a measure of peril, though, when possession is lost, and losing it to Pelé in space only heightens that danger. An attempted exchange of passes between Luis Ubiña and Fontes around the halfway line was rudely interrupted by Everaldo, and the ball ran free to Brazil's number ten with space in front of him. Driving forward, he attacked the penalty area as two, then three defenders closed on him, snapping at his ankles as they trailed in his wake. Finally it was a lunge by Ancheta that tumbled him to the floor. Pelé's momentum saw him fall well inside the penalty area, but the referee's decision to place the resultant free kick just outside was proved to be correct by the replay. The restart came to nought.

Throughout the game, Pelé had noticed a tendency for Mazurkiewicz to hit his goal kicks out short to players midway inside his own half of the pitch, and had been priming himself to capitalise on the observation if opportunity arose. That chance came not long into the second period. Mazurkiewicz drilled the ball towards Maneiro but Pelé had read his intentions, racing forward to intercept. Collecting the ball around 35 yards out, he struck it back on the volley with the goalkeeper having insufficient time to regain his position. It was an inspirational piece of play, deserving of a more tangible outcome, but Pelé's shot was too close to the near side of the goal from where Mazurkiewicz had played the ball, and the goalkeeper managed to scramble across and block the shot with a tumbling save.

Since the restart, apart from all-too-brief flurries from *La Celeste*, Brazil had dominated, pressurising the Uruguay back line. Jairzinho in particular was giving Mujica a torrid time down the right. With the Nacional defender having seen yellow after just five minutes, both he and Jairzinho knew that another rash challenge could bring disaster for him and his team. It gave the Brazilian a licence to run at him almost with impunity. Another Jairzinho thrust down the flank saw him beat the hesitant defender, reach the byline, then cut back, and go round Mujica once more, before setting Pelé up for a shot that flew past the far post.

As the half progressed, Brazil's superior fitness seemed likely to be the telling factor. Uruguay's players were running out of fuel but the *Seleção's* tanks looked to be topped up to full. The combination of Uruguay's travails and Brazil's preparation in the months ahead of the tournament was allowing Zagallo's team an increasingly free rein to display their skills. Another passage of play began by Gérson's short pass to Pelé in the middle of the field set things in motion. An effortless sidestep of a half-hearted challenge and a simple pass out wide to Carlos Alberto, advancing on the right, looked casual and comfortable, because it was. The captain then swiftly altered the point of attack with a cross-field pass to an unmarked Rivellino on the halfway line. The winger turned and advanced into space as the defence sank deeper. This was almost football with a swagger. A forward pass found Tostão around 25 yards from goal. He was marked by Ancheta, but more so in theory than practice. Control and a neat swerve of direction easily took him past the defender to the edge of the penalty area, but his shot was scuffed and Mazurkiewicz gratefully fell on the ball, although it may well have been slipping wide of the near post anyway. There was little panic in Brazil's attacks, despite Uruguay's defence offering typically stubborn resistance and the minutes ticking by. Illogically, as they passed, *Seleção* confidence and belief grew.

With a little more than 15 minutes to play, Hohberg played the card that had turned up trumps against the Soviet Union, Espárrago replacing Maneiro. A forward for a midfield player suggested that the coach was gambling on scoring a late goal to steal the game, as had been the case in the quarter-final. Ironically, Espárrago was involved when a goal arrived just a couple of minutes later, but it was hardly in the way Hohberg had hoped would be the case. The substitute advanced on the right in a rare Uruguay attack but a challenge saw the ball run loose to Fontes who tried to sweep it to the left, but his wearily misplaced pass across the face of the Brazil penalty area fell to Jairzinho. The powerful winger was some 80 yards or so from goal as he controlled, then set off on a run.

Striding forward, he played a pass towards Pelé on the halfway line before sprinting onwards. A first-time flick from Pelé evaded Castillo and landed at Tostão's feet just a couple of yards away from him, but with space to advance into. The invitation was accepted. Two strides drew Uruguay players towards him before an incisive pass precisely met up with Jairzinho's run. Roberto Matosas tried to close but it was a forlorn effort. The hint of a feint with a drop of the shoulder unbalanced the defender as Jairzinho powered past him and into the area. Any efforts to impede his progress, by fair means or foul, were brushed aside.

Mazurkiewicz advanced but a low right-footed shot offered the goalkeeper little chance of any meaningful intervention as the ball arrowed into the far corner of the net. It was a sumptuous goal. Yes, by this time the blue-shirted players were struggling against fatigue as much as against those in *Canarinho*, but this was a goal that any defence would have been hard-pressed to deny. There was power, pace, precision and a sure-footed finish that brooked no argument.

Jairzinho ran to the sidelines before falling to his knees and crossing himself in thanks to unseen powers above. The first to join him was Tostão, whose perfectly weighted pass had been the *hors d'oeuvre*, before Jairzinho feasted on the finish. Next was Pelé, who had provided the *amuse-bouche* of a flick to Tostão. The best parties include the tastiest of fares, and this goal was sufficient to tickle the tastebuds of all lovers of the beautiful game. If the outcome of the semi-final was now decided, the final score was not. There remained the sweetest of sweets to follow although there would be a moment of footballing indigestion to endure first.

Before that though, there was still time for Brazil to confirm that inside their velvet glove there was plenty of steel. A half-hearted Uruguay attack down their right came to nothing and Pelé escaped with the ball, haring down the touchline with Fontes in pursuit. The talismanic forward's ankles and shins had suffered plenty of attention from uncompromising challenges and perhaps fearing the imminent delivery of another one, Pelé flung his right elbow back into Fontes's face just as the scything tackle – although 'tackle' is hardly an apt description of the Uruguayan's intention – was delivered. Pelé ended up crumpled in a heap on the touchline as Fontes gently fingered his nose for signs of damage.

Pelé insisted that the elbow had in fact impacted Fontes on the forehead rather than the nose, and little damage had been caused to the Uruguayan. Fontes contended that the contact was with his eye, but he refused to go down and writhe about on the floor as he didn't want to give the Brazilian the satisfaction of knowing that he had hurt him. It may have been a forlorn gesture of bravado, with Pelé's attention very much concentrated on his own pains as he lay in a crumpled heap on the floor. Later he would confirm that although Fontes's challenge caused some pain to his leg, it quickly passed, in comparison to the discomfort sustained to his elbow as it impacted with the Uruguayan's head.

Pelé's charge forward had left the Spanish official trailing in his wake and the linesman was policing the opposite touchline. It meant that neither official had seen the Brazilian's aggression and, as Fontes stood over the fallen Pelé with the ball in his hand, Ortiz de Mendibil belatedly arrived on the scene, took possession of the ball and awarded a free kick against Uruguay. Perhaps having accepted that he had already delivered revenge of his very own preference, Fontes offered little dispute to the decision and trotted away to take up his defensive position. In modern times, VAR would surely have delivered a different outcome, although it could be the case that knowledge of such things may well have prevented the incident occurring anyway.

There was little chance of Uruguay fighting back now, and if another goal was going to arrive, it would surely be for a rampant Brazil. After a scramble on the edge of the Uruguay area the ball broke out to Gérson, but his 25-yard shot towards the top right-hand corner merely offered Mazurkiewicz an opportunity to display his agility once more. Throwing himself to his right, both feet clear of the ground, he snatched the ball from its trajectory, landing safely with it in his grasp as if he was picking apples from the low-hanging branches of a tree.

Outstanding goalkeeping wasn't going to save Uruguay from defeat, but an obstinate refusal to bend the knee when faced with overwhelming odds came close to doing just that. Time was nearly up as Hohberg's team hurled their last reserves of energy into a series of high crosses into the Brazil box, testing Brito, Piazza and the handling of Félix. Most were dealt with effectively, but when a weak punch from the goalkeeper fell to earth around the penalty spot it was recycled by Castillo to Mojica, who returned it to the area.

If the defender had spotted Cubilla in space on the far post, it was a cross of devilish design. The Brazilian centre-backs had been drawn into the middle of a posse of players, but the flight of the ball passed over them all to find the diminutive winger unchallenged with just Félix to beat from five yards. His header was firm and true, targeted just inside of the post. If the Brazil defenders had fallen prey to one of their lapses of concentration, however, they would be grateful to their goalkeeper for saving the day. His flapping contact with the ball had led to another Uruguayan cross, but Félix redeemed himself by denying Cubilla with a diving save to his left that pushed the ball away. It was a far clearer opening than when the same player had scored in the first half, but with no issue about guarding his near post to cloud his thoughts, Félix's reactions were sharp enough to make the save. Cubilla chased the ball as it ran away but, although his turn and cross evaded Félix's attentions, there was no blue-shirted player to take advantage and it was gratefully thumped clear. Moments later the *coup de grâce* was delivered.

With players committed forward in hopeless endeavour of the equaliser, a long Brazilian clearance was met by a weak defensive header around the halfway line by skipper Luis Ubiña, challenged by Tostão. The ball dropped to Rivellino, who quickly played the ball forward to Pelé, before continuing his forward run in support. Uruguay's desperation for an equalising goal had been akin to playing with fire and they were about to get their fingers burned. Pelé collected possession on the edge of the centre circle and quickly advanced as alarm bells rang out an ominous warning in Uruguayan ears. Entering the penalty area, and faced by a recovering Ubiña, he stopped. Was it a pause before slipping past his opponent? No, he was waiting for Rivellino. In a move that would famously be repeated a few days later, he touched the ball twice before gently rolling it a few yards to his right. The winger arrived and hit in a low left-footed shot that squirmed under Mazurkiewicz's dive and into the net. Even the unbeatable goalkeeper was now beaten.

Rivellino had confirmed the *Seleção*'s place in the World Cup Final, and as he charged around the pitch his face bore every trace of unbridled elation. Walking, striding, rather than running, he pumped his arms up and down shouting as if it was simply too much emotion for his body to contain. Eventually he was swamped beneath a *Canarinho* avalanche of team-mates, and tracksuited support staff, drawn from the bench by the irresistible magnetic pull of triumph.

It was almost all over with time up, but the most sublime moment of the game was still to come. In what was a play-action equivalent of a lap of honour, Pelé had one more trick to perform, an encore *par excellence* – well, so nearly anyway. A cacophony of shrill whistles from the Brazilian fans in the crowd insistently demanded that Ortiz de Mendibil end the game and confirm what was now inevitable. Fortunately for all lovers of football, the Spanish official would not be swayed.

On the right flank of the halfway lane, Jairzinho teased his marker, feinting first this way, then that way, before rolling a pass inside to Tostão. Driving at an exhausted and beaten defence, a simple ball scythed through the blue-shirted wall and met up with Pelé's unchallenged run. With Matosas vainly chasing back, the ball arrived at the feet of the forward just inside the penalty arc, at the same time as Mazurkiewicz's dart from the goal line to cut down the angle. Expecting the obvious attempt to clip a shot over him from the Brazilian, the goalkeeper slid forward with his arms raised. Pelé wasn't about to conform to the obvious though; very far from it. Rather, it was time for another of his party pieces. Offering mere disdain for the ordinary, he stepped over the ball, allowing it to run past Mazurkiewicz and wide to the right as he scampered past to the left. Turning sharply, he then circled behind Mazurkiewicz, collecting the ball once more. It was a moment frozen in time as the world drew breath and watched in awe.

Four years later, at the next World Cup, Johan Cruyff would display to the planet a move that would forever bear his name when he turned and sent a Swedish defender so far in the wrong direction that not only was he required to buy a ticket to get back into the stadium, he needed to hire a taxi first to get him back there. From that moment, as Cruyff scampered clear, a cross with the outside of his foot came to nothing. Poetry has its own beauty. There is no requirement for the mundane pay-off, of a ball in a net, that may detract from the beguiling beauty of what had preceded it. And so it was with Pelé against Uruguay.

Noticing Ancheta racing back towards the goal line, the magician paused for a split second, hoping to allow the duped Uruguayan to run too far too quickly and eliminating any possible intervention. Immortality, though, is a characteristic jealously guarded by the gods. Pelé stroked the ball towards goal but the slightest touch by the heel of Ancheta's boot was enough to divert its trajectory, and it slipped agonisingly wide of the far post. The insertion of Ancheta's heel into the story of what would surely have been the most audacious, if not simply the downright greatest, goal of World Cup history was like a heckler at an operatic finale; unwelcome, unwanted and almost churlishly selfish. At least for the fans in the stadium and the millions granted the privilege of watching on television, as would be the case with Cruyff in West Germany, there was the rarest of glimpses of a human being like us all, well almost like us all, reaching up to touch the sky.

Moments later, it was all over. Ortiz de Mendibil brought the game to a close and Brazil had reached the World Cup Final for the third time in four attempts. Beauty had slain the beast. Poetry had overcome the prosaic, and artistry had prevailed against the artisan in a game that had offered the *Seleção* the sternest of tests and yet had also inspired them to deliver with the utmost of flair. Pelé was in no doubt about the justice of the result, 'We were a better team than the Uruguayans, just as we had been in 1950; the difference now was that, 20 years on, it was the better team that won.'[71]

---

71 do Nascimento, Edson Arantes, *Pelé – The Autobiography* (London: Simon & Schuster UK Ltd, 2006)

In *The Times* the following day, Geoffrey Green lauded the *Seleção*'s success and celebrated their play. 'The world that loves attacking football will applaud this result,' he enthused. 'As the children of the Samba game sometimes dissolute in their poetic arrogance, but always a joy to watch – have now reached the climax of this global tournament.' He went on to add, 'Uruguay could not face the final hurricane. Brazil had too many options and too great an insinuating rhythm which even the enmeshed Uruguayan defence had to bow to in the end. Viva Brazil!'[72] That Samba rhythm would be beaten out even after the game, as Pelé recalled, 'We left the stadium with our instruments and we didn't stop singing until we got back to the hotel. Then we kept going on the terrace.'[73] For now, the party was in full swing, but there was one more game to play before the real celebrations could begin. At high noon on 21 June in Mexico City's Estadio Azteca, Brazil would face off against Italy to decide who would lift the Jules Rimet Trophy. They had come through a battle to beat Uruguay. If anything, however, the *Azzurri*'s passage to the final had been even more dramatic.

---

72 'Brazil in World Cup final again', *The Times*, 17 June 1970

73 Downie, Andrew, *The Greatest Show on Earth* (London: Arena Sports, 2021)

Part 4 – Here comes the sun. And I say, 'It's alright'[74]

74 From the song 'Here Comes the Sun', *Abbey Road*, the Beatles
    (Apple, 1969)

A Roll of Blue Thunder

After finding their form, Luigi Riva finding his shooting boots, and Ferruccio Valcareggi deploying his *staffetta* with devastating effect against Mexico, it was an increasingly confident *Azzurri* that moved from Toluca's Estadio Luis Dosal, where they had played three of their four games to date – the other being staged at the Estadio Cuauhtémoc in Puebla – to Mexico City, and a meeting with West Germany for a place in the World Cup Final. Even with the obvious boost of playing against the hosts, the attendance for Italy's quarter-final was less than 27,000. It meant that even if all of the attendance figures from the *Azzurri*'s group games were added to that sum, the total would still be subsequently short of the number that would attend the semi-final in the Estadio Azteca, when they faced the Germans. Toluca had the highest elevation of all the World Cup venues, sitting at a height of 8,730ft above sea level compared to the capital's 7,350ft. The altitude would not require a step up for the Italians, but the attendance, atmosphere and heightened importance of the game certainly would.

The Germans had played all of their games so far at León's Estadio Nou Camp and, although they had performed in front of similarly small crowds, their results had been far more consistent than those of Italy. A 2-1 win over Morocco was just about satisfactory but, from there, they accelerated when netting five times against Bulgaria, before adding three more against Peru and the same number when they came back from two goals down to eliminate England in the quarter-final, albeit after extra time. Not exactly the ideal preparation before heading into a World Cup semi-final. At 5,995ft above sea level, the German change to playing at Mexico City's altitude would also not be too much of a step up, especially when compared to Brazil moving from Guadalajara's 4,920ft. Their carefully planned altitude training would be of great benefit to the *Seleção*.

Approaching the semi-final, both Italy and West Germany would have reason to feel confident. The Italians were reigning European champions and looked to be striking form at precisely the right time, especially as their performances across the previous four years had included the type of switchback that would send anyone's head spinning. The 1966 World Cup had seen the team endure the humiliation of a 1-0 defeat to North Korea when Pak Doo-ik's goal at Middlesbrough's Ayresome Park had sent the *Azzurri* to elimination at the group stage and the indignity of arriving home to face the *vaffens* and insults, with pelters of rotten fruit from the *tifosi* and copious lambastings in the press.

Unlamented manager Edmondo Fabbri was understandably removed from his post shortly afterwards, and the Italian federation decided that the old maxim of two heads being better than one was the way forward. In a move that always threatened to have a limited lifespan Fabbri was replaced by what was labelled a 'Technical Committee', made up of the highly experienced Argentine

Helenio Herrera – the former manager of Barcelona, Inter Milan and Roma – and Ferruccio Valcareggi, previously in charge at Atalanta and Fiorentina. There's another old phrase that perhaps should have been considered at the same time, that of a camel being a horse designed by a committee. Fortunately, the structure didn't last long, calmer heads prevailed and Valcareggi was put in sole control, with his first task to capitalise on the final stages of the 1968 European Championship being staged in Italy, which at that time meant two semi-finals and a final for the qualifying teams.

Italian qualification was achieved with some comfort. Placed in a group with Switzerland, Romania and Cyprus, the *Azzurri* eased through their programme, winning five of the six games, as Cagliari's Riva emphasised his promise by scoring six times in the final three matches. The reincarnation of victorious legions under the guidance of Valcareggi were on the march to Rome. A coronation was expected or, more accurately, demanded, when Italy were paired in one semi-final with the Soviet Union, and world champions England faced Yugoslavia in the other. The path to victory was hardly smooth though.

After a sterile goalless draw against the Soviets, Italy progressed to the final on the spin of a coin. Any accusations of the decision being influenced by the game being staged in Italy is difficult to sustain as the coin spun through the air, but it landed blue side up, rather than red. Perhaps it was a portent for the future. In the other game, Yugoslavia triumphed 1-0 as Alan Mullery became the first England player to be sent off.

In an innovative move, the third/fourth play-off was played in the same stadium just hours ahead of the final. It meant that the official crowd, although some didn't arrive until it was time for the final, still broke records for such a meaningless and unloved fixture. The script for the final, now that England had been removed from the equation, was for a comfortable stroll to victory for Valcareggi's team, but a goal from Dragan Džajić after 30 minutes suggested that the old soldier's lament that a battle plan remains intact until any initial contact with the enemy was borne out once more.

It could even have been worse had Swiss referee Gottfried Dienst, who had officiated in the 1966 World Cup Final at Wembley and awarded Geoff Hurst's controversial second goal, not taken a lenient view of what looked a certain penalty when Giorgio Ferrini charged Vahidin Musemić in the back inside the area. Fortune again favoured Italy, though, and Angelo Domenghini levelled the score with ten minutes to play. Fortunately, such an event had been foreseen with provision for a replay rather than the referee dipping into his pocket for another coin to decide who would be European champions. Days later, perhaps deflated by being so close to victory before seeing it snatched away, the Yugoslavs offered small resistance and goals from Riva and Pietro Anastasi saw Italy home. From the outright embarrassment of 1966, a team bolstered by the success of AC Milan, and still containing many of the players from the *Grande Inter* sides of Herrera, and proud champions of their continent had travelled to Mexico with dreams of emulating the famous Julius Caesar *'Veni, vidi, vici'* phrase, of coming, seeing and conquering.

The Germans had lost in the World Cup Final four years earlier and their squad contained many of the players from that Wembley encounter with England, feeling they had a point to prove. They had also tripped up in qualification for the European Championship. Travelling to Albania for their final game needing a win of any description against one of the eternal minnows of European international football, who had failed to find the net in any of their qualification fixtures and had been averaging a four-goal-per-game concession rate, to take them to Italy, uncharacteristically they drew 0-0. Yugoslavia profited from the slip-up.

Surely determined to avoid any such repeat on the path to Mexico, West Germany had the best qualifying record of all the European countries that journeyed out to Mexico with their haul of 11 points from six games, albeit in a group containing neighbouring Austria, Scotland and Cyprus, outstripping any other. They could also call on the services of the tournament's ace marksman. Going into the semi-final, Gerd Müller had scored eight times in the four games played for a total almost double that of the entire Italian team. The diminutive Bayern Munich poacher had also scored six times across the qualifying tournament and, as was the case with Riva, would be his nation's top marksman for a long time with 62 goals in just 68 internationals. He was eventually overtaken by Miroslav Klose, although it took him more than twice as many games as Müller to get there.

At this time, only one nation had won the trophy outside its own hemisphere so two European teams playing for the honour of reaching the World Cup Final, in a stadium, country and conditions alien to them, promised to be an intriguing contest, and that's what happened – eventually. The plaque outside of the Estadio Azteca pays homage to the outcome, proclaiming, 'El Estadio Azteca rinde homenaje a las selecciones de: Italia y Alemania protagonistas en el Mundial de 1970, del "Partido del Siglo" 17 de junio de 1970.' Or, in English, 'The Azteca Stadium pays homage to the national teams of Italy and Germany, who starred in the 1970 FIFA World Cup, the "Game of the Century" June 17th 1970.' It feels perhaps a little strange that one match, merely a prequel to what is widely regarded as the greatest World Cup Final of all times, is so lauded, especially so when, for so much of it, the outcome looked destined to be a less-than-inspiring, lukewarm 1-0. But, like a kettle that takes a while to come to the boil, eventually it reached a scalding point.

Flushed with the success of the *staffetta* delivering Italy's best 45 minutes of football in the tournament to date, a repeat of the tactic looked to be on the cards for the *Azzurri* as Valcareggi selected the same 11 who had started against the Mexicans to take the field for the semi-final. Sandro Mazzola was in midfield with Gianni Rivera primed and waiting to make his half-time appearance from the bench.

In contrast, German coach Helmut Schön made four changes to the team that had overcome England. Only Berti Vogts and Karl-Heinz Schnellinger retained their places in the back four. The latter, who had just completed his 11th season in Serie A before returning to his homeland, having enjoyed nine trophy-laden seasons with AC Milan, would have an extremely rare but vital role in the game's outcome. The unfortunate Horst-Dieter Höttges, who had been substituted at half-time against England, was unavailable and was replaced by the experienced 1860 Munich defender Bernd Patzke. The other change brought long-serving Hamburger SV centre-back Willi Schulz into the middle of the defence to partner Schnellinger in what would be his final appearance for the *Mannschaft* before retiring from international football.

In the centre of midfield, the established pairing of the majestic Franz Beckenbauer and 1. FC Köln's Wolfgang Overath had started every game of the tournament and retained their slots to face Italy. The introduction of substitute Jürgen Grabowski against a tiring England defence had been key in turning the quarter-final in West Germany's favour and the Eintracht Frankfurt winger was rewarded with a starting berth for the semi-final on the right of the attack, replacing Reinhard Libuda, who dropped to the bench but would join the action early in the second half. Hannes Löhr retained his starting place on the left, but it would be the Köln forward making way for Libuda's introduction. In the centre of the forward line, veteran skipper Uwe Seeler, who was also making his final appearance for the national team, was accompanied by the prolific Müller, destined to be the tournament's top scorer with ten goals. The scene was set for a game that, for so long, appeared destined to deliver stodgy fare while, over in Guadalajara, Brazil were playing champagne football, but burst into life in a 30-minute extra-time period of pulsating and intense drama.

The opening minutes had been filled with less than fully committed forward probes as the teams shadowboxed, fretful of any errors compromising their ambitions of reaching the final. And yet the first goal came as early as the eighth minute. Inter Milan's Roberto Boninsegna had been fishing at a lake where his family owned a small holiday home when his wife had called to him that he must leave immediately for Milan to take a flight to Mexico. Pietro Anastasi had been selected for the final 22-man squad but, when an injury forced his withdrawal, Valcareggi turned to the *Nerazzurri* forward – but he wasn't the only one.

Arriving at the airport he met up with AC Milan's Pierino Prati, who had received a similar late summons to fly to Mexico after being left out of Valcareggi's 22. Had it been a communication error? The players both thought that at least one of them would be on a return journey back to Italy soon, but that wasn't to be the case. Instead the coach retained them both for the tournament and opted to jettison Prati's *Rossoneri* team-mate Giovanni Lodetti.

The midfielder had suffered the ignominy of being part of the Italian squad eliminated by North Korea in 1966, although he hadn't been selected for that game after featuring in both the victory over Chile and the defeat to the Soviet Union. A measure of redemption had been achieved as part of the team that drew 1-1 in the final of the 1968 European Championship, but he was then omitted for the replay when the *Azzurri* lifted the trophy. Lodetti had won Serie A titles in both 1961/62 and 1967/68 and enjoyed further domestic success with a Coppa Italia victory in 1967/68. On the continental club scene, European Cups in 1962/63 and 1968/69, plus a Cup Winners' Cup the previous year, had stamped his pedigree and defeating Argentina's Estudiantes in the Intercontinental Cup of 1969 was a global success.

World Cup redemption would be denied him though. After selection for the final squad in Mexico had been reversed by Valcareggi to accommodate both Boninsegna and Prati, the heartbroken Lodetti was sent home. More than a little frustratingly for the rejected Lodetti, Prati wouldn't feature at all in the tournament, while Boninsegna played every minute of every game, except for a late substitution in the final when it was already lost. Casting aside his fishing tackle back at that lake in Italy proved to be worthwhile as, with eight minutes played against West Germany, it was the ball, rather than fish, that he was putting into the net, and that was even more the case when he profited from a Brazilian midfield muddle to snatch the equaliser in the final.

Boninsegna had made his debut in a European Championship qualifier against Scotland back in 1967 but hadn't featured since. He arrived in Mexico with just that single cap to his name but, despite the late call-up, the coach's decision to play him in each game would bring rich rewards in the latter stages. Now with the five caps earned in Mexico to add to his international CV, Boninsegna was about to open his goalscoring account for the *Azzurri*. Advancing with the ball, he played a forward pass to Riva on the edge of the box. The Cagliari frontman was tightly marked and could only bobble a return pass as Boninsegna brushed aside a half-hearted challenge to collect the ball, control and then fire left-footed past Sepp Maier in the West German goal. If you're going to score your first international goal, a World Cup semi-final is a more than adequate stage on which to deliver it. His second would come four days later, on the ultimate stage.

In some games, an early goal can be akin to lighting the blue touchpaper on a firework as a game becomes more open. In this case, however, it would provoke more of a damp squib than pyrotechnics. Despite occasional flurries forward, Valcareggi's team adopted the plan that had seen them progress from the group stages. One goal had been sufficient then, and the approach seemed to be that they believed a similarly slender advantage could take them to the final.

The Germans pressed forward but, despite a few openings, goalkeeper Enrico Albertosi and his defence, fortified by an ever deeper-lying midfield, coped with the threat. With the confidence of a steady flow of goals from the earlier games to sustain their ambitions, the Germans pressed forward enthusiastically. A corner from the left saw Seeler leap and head towards Albertosi's top-left corner, but the grey-shirted Cagliari man flung himself acrobatically to push the ball away. It was to set the pattern for much of the remainder of the 90 minutes. Years of playing attuned to the stifling rigours of disciplined *catenaccio* defence in Serie A had produced a streetfighter of a team, well used to taking an early lead and seeing out the rest of the game to achieve the desired result.

A dubious challenge by skipper Giacinto Facchetti on a charging Franz Beckenbauer brought a heart-in-the-mouth moment as the German tumbled inside the box, but referee Arturo Yamasaki – he of Garrincha dismissal fame/infamy in 1962 – recognised no offence. As the half wore on and the Italian 'bolt' appeared to have firmly locked their back door, the German attacks became frustrated and increasingly ragged. Italy were a case-hardened, well-drilled team and the tactic of drawing the Germans on and looking for a killer second goal was perfect for them. After Boninsegna had rifled the ball past Maier, the *Azzurri*'s task was to hold on to their lead for a further 82 minutes. As Yamasaki brought the first half to a close there were just a further 45 remaining for the blue shield to hold firm.

At the break the German players would have been reminded that they had fallen two goals behind to England and still triumphed in the end, and with the razor-sharp cutting edge of an in-form Müller leading the line, a goal from nothing was always possible, if not likely. For all that England had been described as having a strong defensive unit as their major asset, however, it was Italy, rather than the Three Lions, that the Germans now had to overcome, and for the *Azzurri* stoic defence was less a trained function than a way of life. Across in the Italian dressing room, despite holding the lead, Valcareggi chose to stick by the *staffetta* tactic and introduced Rivera for Mazzola. It would turn out to be the right decision but there was plenty of the game to play before the denouement delivered that verdict.

The second half quickly developed into the same pattern as the opening 45, with frequent German attacks interspersed with occasional Italian sallies forward from their defensive redoubt. Frustratingly for Schön's team, even when they could prise open a chance, either wayward shooting or the reassuringly confident Albertosi denied them. Overath struck the top of the crossbar from around 12 yards as he sought to avoid a crowded goalmouth, but his aim was inches too high. With each opportunity spurned, frustration, and the growing fear that Italy would see out the game, began to nag insistently at German belief.

Schön replaced Löhr with Libuda but, unlike against England when introducing a winger against a tired defence had been so effective, seeking a similar outcome when pitted against the disciplined back line and midfield of Italy was an entirely different matter. Albertosi flung himself right, left and centre into the air to deny the rare German shots bound for the goal and another couple of penalty shouts were brushed away; time drained away, and German faith was following suit.

Inside the final quarter of the game, Beckenbauer drove towards the Italy penalty area with the ball before being tumbled by Pierluigi Cera. Of all the penalty claims so far this was perhaps the one with the best chance of being confirmed by the referee. The contact was clear and indisputable, but only the location of it was left to furious debate as Yamasaki was surrounded by players. Blue-shirted ones pointed insistently to a spot outside the area. White-shirted ones stood inches further forward on the other side of the white line. The Italian claims won out and, as the ball was tapped sidewards to try and avoid the solid blue wall obscuring any direct shot on goal, Sigi Held, who had just joined the fray for Bernd Patzke, scuffed his shot tamely wide. The free kick had been won at a cost. Beckenbauer's tumble into the area had seen the midfielder fall awkwardly on his shoulder. Some reports suggest a broken collarbone resulted, others say it was a dislocated shoulder. Whatever the correct diagnosis, Beckenbauer was now little more than a passenger in the team. With Schön having used up his allotted two substitutions, West Germany now had to chase that elusive equaliser with just ten effective players.

After so much attacking, a bizarre moment almost brought a German equaliser when Albertosi's kick from hand struck Seeler on the back and rolled towards the goal line. The goalkeeper eventually just reached the ball before the predatory Müller and slid it clear. Even fate was turning its smile away from the Germans, but with mere seconds remaining it was time for an unsung hero to take the stage. Out on the left flank, Grabowski slung yet another cross into the Italy area. So many had been headed clear, clutched by Albertosi or resulted in unsuccessful headers on goal. This time was different. With nothing to lose, Schön had urged his defenders forward and, when the cross dropped on the edge of the six-yard line, it was the rarest of rare sights as Schnellinger threw himself forwards, right foot outstretched, to divert the ball past a stationary Albertosi.

In an international career spanning 14 years, it would be Schnellinger's only goal for the *Mannschaft*. On German television, commentator Ernst Huberty exclaimed, 'Schnellinger, ausgerechnet! Schnellinger!' (Schnellinger, of all people! Schnellinger!). Later, the man who had saved the day for West Germany would confirm that, at the time, he thought the game was lost and had wandered forwards as the access to the dressing rooms was behind the goal that the Italians were defending. He was positioning himself to make a quick exit at the final whistle.

In the end, his journey into the penalty area served to delay that departure from the pitch for a further 30 minutes. The man who had plied his career in the Italian league for so many years had broken *Azzurri* hearts and opened the door for 30 minutes of football that would tug cruelly at heartstrings, burn the lungs and render asunder the emotions of the players on the pitch, and the millions of fans watching. The first 90 minutes of the game had done precious little to earn the acclaim of that plaque outside the Azteca. That was all to come in the next 30 minutes.

The break before the first period of extra time gave the German bench a chance to patch up Beckenbauer as best they could, strapping his arm inelegantly to his side, with untold yards of bandage as he held firm to his shirt, beneath the German badge, to keep the damaged limb as stable as possible. It was all they could do but it served little in aiding his movement or contribution. Despite that, at the start of extra time, logic suggested that momentum should lie with the Germans. After so late a goal, the Italians would surely feel as deflated as the Germans were elated, and yet the true advantage probably still lay with the *Azzurri*. Despite the kick-off coming in mid-afternoon, the temperature was in the high 40s and, with a yellow mist of smog also covering the city, breathing was becoming a task in itself. Italy had enjoyed a fairly comfortable passage past Mexico in the quarter-final, easing three goals clear in the second half, while West Germany had been extended into extra time against England, and would have the effects of that game in their legs. Logic doesn't always apply in football though.

Held had already extended Albertosi, requiring a plunging save low to his left as the forward's header dropped towards the corner of the net, when within four minutes of the restart Müller did what he always did, profiting from a moment's hesitation between Fabrizio Poletti and Albertosi as the defender sought to chest the ball back to his goalkeeper. 'He who hesitates is lost', as the old saying goes, and it was true here. His poacher instincts screaming in his head, Müller forced himself into the smallest gap between the pair, securing just enough contact on the ball to divert towards the goal line. Even then there was a chance that either of the Italians could save the day but, in their urgent but brief chase, they tangled legs and the ball rolled on. Agonisingly, slowly, oh so slowly, it trickled almost apologetically over the line and barely reached the back of the net. For the first time in the game, West Germany were ahead. It was the fourth time they had come back from behind to take the lead in the tournament but their advantage would last for all of four more minutes. West Germany had found their unlikely hero in Schnellinger and now it was time for an unsung hero in blue to answer the call.

Rivera lifted a hopeful free kick into the area and Held, caught in two minds as to whether to head or control and kick the ball clear, merely let it hit him. Inter Milan defender Tarcisio Burgnich had an international goalscoring record akin to that of Schnellinger; in 66 games for the *Azzurri* he would find the back of the net just twice. His first goal had occurred almost precisely four years to the day earlier, securing a 1-0 win in a fairly meaningless friendly against Austria on 18 June 1966. His next goal was far more important. As the ball hit Held, it dropped perfectly into Burgnich's path no more than seven yards from goal and he despatched his shot past Maier with the aplomb of a seasoned striker.

After waiting 82 minutes for a goal following Boninsegna's strike, two had now arrived within just eight minutes of the restart. A further six minutes later and Italy were ahead again as a more regular goalscorer put his name on the scoresheet. Both teams had delivered haymaker punches flush on the chin of their opponents. Each had staggered under the blow before climbing to their feet and fighting back. It would set the pattern of the final period of the game. With just a minute to go before the break, Domenghini crossed in from the left. The ball found Riva on the edge of the area. He controlled with practised calm before driving a left-footed shot across Maier and into the far corner of the net. Should you ever have an opportunity to listen to the commentary by Nando Martellini, as he described the goal, please don't miss out. The rising scream, driven by passion, of 'Riva, Riva, Riiiivvvaaaa!' offers a portrayal of relief and exultation as he draws out a four-letter name into something worthy of a Latin schoolmaster conjugating an irregular verb.

In the exhausting heat and breathless atmosphere, fuelled by the importance of the occasion, Italian hearts had swelled only to be broken as German relief broke the dam of frustration. Then Müller's stiletto strike had plunged a dagger into *Azzurri* hopes before Burgnich breathed new life into them. Now Riva had all of Italy dreaming of adding a world title to their European crown. Too early, far too early. There was another 15 minutes of drama to follow as the two teams, like a pair of bone-weary heavyweight boxers dragging themselves from their stools for a final round of a brutal slugfest, began the second period of extra time to determine who would return, in four days' time, to contest the World Cup Final. The outcome would rest as much on the force of will of the players to resist the demands of tired limbs and burning lungs as on the skills they possessed.

Seeler had a header guided over the bar by Albertosi, but with five minutes played after the restart his next header, resulting from the *Mannschaft*'s 17th corner of the contest, would bring the teams level once again. Grabowski played the corner short to Libuda, altering the angle of the cross slightly. It found Seeler, whose ability to leap high to meet such deliveries belied his 5ft 7in frame. He directed the ball back across goal, leaving Müller to throw his body into the air at a jagged angle to divert it towards the target. Guarding the post, Rivera was caught in two minds. The ball was too high to block with a leg and too low to head. It evaded a lunge with his hip and sneaked inside of the post. On another day, he could easily have blocked the shot. Albertosi screamed at him in frustration, and the downcast demeanour of the midfielder suggested that the burden of responsibility for the goal was weighing heavily on him. The only chance for redemption was to go and score at the other end. German limbs may have been weary, but the heart and desire were still there. The shape of things now was that *Der Bomber*'s diagonal jump had squared things up again.

Energy banks that had been overdrawn for many minutes were drawn on again for celebration, before adrenalin could no longer deny reality. The two teams dragged themselves into position for kick-off again.

There are only so many times you can go to the well before the bucket comes up empty. For West Germany, Müller's goal may have consumed the last drops of water, but the Italians had one more swallow to come to make their summer. Riva took the restart, rolling the ball sidewards to Giancarlo De Sisti. Almost all of the play was now at walking pace. De Sisti then passed on to Rivera. Having only arrived into the game after the first 45 minutes had been completed, despite still having heavy legs his energy levels were less depleted than many others, and he summoned up the resolve to jog forwards feinting right, then left as he was closed down, before shipping the ball back to Domenghini. Looking forwards and hoping for a run by a team-mate was a forlorn pursuit and the ball was played wide to Facchetti. Arcing the ball forward, the Italy captain's pass met up with the ambling run of *Nerazzurri* team-mate Boninsegna. Turning away from a tired challenge by Schulz, the forward drove into the penalty area, looking up for options. Seeing Rivera making a run from midfield untracked by defenders, Boninsegna cut the ball back towards him and, opting for accuracy rather than pace, he side-footed low past a despairing Maier. The Germans had been level for a mere 20 seconds. It was the knockout blow. There were still nine minutes to play but the well was as dry as their gaping mouths. They had given their all, and then some. At full time the pitch resembled a battlefield, full of combatants who had perished in pursuit of national honour.

To the victors the prize of a World Cup Final. To the losers the honour of being part of *El Partido del Siglo* and falling short by the narrowest of margins, but that was surely of little compensation. After the game, Valcareggi would have nothing but praise for the Germans when questioned by Roger MacDonald of *The Times*, declaring that he was 'proud to have beaten a great team, a team with five world-class players – Schnellinger, Overath, Beckenbauer, Müller and Seeler. If Beckenbauer hadn't injured his shoulder in extra time, the game might have gone against us.'[75] MacDonald had also been impressed by the way that Valcareggi's men had flourished after the stodgy fare of the group stage, with the win over Mexico and now overcoming that 'great team', not necessarily by individual flair, but by the collective will and effort of all wearing the iconic blue shirt. 'Now that the star cult has been subordinated to team effort,' he suggested, 'the Italians will give even Brazil a run for their money.'[76]

Combinations had certainly been a key factor in the victory. Had Valcareggi's *staffetta* been the deciding factor? Certainly, that last goal showed that starting at half-time had been advantageous for Rivera, with many other players having played since the start of the game in the increasingly hot and humid conditions. And would he persist with the plan when facing Brazil in the final? The Italian press cared little for such ponderings in the following morning's editions, as they basked in glory. One leading newspaper, lauding the *Azzurri*'s triumph, threw out the banner

---

75   'Seeler: Half a team', *The Times*, 18 June 1970
76   'Seeler: Half a team', *The Times*, 18 June 1970

headline 'Italy rediscovers the Tricolour!'[77] Surely, after such a titanic struggle, anything was now possible.

It's impossible to tell the full story of the 1970 World Cup Final without including *El Partido del Siglo* as a contributory factor. The Germans' struggle and extra time against England, compared to Italy's win over Mexico, had been to the detriment of the *Mannschaft* in the semi-final, much as Brazil's win over Uruguay compared to the titanic battle the *Azzurri* endured against West Germany would favour the *Seleção* in the final. It's not the complete story, far from it, but without giving it due attention, any appreciation of the final would be incomplete.

* * *

Do Brazilians Only Dream in Canarinho?

If the final of any World Cup is the generously gifted, precocious child that demands everyone's attention and bathes in their adulation, then the play-off for the theoretical honour of finishing in third place is the shuffling, self-conscious and downcast sibling, sitting quietly in the corner, hoping no one notices them and that everyone just leaves quickly. The day before the final saw the two beaten semi-finalists – Uruguay with little argument to offer, West Germany with huge and undiminished pride from their defeats – arrive at the Estadio Azteca to complete the necessary formalities.

In 1958, more than 32,000 fans had turned up at the Ullevi in Gothenburg to watch a pulsating game between France and West Germany, with *Les Bleus* running out 6-3 winners. Four years later there was the massive boost

---

77 *CHAMP10NS*, Netflix

as Chile played off for the bronze medal position against Yugoslavia in Santiago's Estadio Nacional, and a partisan crowd of 66,697 saw the hosts to a 1-0 victory. Fewer than 2,000 more fans attended the final on the following day. In the 1966 event, it was Portugal winning 2-1 over the Soviet Union in front of more than 87,000 at Wembley. Tickets for any World Cup game are bound to sell well, but outside those attending for the atmosphere and an opportunity for a very hipster 'I was there' claim, there's little interest outside of the stadium itself, or often even in the competing countries, for the third/fourth play-off. Rather than the more usual description of an anti-climax following the big event, it's very much a case of being 'before the Lord Mayor's show'.

In the respective German and Uruguayan camps, however, there was a clear desire to end the tournament on a high and, at least to some small measure, dilute the disappointment of missing out on the big day. Both Helmut Schön and Juan Hohberg selected strong sides, and five yellow cards across the piece suggests a decent level of competitiveness. The issue was decided midway through the first period when Wolfgang Overath drove home the only goal of the game after Gerd Müller had controlled a cross from the left and laid the ball back to the edge of the area for the 1. FC Köln midfielder to fire low past Ladislao Mazurkiewicz. A header by Julio Montero Castillo that struck the post following a corner was the closest Uruguay came to levelling things up before the break.

In the second period, despite West Germany seeking to control the momentum of the game, Uruguay refused to be denied possession and, with typical belligerent insistence, pressed for an equaliser. Luis Cubilla, Julio Morales and

270

Ildo Maneiro all went close only to be denied by last-ditch clearances as the German defenders protected goalkeeper Horst Wolter. Perhaps offering a little bit of sentimentality to the occasion, Schön had selected the Eintracht Braunschweig stopper, instead of Sepp Maier, to play his 13th – and final – game for the *Mannschaft*. The coach was rewarded with a clean sheet and, despite having to rely on his defenders' clearances on numerous occasions, Wolter performed competently, particularly with a punched save to deny a late fierce header from right-back Atilio Ancheta who had joined the attack. West Germany finished third, to go with their runners-up position in 1966 and four years later and playing at home they would round out their run of covering all three of the podium places across successive tournaments. That was for the future though. With the overture completed, it was time for football to put on its magnum opus.

With both Italy – in 1934 and 1938 – and Brazil – in 1958 and 1962 – being dual winners of the World Cup, whoever triumphed in the final would take possession of the Jules Rimet Trophy in perpetuity, with a new one required to replace it for the next tournament. While there would surely have been noises from the very top of FIFA to honour their existing president by according him the same privilege granted to Rimet when naming the first trophy after him, political machinations within the organisation may have stymied that suggestion.

Other ideas apparently included 'The Winston Churchill Cup', reportedly a suggestion that came from Brazil. How that would have gone down in West Germany or Italy is up for debate. Another potential name was inspired by the success of South American countries, and particularly

Brazil, across the World Cup, calling it 'The Amazon Trophy'. Such an appellation was always unlikely to find favour with European associations, let alone those with growing influence in Africa and Asia. Had it been chosen though, and bearing in mind FIFA's propensity to protect its branding, perhaps a certain online marketing platform may well be known by a different name today.

Eventually, Italian artist Silvio Gazzaniga was commissioned to design the new trophy and, despite all the exotic and often Quixotic suggestions, it was the more prosaic 'FIFA World Cup' name that won the day. The longevity of the new trophy may well comfortably exceed that of its predecessor as, rather than the winning team keeping it until the draw for the next tournament, after the ceremonies are completed it returns to FIFA's possession and stays at their headquarters, with a bronze replica given to the newly crowned world champions. In June 1970 the final destination of the Jules Rimet Trophy was still to be decided.

On 18 June, three days before showdown against the *Azzurri*, the Brazilian party left their headquarters in Guadalajara and flew the 350 miles south-east to the Mexican capital and their date with destiny. If there was any sense of trepidation among the players, it hardly showed, as was reported by the journalists accompanying them on the flight, despite a storm making it a bumpy journey. 'Whilst the aircraft rocked its way through a storm of thunder, lightning and rain, most of them sang and beat out their happy Samba rhythms. Meanwhile, Pelé, also without an apparent care in the world, closed his eyes in deep slumber,' *The Times* reported.[78]

---

78 'Brazilian flair should overcome Italians', *The Times*, 19 June 1970

The same could hardly be said for many of the millions of Brazilians back home, now seeing their dream of a third World Cup victory tantalisingly close to becoming reality. A Reuters report on the day before the final related that doctors across the country had sent out an urgent, if surely forlorn, appeal for any Brazilian suffering with a heart condition to avoid watching the big game. Apparently, authorities in Rio de Janeiro had reported that the heart attack rate had increased by 40 per cent above normal during the semi-final against Uruguay. With the final demanding an inevitable increase in tension and stress for those watching, there was clear concern.

The day before the final suggested anything but sunny weather in prospect for the big occasion as rain and heavy clouds filled the Mexican sky. The weather hardly dampened the appeal for the *Seleção*'s Mexican fans though, with plenty of local partisan desire to see Brazil triumph. Thanks to their open approach to the local fans, there had already been support for the South Americans, something that was built on by their performances in reaching the final, especially when they got the better of England and the reviled Sir Alf Ramsey. The fact that it was the Italians facing them, the team who had eliminated *El Tri*, only cemented the desire for Brazil to lift the trophy. It was a situation abundantly clear to the players, as Jairzinho recalled, 'When Mexico went out, the whole of Mexico supported Brazil. Italy had put them out, so they wanted us to win.'[79]

The Mexican newspapers fed the frenzy, suggesting that Mário Zagallo's team were overwhelming favourites to win, with the coach keen to keep such opinions away

---

79   Donald, Michael, *Goal!* (London: Hamlyn, 2017)

from the players lest they distract from his preparations. Overconfidence, which had so nearly been costly against Romania and delivered what Pelé described as the team's 'worst performance', was to be avoided. Despite their earlier struggles in the tournament, the Italians had earned their place in the final, as Zagallo was keenly aware, 'I myself didn't believe we'd win by much more than 2-0 or 2-1 and I wouldn't have been surprised if it had been a draw.'[80] It was the first World Cup Final to be contested by two previous winners of the trophy, with little wonder that Zagallo thought it was anything but a done deal before a ball had been kicked.

England's game against Brazil in the group stages had been portrayed as a battle between opposites. The fluid attacking play of the *Seleção* against the organisation and defensive security of the reigning world champions. The 1970 final would be a similar conflict but, if it had been easy to cast England in the role of the 'defence' against Brazil's 'attack', the *Azzurri* were past masters of the defensive approach, schooled in the dark arts of a stifling *catenaccio* that had brought success not only to the national team, but also to the Serie A clubs that prospered in European competition. Across the previous seven years, no fewer than five Italian clubs had contested the final of Europe's premier club competition with one or the other of the two Milan clubs lifting the European Cup in four of those five showdowns, and Inter Milan going on to win the Intercontinental Cup against the champions of South America twice in the same period. More than half of the players who would feature in

---

80 Downie, Andrew, *The Greatest Show on Earth* (London: Arena Sports, 2021)

the final would come from the two Milan clubs; players who had been tested, and then prevailed, at the highest levels.

On the day of the final, inevitably nerves began to gnaw away at the Brazilian players. With the game scheduled for a midday kick-off, the players were woken at 7am – although, understandably, few had slept much – for a breakfast of strong coffee and little else. Food would have to wait until after the game. Then it was into the regular routine on a World Cup matchday as Carlos Alberto recalled, 'When we left the hotel to go to the stadium, we had our traditional Brazilian dance percussion group on the bus. We were the band.'[81] The Samba rhythm, the regular accompaniment for the *Seleção* on the way to a game, helped to ease the tension. They played a *pagode* (a celebratory Samba), not out of overconfidence but fuelled by a belief that it would be their day, and help to keep the positivity topped up. All of the party were involved. Of the players, Jairzinho was on the drum, Gérson slapped the tambourine and Pelé shook his maracas. Some tapped the window and tables, clapping in time with the rhythm, while others sang. Everyone was involved. Not to be part of the 'band' was not to be a part of the *Seleção*. As well as calming nerves, and setting the rhythm for the game ahead, it was a statement of unity. The party were all in tune with each other, bound together by the Samba.

With the rain now cleared, conditions were in Brazil's favour. The midday start placed the now clear and bright Mexican sun at the centre of attention. Temperatures of around 93 degrees Fahrenheit were perfect weather for a Brazilian beach party. For the Italians, however, especially

81   Donald, Michael, *Goal!* (London: Hamlyn, 2017)

following their tortuous semi-final against West Germany, the heat would be far less favourable.

As the Brazil coach wound its way towards the stadium, the crowds of fans lining the route grew larger, and more vociferous in favour of the *Seleção,* compressing the space on the road and slowing traffic. It made the journey more difficult and longer than would otherwise have been the case, but at least the fans were there to support Brazil. The Italian journey to the Azteca was much less heralded. Unplanned, the two coaches arrived at the same time. Roberto Boninsegna remembered the moment, the atmosphere and the difference between the two teams, Italy focused and quiet while the sound of music and singing from the Brazilian coach illustrated a much more relaxed approach.

After reaching the stadium the Brazilians took to their dressing room, where some rested and a few even tried to sleep, a pursuit hardly aided by the offers of more coffee to follow up the early morning intake. After a while they ventured on to the pitch to examine the surface. The rain from the previous day had continued into the early morning and, although even the last light drizzle had now drifted away, the weather had dictated a change in footwear. After returning to the dressing room and gearing up for the game, the players went back to the pitch in boots with long aluminium studs, rather than footwear with moulded rubber ones that they had played in up to that point. There would still be some slips and slides on the wet surface of the pitch though. A tournament that had begun in the brightest days of the Mexican summer looked to be bowing out under slate-grey skies with a high humidity that suggested more rain may be on the way. Up above it was a damp squib of a day, but there would be plenty of sunshine on the pitch as the *Seleção* painted the canvas in bright shades of *Canarinho*.

By now, many of the 107,000 fans who would watch the game from the stands were in place and, across the globe, countless others were seated in front of their television sets, ready for the first World Cup Final to be shown in full colour, something that simply could not be missed. It was time to take to the field and, awaiting the signal to follow East German referee Rudi Glöckner and his officials out into the comparative sunlight, as the clouds were chased away, the two teams lined up side-by-side in the tunnel. The *Seleção* stood behind captain Carlos Alberto and the Italians behind their skipper, Giacinto Facchetti. At such moments there are emotional battles to be won and Brazil secured their first triumph. Jairzinho remembered standing in that line next to the Italians, 'We looked at them but they wouldn't look at us. We were stamping our metal studs. It must have been quite intimidating because they looked very tense.'[82]

The Italians were indeed tense and, if some of the *Seleção* players were nervous and unsure, that was even more the case for those wearing a blue shirt. Valcareggi had the onerous task of having to lift a team that had gone through a physical and emotional wringer against West Germany just three days earlier, and now they were pitted against the tournament's outstanding side, in conditions that favoured their opponents and in front of a fiercely partisan crowd, overwhelmingly ranged against them. On top of that, if Brazilian preparation for the tournament and the track to the final had been planned with precision, the Italians

---

82 Donald, Michael, *Goal!* (London: Hamlyn, 2017)

had precious little similar comfort. The midday start was unusual for them and their normal preparation for a game was ill-suited.

Whereas the Brazilians had risen to be welcomed with stimulating coffee, Valcareggi's team faced spaghetti for breakfast before the uncomfortable journey to the stadium, running a gauntlet of barracking fans doing everything they could to help the *Seleção*. The Italian party had even been compelled to pack their bags on the previous evening before sleeping. It seems strange to relate, but arrangements had been made that they would not return to the hotel following the game and after any ceremonies had been completed. Instead they would travel directly from the stadium to the airport and the flight home. It's perhaps little wonder that, in the tunnel with the piercing light and sound of a packed Estadio Azteca, plus untold millions of eyes glued to television sets awaiting them, while Brazil looked keen and confident following the uplifting win over Uruguay, the Italian demeanour, fatigued by battle and bedevilled by poor logistics, was much flatter.

Fate also seemed to favour Brazil in matters of team selection. Aside from the hamstring problem that Gérson had brought with him into the tournament, and Everaldo's substitution against Romania and subsequent absence for the quarter-final against Peru, Zagallo had largely escaped concerns about absences from his preferred 11 through injury. Some may say that the coach enjoyed the good fortune of a smile from the fates, while others would point to added benefits accruing from a studied and scientific preparation. It's difficult to acclaim credit to either source exclusively, but it's surely obtuse to suggest that the preparation had no material benefit in this situation.

With no injury concerns following the win over Uruguay, Zagallo asked the same starting 11 from that game to go out and win the World Cup Final. Despite various comments about his consistency, or perhaps more accurately a perceived lack of it, Félix had played every minute of every game in the tournament so far and was unchallenged for his place in the final. In front of him, the firmly established back four of captain Carlos Alberto on the right and Everaldo on the left flanked the central defensive partnership of Brito and Piazza. The diligent Clodoaldo paired up with the wonderfully expressive talents of Gérson in midfield, with Jairzinho on the right of the front four, outside of Pelé and Tostão. Rivellino had the other flank when Brazil attacked, but would drop deeper to complement Clodoaldo and Gérson when possession was lost.

In contrast to the man who Zagallo had between the sticks for the *Seleção*, Cagliari's Enrico Albertosi was the very model of consistency behind an obdurate and uncompromising defensive machine. While Riva had been banging in the goals at the other end of the pitch, Albertosi was also a key factor in Cagliari's Scudetto-winning team, conceding a miserly 11 goals, with the newly crowned champions losing just twice across the 30-match Serie A programme. Albertosi would carry that form into the World Cup and three successive clean sheets in the group stage meant that the single goal the *Azzurri* notched was sufficient to send them into the knockout rounds. Even then, the lone goal conceded against Mexico was the only blot on Albertosi's copybook before the last-minute Schnellinger strike, and consequent carnage, of the semi-final's extra time.

It almost goes without saying that while an outstanding shot-stopper is a fundamental element for a team built on

its ability to concede one fewer than their opponents do –
something diametrically opposite to the ethos of the *Seleção*
– that can only work if there's a strong defence in front of
the goalkeeper. Italy certainly had that. The full-backs,
skipper Facchetti on the right and the imposing physique of
Tarcisio Burgnich, known in Italy as *La Roccia* (The Rock),
were a formidable partnership who both played for Inter.
At 27 and 31, respectively, they were at the peak of their
powers and, with more than 80 *Azzurri* appearances behind
them, many times as a pair, they were case-hardened in the
international arena. It's of little surprise that, along with
Albertosi, both Facchetti and Burgnich had been manning
the Italian defensive ramparts consistently through the
World Cup.

Inside of them Valcareggi paired another Inter defensive
stalwart, Roberto Rosato, with Cagliari's Pierluigi Cera.
While the latter went into the tournament with just two
caps at the age of 29, he would join his Cagliari team-mate
and goalkeeper, plus Facchetti and Burgnich, in being an
ever-present for Italy throughout. The same could not be
said for Rosato. In the *Azzurri*'s opening game, against
Sweden, Valcareggi had selected the Cagliari centre-back
Comunardo Niccolai to play alongside Cera at heart of
the defence, preferring a triangle of Cagliari players –
Albertosi, Cera and Niccolai – in the centre, flanked by
the two Inter full-backs. As with Cera, Niccolai was fairly
new to the international stage, having just a single cap to his
name before the World Cup, but the coach still decided to
transfer the defensive solidarity of the Serie A champions'
back line into the *Azzurri* setup. Sadly, for both Niccolai
and Valcareggi's plans, the defender suffered a knee injury
after just 37 minutes against the Swedes and was out of the

tournament. Cera replaced him in that game and would retain his newly won position all the way to the final. Although Niccolai would collect a World Cup runners-up medal, it would have been scant compensation for a dream foreshortened by injury, and he would only play once more for Italy.

Mario Bertini was another member of the Inter contingent consistently chosen by Valcareggi across the tournament. Although sporting the number ten shirt, his role was far removed from that of the future *fantasistas* of Italian football such as Roberto Baggio, Alessandro Del Piero and Francesco Totti. Although he would score 32 times for the *Nerazzurri* in a nine-year career spanning more than 200 Serie A outings, his main role was to be a destroyer, a ball-winner, a solid and dependable ally for his defenders. In the final he would find himself with the onerous task of seeking to subdue Pelé.

Italy's midfield was completed by Sandro Mazzola, Fiorentina's Giancarlo De Sisti, and Angelo Domenghini of Cagliari, who had scored the *Azzurri's* only goal in the group stage. Mazzola was again selected ahead of Rivera, and looked primed to be the lead-off man should Valcareggi go with the *staffetta* once more. The midfield four had started every game in the tournament so far and, although they only completed the full 90 minutes as a unit once – in the opening encounter against Sweden – it was clearly a quartet that the coach had confidence in. The forward line was made up of Riva, who had struck goalscoring form in the knockout stage, and the late-arriving Boninsegna, reviving the partnership the pair had enjoyed at Cagliari until Boninsegna moved to Inter in 1969. His first-half strike would put Italy on level terms going into, and beyond, the half-time break, before the irresistible *Canarinho* wave washed away *Azzurri* aspirations.

As well as the battle on the pitch between the players, there was also a tactical battle between the two coaches. Ferruccio Valcareggi was hugely experienced, having coached clubs in Serie A for more than a decade, and had led the *Azzurri*, in one form or another, since 1966. Four years in charge of his players, and winning the European Championship, vastly outweighed the mere months that Mário Zagallo had been in charge of the *Seleção*, but the man who already had two World Cup winner's medals as a player was bright and innovative. The Italian mode of play was well established, with surprises unlikely, but Zagallo wanted to establish whether the Italian coach was planning to deploy a man-marking system on Jairzinho and Rivellino.

At the start of the game, he instructed his two wide attackers to switch positions. Gérson later revealed the plan, 'If their markers followed them, then we knew they were really man-marking. So, he switched them again – Jairzinho on to the right wing and Rivellino on to the left wing.'[83] It quickly became clear that, with Bertini having the unenviable task of policing Pelé, he was often being drawn away from his position in front of the back line and Burgnich's task of marking Rivellino was made difficult by the Brazilian's tendency to drop deeper into midfield leaving the defender to decide whether to follow him and risk exposing the right flank of the Italian defence, or let him roam. Only Facchetti's role of marking Jairzinho seemed less troublesome, but his well-drilled and cussed

83 Donald, Michael, *Goal!* (London: Hamlyn, 2017)

adherence to the task would be key to opening up space for Brazil's second goal just past the hour mark.

Effective marking of opponents was second nature to Italian defenders, raised to operate in the *catenaccio* system that required such a discipline, but there are only so many players you can deploy in such a pursuit. As soon as the final got under way it appeared clear that any analysis that the Italian coaching team had studied from Brazil's semi-final win over Uruguay had failed to take note of one of Juan Hohberg's key tactics in nullifying them for so long. In the semi-final, the Uruguay coach had identified Gérson as one of the key elements in Brazil's attacking movements and deploying a marker to restrict his freedom had caused the *Seleção*'s forward line to splutter ineffectively in the early phase. Despite having players mark other Brazilian forwards, the balding figure of Brazil's puppeteer in midfield was allowed free rein. Initially, the price paid was relatively low, as the midfielder played a subdued role in the first half, but as the game progressed that would change significantly.

As Sam Kunti explained, he considered the outcome almost inevitable, 'Carlos Alberto Torres always said that Pelé was the best of all time but that Gérson was the key player of the team and who am I to disagree with the eternal captain? It says quite something about Gérson when some of his colleagues call him the cog of the team. Every attack ran through Gérson. His *lançamentos* [releasing of passes] were famous. He had a good tactical vision and, in a way, he was Zagallo's right-hand man. They had a relationship from their time with Botafogo. Gérson didn't play against England and some argue that he would have been too slow against the English who pushed up. Perhaps, but then Gérson always sought to find space for himself, as he did in the final against Italy. It's incomprehensible that the Italians didn't mark him. To give Gérson space was to give Brazil the match and the World Cup. He operated from deep in midfield and orchestrated Brazil's many attacking moves. In the second half he restored Brazil's lead. It was a fine strike and a fine moment for one of the unforgettable stars of that team. He simply had the best left foot in Mexico.'

As the clock ticked around until both hands were pointing directly upwards, indicating that it was time for the 1970 World Cup Final to begin, large balloons bearing the tournament's logo floated up into the sky. Back on ground level, banks of photographers, clicking furiously, plied their trade as the *Seleção* stood in two banks of *Canarinho*. As the lines broke up and the players selected by Zagallo to return the Jules Rimet Trophy to Brazil skipped and trotted around, as much to relieve tension as to warm up muscles, the phalanx of cameras was transferred to the other side of the pitch where the blue walls of the *Azzurri* were being lined up for their turn to look both confident and assured when, inside, the emotional turmoil of realisation that the defining moments of their careers, and indeed their lives, was about to be played out shredded nerves. Sunshine and Samba on one side, ebullient and entertaining, with wonderful individual skills woven into a team, like notes in a piece of music. On the other, the blue of Italy, a Puccini opera of a team, rehearsed and organised, a libretto to follow, peppered with moments of soaring heights and passionate drama.

Interminable preliminaries completed and the pitch cleared of those not wearing blue, yellow or black, Rudi Glöckner prepared to get the main event of the footballing calendar under way. Understandably, the occasion may well have got to Glöckner as well as the players. Despite officiating in the 1964 Olympic Games and taking charge of cup finals in his own country, this game was to be the undisputed highlight of his career as well. A realisation probably betrayed by the fact that, standing next to Boninsegna and Mazzola as they awaited the signal to kick off, Glöckner's whistle escaped his grasp, and fell to the floor. Quickly retrieving the key piece of his equipment, a furtive look around and glance at his watch was followed by raising his left arm high into the air. Then a shrill whistle signalled the moment when all things were still possible, when dreams and nightmares lived side-by-side. Boninsegna rolled the ball to Mazzola before trotting forward and the World Cup Final was up and running.

In matches where the highest honours are at stake, a gentle introduction to the game, where each of the teams only venture forward cautiously and defend with determined concentration, is common. That was hardly the case here. After quickly snaffling away possession the Brazilians moved the ball around, offering the chance for each player to feel involved as they eased forward before an over-hit pass saw the ball run into the welcoming arms of Albertosi. Brazil had made their intentions clear and Italy were quick to respond. Still inside the first 100 seconds, the *Azzurri* pushed forward with Burgnich overlapping on the right before playing the ball inside to Riva. Touching it away from a fairly insipid challenge by Clodoaldo, Riva launched one of his thunderous left-footed shots that homed in on the Brazilian goal, drawing a full-length flying save from Félix to tip the ball over the bar for a corner. If this was to be the pattern of the game to come then it would be a feast of fluid, flowing football. Both of these would prove to be the case.

For the next few minutes the play moved one way, then the other as both teams took a front-foot stance when in possession. The Brazilians were languid with the ball at their feet, comfortable and confident as they probed forwards with eager darting runs off the ball by Tostão and Pelé, as Jairzinho and Rivellino pulled at any loose threads in the *Azzurri* defence by drawing their markers into spaces they didn't want to go. In contrast, Italian possession was more direct with fast counterattacks seeking to exploit any gaps in the Brazil defence created by an overconfident impulse to attack.

There was still time to revert to type, however, and, it felt somehow inevitable that when Glöckner's whistle signalled the first free kick of the game, it was for a foul by Bertini on Pelé as the iconic forward sought to spin clear of his marker. A ten-on-ten offence but zero out of ten in surprise value. Rivellino's effort from the free kick was bent accurately towards the far post, but a slip on the greasy surface as he struck the ball meant that the shot was tamely bouncing towards goal as Albertosi coolly collected. The Italian mentality of doing whatever was necessary to prevent threats on their goal next appeared just minutes later, when a tumbling challenge by Facchetti brought Jairzinho to the ground as he tried to power through the centre of the *Azzurri* defence with the ball at his feet. The Italian skipper was having none of it and when Rivellino hit the free kick over the crossbar and into the crowd, the fates had clearly forgiven Facchetti's indiscretion.

Passing quarter of an hour, Brazil had been enjoying the majority of possession but, with the Italians happy to sink back into a deeper defensive formation, many of the *Seleção*'s attacks broke down on the resolute blue wall in front of Albertosi. The scuttling runs from the flanks of Rivellino and Jairzinho, inside to create spaces for Everaldo on the left and more regularly Carlos Alberto on the right, looked to offer promise of some tangible reward. Mazzola later recalled the growing concern among the Italian defence that gaps were being opened as players were being dragged out of position, and calls began to be sent to Valcareggi to make changes. They would be but, ironically, as they were being carried out, Brazil would take the lead.

Before that, though, Italy offered another threat on Félix's goal. From a free kick around 30 yards out Mazzola ignored the siren calls in his head to try a shot and, instead, clipped the ball towards the far side of the area where Riva charged in from the left, leaving his marker trailing his wake and rose, scandalously unmarked, to head powerfully on goal. Félix hurled himself towards the ball as it threatened to dip under the crossbar but, with the goalkeeper struggling to make contact, he was relieved to see it narrowly pass over the bar. Since Riva's powerful shot in the opening minutes of the game, it had been the first threat on goal carrying any meaningful menace. It was a fortunate escape and, given the amount of space afforded to Italy's ace marksman, Brazil would have little recourse to complain about injustices had the ball found the back of the net. On such moments do games turn, however, and less than three minutes later Italy would pay a price for the missed chance.

With 18 minutes played, a driven cross into the box from the left by Tostão was headed clear by Facchetti for a throw-in. According to Mazzola's account, this was the moment that Valcareggi chose to rejig his defensive marking. With the changes happening, Rivellino was suddenly free, and a quick-thinking Tostão, still out on the left flank, grabbed the ball and found the Corinthians forward in space as Burgnich had left him to take over the marking job on Pelé. Rivellino crossed, with Burgnich sprinting to close down on a newly instructed target, before the ball arrived with Pelé. He lost the race. *O Rei* rose salmon-like and headed firmly past Albertosi to put the *Seleção* ahead.

It's often said that in battle your greatest strength is also your greatest weakness. Italy were masters of defensive organisation with players finely tuned to negate the effectiveness of opponents with claustrophobic marking. On this occasion though, application to that particular task had been their undoing. Pelé spun around in celebration, leaping into Jairzinho's arms and punching the air, as blue-shirted players pointed here and there in forlorn analysis of what had gone wrong. The Italian defence had been breached the first time that Albertosi's goal had been genuinely put under pressure and the *Azzurri* now faced an uphill task to get back on level terms. Throughout the tournament to date, Brazil had fallen behind on a couple of occasions. Once in front, however, they had not yet squandered a lead. In fact, that statistic had been the case since Zagallo had taken charge of the team early in the year.

Up to that point, the game had been fairly even with each team comfortable playing in the style they were accustomed to, and Italy were far too experienced a side to abandon their tried and trusted approach in favour of some cavalry charge in search of a rapid equaliser. Less than 20 minutes had been played and the chances the *Azzurri* had already created, calling Félix into action on a couple of occasions, suggested that more would follow if they continued along the same path. The Yin-like passivity of Brazil's defence was the inevitable counterbalance of their Yang penetrative attack. The latter had delivered, but inside five minutes later the former would be exposed.

Brazil had been passing the ball around with their usual composure, looking for a gap to exploit, while the Italians sat deep, waiting for a chance to break forward. Left to right, and back again, forward, and then back, the ball was transferred confidently. A throw-in on the left was moved back to Everaldo, who rolled a pass to Brito waiting on the edge of the centre circle in the Brazil half. A simple pass on to Clodoaldo looked the obvious next move, and it was. So obvious, however, that Boninsegna had anticipated it and strode forward to intercept, prodding the ball into the acres of empty pitch behind the defender.

Sprinting after the ball, had Boninsegna reached it first there would only have been Félix to beat. The goalkeeper thwarted the run, dashing out of his penalty area to hack the ball clear. There was no cost to pay for Brito's error other than Félix gesticulating angrily at the culprit. It was an ominous warning that a lack of concentration, and Brazil's proclivity towards defensive lapses, could open the door for Italy to strike back. The warning wasn't heeded and, 15 minutes later, that's precisely what happened.

The opening, albeit coming from a defensive error rather than an attacking move, offered encouragement to the *Azzurri*. For the next few minutes Brazil were pushed back as Mazzola buzzed busily around the midfield demanding possession and looking to feed passes into his team-mates' runs until a foul by Bertini on Rivellino, six yards from the edge of the penalty area, disturbed the run of blue-dominated possession. A shot from distance by the

Corinthians forward looked the likely outcome as he and Pelé stood ten yards or so behind the ball, primed for a run-up. Rivellino strode forward first but, instead of unleashing one of his thunderous left-footed strikes, he stepped over the ball and trotted past the left side of the blue defensive wall constructed by Albertosi. So it was seemingly Pelé to shoot. But no. Instead, reaching the ball, he gently clipped it over the wall and into the path of Rivellino who now accelerated into empty space inside the box. Nudging the ball forward with his knee, Rivellino shaped to square across goal to where Gérson, Tostão and Jairzinho had taken up position, fully aware of the plan. The move had taken the Italy defence by surprise but was confounded by the early morning drizzle as Rivellino's feet slid from underneath him at the critical moment, and the ball ran harmlessly out of play.

Italy were looking more aggressive as time went on, and not only in an attacking sense. Just minutes later a throw-in around halfway by Carlos Alberto had Pelé turning past Burgnich, now in constant close attendance to the Brazilian, and skipping clear, but his run was rudely halted by the defender who took both of his legs from under him with the ball a clear yard away. A raised arm in contrition and a couple of apologetic pats on the back of the fallen star were clearly aimed at dissuading the referee from applying any sanction other than the obvious free kick, but came to nought, as Glöckner brandished the fully merited yellow card.

After incurring the wrath of the Italians, the official then did the same to the Brazil players by refusing access for the medical team to administer the magical healing properties of the cold sponge to Pelé, dismissing them from the field with fluttering waves of hands on outstretched arms. Pelé struggled to his feet and hobbled forward as Rivellino took a more orthodox approach to the free kick by firing in a shot from fully 35 yards. The effort flew high over the bar, and on upwards, with the Telstar ball appearing destined to take the place of the satellite that had borne the same name when orbiting the earth seven years before. Commentating for FIFA's official film of the game, all Alan Parry could offer was a sigh and a resigned comment of 'Oh, dear.'[84]

Less than 60 seconds later Italy were awarded a free kick on the edge of the Brazil box for an offence unseen by everyone save the East German referee. In contrast to Rivellino's strike moments earlier, Riva fired his shot low, but with equal lack of effect. The ball cannoned off the defensive wall and a shot from the rebound drifted well clear. The next effort on the Brazilian goal, a shot on the turn from Boninsegna, was closer but lacked power and Félix was happy to watch it roll wide of his post.

Thirty minutes had now passed and still Brazil, despite dominating possession and playing wonderfully fluid football, had only offered a serious threat to Albertosi's goal on the sole occasion when Pelé had headed past him to open the scoring. Much as a Brazilian defensive error always appeared likely, the *Seleção*'s dynamic forward play could not be stifled forever. For the moment, however, it was Italy pushing forward with increasing menace as the half-time break loomed. Mazzola, ever busy, exchanged passes with Boninsegna as he drove into the area to collect the return, and it took a lunging tackle from the recovering Gérson to block the Inter midfielder's shot, diverting the ball for a corner which came to nothing.

---

84 https://www.fifa.com/fifaplus/en/watch/1PWVyYB9n0irNo8j8ndgTL

Even for a seasoned defence such as that of the *Azzurri*, blunting the sharp cutting edge of Brazil's inventive play was becoming an increasingly difficult task as Gérson's role in midfield grew in influence. A ball on the right to Clodoaldo brought a cross into the box and another leap by Pelé saw him rise clear of his marker. This time, however, he couldn't direct his header downward and the ball cleared Albertosi's crossbar. The next thrust had Jairzinho powering through the Italy midfield. He exchanged passes with Tostão as he neared the blue wall of defenders on the edge of the penalty area but was foiled by a solid challenge by Facchetti. The ball ran loose to Pelé who coolly picked a pass to Tostão across the edge of the area, but the ball ran on too far and, from an ever-tightening angle, the Cruzeiro forward could only manage a tame shot, with his weaker right foot, that was drifting wide anyway, before being comfortably blocked. The play was far from being one-sided though. As Parry commented, it was now 'a wonderfully open game, more like a basketball match at the moment – you attack, we attack'. A goal was on the cards, but would it come from one of Brazil's flowing attacks or Italy's counters? As it turned out: neither.

Brazil were now dominating with the space afforded to Gérson by Valcareggi's decision not to put a marker on the midfield maestro increasingly looking like a costly error. Rivellino was increasingly popping up on the right flank, pulling his marker out of position, as another astute Gérson pass found an advanced Carlos Alberto who quickly moved the ball on to the erstwhile left-winger, on the opposite side midway into the Italy half. Cutting inside, he skipped past Mazzola and, unable to resist the sight of the whites of the goalposts, he hit a left-footed shot that flew harmlessly wide.

But then came the goal that seemed on the cards, albeit in a way few expected.

A Brazil attack broke down as Pelé tried to wriggle free in the penalty area, but Burgnich hacked clear upfield. Everaldo chased down the ball, playing it inside to Piazza. A lofted pass across the field required Carlos Alberto to stoop and head towards Clodoaldo who attempted a back-heel pass back to Everaldo. Having already capitalised on one case of defensive overconfidence, Boninsegna sensed an opportunity. He closed down on the Brazilian midfielder, blocking his attempted pass and chased after it as the loose ball ran forward. Unlike the earlier occasion, when a rapid reaction from Félix had saved his defender's blushes, there would be no escape for Clodoaldo.

Collecting the ball just before a lunging tackle from Piazza failed to clear, the Inter forward ran on with Riva in support to his left. Brito approached to deliver a sliding tackle, and Félix advanced to close down space. Boninsegna flicked the ball to the left at the perfect moment to evade the tackle, as goalkeeper collided with defender. The route to goal was now clear, with the potential of a collision with Riva the only thing stopping Boninsegna scoring. The disaster was averted and Boninsegna rolled the ball into the net. Months earlier he had been sitting by a lake in Italy, dropping fish into his keep net, and lamenting that he had missed out on a trip to Mexico. Now, it was the ball, rather than fish, in the net and the 26-year-old was the *Azzurri's* saviour. At the moment he probably felt like he could walk on water, as well as fish in it.

For Everaldo, the emotions were entirely different and, later, Zagallo revealed that he had made his anger clear to the player about where and when to try such tricks and flicks. He also admitted that he put his arm around him. It was a single mistake, rather than a catalogue of errors. In a strange way, the manner in which Brazil had conceded was less concerning than if it had come at the end of a flourishing attack. Regardless of the lead now being lost, the Italian attack had still not breached the Brazil defence due to any creative play. The goal came from an error by a Brazilian, not from a moment of magic from an Italian. If that fact gave a little reassurance to the *Seleção*, it mattered little to the *Azzurri* who suddenly had found a couple of yards of extra pace and an injection of adrenalin that boosted belief.

In the remaining minutes ahead of the break, Gérson had a mishit shot go wide, Domenghini's effort from distance was saved by Félix, and Rivellino was booked for retaliation after a foul by Bertini. It led to a bizarre moment. The winger slipped as he hoisted the ball into the Italy penalty area but, as it was in the air, Glöckner whistled for half-time – ten seconds early according to the clock on FIFA's film of the game. It was clear that some of the players had heard the whistle, but less so about others. As the ball drifted towards the line of the six-yard box, Burgnich threw up a hand to stop it reaching Pelé, standing a couple of yards behind him. It was only partially effective. Burgnich fell to the floor and the ball dropped to a startled Pelé. Unsure whether to appeal for a penalty or put the ball into the net, he did both. After a few moments of confusion, the reality of the situation was revealed as Glöckner placed the ball under his arm and walked from the field, followed by the players. After 45 minutes of riveting football the 1970 World Cup Final was deadlocked, 1-1 at half-time, with both managers having things to be happy, and concerned, about.

Zagallo would have been pleased that his team had controlled much of the game, with the freedom allowed to Gérson becoming more and more important as the final went on. Unless Valcareggi changed things in the second period, that would only increase in importance, especially as gnawing fatigue would eat away at the Italians' ability to man-mark with such suffocating efficiency. The goal had been annoying more than worrying, in that aside from defensive lapses and Italian shots from distance the *Azzurri* forwards had created little. Additionally, throughout the tournament Brazil's well-planned preparation had meant that their second halves had always been an improvement on the first 45 minutes of each game played. Brazil had scored six first-half goals while conceding four. After the break, that record improved to nine scored with just two conceded. That pattern would continue after the final restarted.

In the Italy dressing room, Valcareggi would surely have been aware of the *Seleção's* record of improvement after half-time, and that may well have influenced his decision as to whether to proceed with the *staffetta* approach, sacrificing the studied application of Mazzola for the more flamboyant but less disciplined skills of Rivera. After Pelé's goal, the new marking assignments had been far more effective, restricting Brazil to a mere handful of opportunities. Open up too much, concede again, and another fightback would be required. It may have felt too much of a risk. Instead, remaining true to years of depending on defensive familiarity, he left AC Milan's Golden Boy on the bench.

The second half began under a milky sun as Pelé tapped the ball to Tostão, who then rolled a pass back to Gérson to begin another Brazilian attack. It was a symbolic moment. For much of the coming 45 minutes, the balding midfielder would control the game and be the fulcrum of almost everything that the *Seleção*'s attack did, and they would do plenty. The first few moments would show whether Valcareggi had taken note of Gérson's growing influence as the first half had drawn to a close and adapted his system to allow closer marking of the player often described as the 'brains' of the Brazilian team. As Brazil passed the ball among themselves, with Gérson frequently taking up possession, it seemed clear that the Italian coach had not done so. Even when Gérson picked up possession from Félix after a half-hearted Italian sally forward had broken down inside the first minute, the ball found him in acres of space. Advancing into a trot and then a sprint, the Italian defence backed off until he was nearing the penalty area and a desperate challenge from Mazzola skewed the ball away from his feet. It was an early indication that there would be a price to pay for Valcareggi's decision. Later Mazzola would describe it as 'one of our biggest mistakes'.[85] He was correct, and it may well have cost the *Azzurri* the World Cup Final, but other factors would increasingly come into play as the second half progressed.

The early minutes began very much as the closing phase of the first half had played out. Brazil dominated possession, probing for openings with their intricate play and darting runs, while the *Azzurri*, with caution to the fore, patiently awaited opportunities to counterattack. The difference was, however, that now there was a sharper cutting edge to the *Seleção*'s attacks. Jairzinho fed an overlapping Carlos Alberto, who reached the byline before cutting the ball back

---

85 Downie, Andrew, *The Greatest Show on Earth* (London: Arena Sports, 2021)

across a crowded goalmouth in front of Albertosi. Almost any touch, be it from a blue or yellow shirt, could have sent the ball into the net, but it passed Tostão on the near post and the lunging glance from Pelé's studs narrowly failed to guide it into the net.

Only three minutes had been played when David Pleat, on co-commentary duty with Parry for FIFA, speculated about the space Gérson was being allowed, and how he was beginning to be the key factor in the game. 'You just wonder whether De Sisti or Domenghini should take a tighter grip on Gérson, because Gérson is dominating a lot of the midfield play,' the man who would become a much-travelled manager pondered, as the midfielder took possession of the ball once more, as if to prove Pleat's point.[86]

As the early minutes passed, the sun that had up to now been shrouded by clouds began to shine more brightly. On the pitch too, yellow also became more dominant. Slowly, almost imperceptibly, the flow of the game was changing. Brazil were taking control and the balance of play, at a broad equality in the first half, was now swinging increasingly in their favour. *The Times* reported the following day that, as Zagallo's team took control, 'Brazil began to raise their game a notch or two and tighten the screw'.[87] The Italian response, instinctively, was both to drop deeper and increase the physicality of their challenges. The rapier attacks of the *Seleção* would be pitted against the *testudo* defence of the *Azzurri* as they raised their *scudi* and manned the ramparts.

Another overly zealous challenge set up a free kick for Brazil following a foul on Pelé by his ever-present shadow

---

86 https://www.fifa.com/fifaplus/en/watch/1PWVyYB9n0irNo8j8ndgTL
87 'Brazil dance their way to victory', *The Times*, 22 June 1970

Burgnich. A full 30 yards from goal, Rivellino drove forward to try his luck. In the first period the moustachioed forward's shooting boots appeared to be on the wrong feet as one effort after another ballooned into the Mexican sky. As with the pattern of the game, the outcome of Rivellino's effort on goal was also changing as his left-footed piledriver homed in on Albertosi's goal, requiring a full-length diving save from the Cagliari stopper to prevent Brazil taking the lead again.

Seconds later, another driving run from Gérson threatened. Approaching the penalty area, he fed the ball forward to Tostão before running on and looking for a return to his feet. A challenge by Rosato into his back, however, unbalanced him and the ball spooned up into the air. As Gérson's run took him underneath, and past, the ball, Cera leapt to head clear but the contact was slight and only dropped the ball towards the edge of the area, and Pelé. With thoughts only on clearing the danger, Burgnich threw himself into a bicycle kick as Pelé tried to head the ball. Any contact between Italian foot and Brazilian head was fortunately slight but the only question in Glöckner's mind would have been whether a penalty or indirect free kick inside the area was the most appropriate. As is so often the case with officials in such circumstances, he opted for the lesser sanction. It was probably the correct decision, despite Everaldo grabbing the ball and placing it on the spot, more in hope than expectation.

It took a full minute for Glöckner to push the blue wall back far enough for him to enjoy a measure of satisfaction. He was never going to manage the full ten yards, and settled for around eight as the best achievable. Pelé stood over the ball, ready to tap it to either Gérson or Rivellino in close attendance. Arm ramrod straight into the air, as it had been since making his decision, Glöckner blew and Gérson stepped up and shot against the wall. Was he hoping for a deflection to legitimise his drive had it found the net? It was an extravagant plan if so and, unsurprisingly, it didn't come off.

As the ball bounced clear, Facchetti collected and powered down the Italian left flank, launching an infrequent counterattack, sprinting past and clear of Rivellino. Reaching the midway point of the Brazil half, and closed down by a backtracking Clodoaldo, the Italy captain fed the ball inside to Boninsegna. The Inter striker was in space, with so many Brazilians stranded upfield by the speed of Facchetti's run. With options available on either side, Boninsegna rolled a pass across the face of the penalty area towards Domenghini. The forward, who had joined Cagliari from Inter as Boninsegna had moved in the opposite direction, struck his shot right-footed across Félix's goal. It may well have been travelling wide of the far post but the goalkeeper was compelled to follow its path just in case, edging away from his near post. It so nearly led to a goal. Everaldo had recovered position and got a half-block on the shot, diverting it back towards the area Félix had just vacated. Looking back, as he fell away to his left, Félix's agonised expression revealed just how close the ball was to creeping inside the post before it clipped the outside of the upright, rippled the side-netting and rolled away. Domenghini thumped his fists out either side in frustration as Everaldo sighed in relief. Maybe Italy's attacks were becoming rarer, but they still carried a threat.

Gérson, the irritating thorn in Italy's side, nearly forced a way through the blue-shirted back line to find Tostão in space before running on for a return, but the ball was smuggled clear. Whereas in the first period the runs and passes of the midfielder were designed to open spaces for others, since the restart Gérson had sought to play a ball and look for a first-time return. The tactic was causing problems for the *Azzurri* defence as so often no one was tracking his run for the return pass. Perhaps the brutal effects of the strength-sapping semi-final against the Germans just a few days earlier was now taking its toll both physically and emotionally on the Italians, and the heat of the now brightly shining sun was also playing its part too. Inevitably though, it was the effect of the *Seleção*'s dynamic play that made Italy look weary. The pendulum had swung heavily in Brazil's favour. If they scored next, there seemed little hope of a second comeback from the Italians.

Gérson was like a ringmaster, standing centre stage, inviting colleagues to perform in turn as he passed them the ball, a karaoke organiser handing around the microphone, and demanding, 'Now sing!' Aways available, always in control, never hurried. A pass from Tostão, dropping deep to join the midfield, invited Rivellino to jink inside of Mazzola and set off on a determined run towards the penalty area. For all the world the number 11 looked primed to fire in a shot, but a scything lunge by the Inter midfielder halted his progress. It was cynical but, in the eyes of his team-mates, simply necessary. No Italian would have condemned Mazzola for the offence. If Rivellino's double-digit number of rolls as he tumbled to the ground was intended to illustrate the aggression of the foul, it may have only served to inject an inappropriate element of humour into the proceedings. After receiving both genuine and affected concern for his health, Rivellino climbed to his feet only to watch Pelé offer up a passable impression of one of his own free kicks from the first half. Another Telstar launched into orbit.

The pace of Brazil's play was showing no signs of slowing. At free kicks, where a shot on goal wasn't possible, they were quick to restart the game and launch another attack. In contrast, the *Azzurri* players saw such incidents as a chance to catch breath. Minutes after Pelé's up, up and away shot, a foul on Gérson just inside the Italy half offered up just such a case. Clodoaldo pounced on the ball and had taken the free kick, playing it forward to Jairzinho, while Gérson was still regaining his feet. The speed of the restart had allowed little time for the Italy defence to organise and the winger had space to advance into. He drew Facchetti to him before slipping a pass to Tostão and racing forward to collect the return. A shooting chance looked likely, but the diligent Facchetti had tracked the run and bundled Jairzinho off the ball. It looked a decent challenge but Glöckner was unconvinced and Brazil had another free kick on the edge of the penalty area. The fact that the official decided it would be indirect only added to the surprise.

Previous attempts from such situations had been mystifyingly squandered or fired high into the air. This time would be different. Gérson tapped the ball to his right and Rivellino decided to try his luck with his weaker right foot and cannoned in a shot that rattled Albertosi's crossbar before dropping behind the goal and out of play. The goalkeeper had launched himself into a dive towards the flight of the ball but was never in serious danger of reaching it. Had the shot been just a few inches lower, the only achievement of Albertosi's flight would have been to give him a close-up view of it ripping into the net.

Seconds later, the hour mark was reached. Italy had done well to deny Brazil as the *Seleção* had assumed control of the game, increasingly so since the break, but the next 30 minutes would see Zagallo's team power on and Italian spirits drain away, their demeanour matching the colour of their shirts. In contrast, those yellow shirts matched the bright sun, and Brazil were about to deliver a period of football to enthral the watching millions. It was show time. It was Samba time. It was party time. 'Here comes the sun. And I say, "It's alright."'[88]

Fouls and frustration were now increasingly apparent as the waves of Brazilian attacks battered the Italy defence. Another edge-of-the-box free kick, this time for Burgnich's errant tackle on Pelé, was launched into orbit by Rivellino. Encroachment by the defenders offered him a second attempt, but that one cannoned into the wall and was hacked clear. A goal was looking increasingly inevitable, however, and it came on 66 minutes.

Zagallo had switched Jairzinho and Rivellino again, dragging markers out of position. Out on the right flank, midway into the Italy half, Carlos Alberto had possession as Rivellino trotted forward, followed faithfully by his shadow. Eschewing the simple lay-off, the Brazil captain clipped the ball into the centre of the field to Gérson. The midfield maestro controlled, turned, and played a pass towards Everaldo on the left. As the full-back advanced, Jairzinho cut inside from the left-wing position he had taken up, opening a passing opportunity that Everaldo readily accepted. As ever, Facchetti was touch-tight to the wide man and, as Jairzinho headed diagonally across, towards

---

88 'Here Comes the Sun', *Abbey Road*, the Beatles (Apple, 1969)

the penalty area, the slightest of contact by the Italian eased possession away. Unable to track the ball as it rolled the other side of Jairzinho, Facchetti could do little to stop it reaching Gérson. With the defence pulled hither and thither, first by Rivellino dropping deeper and to the right and then by Jairzinho's run across goal from the left, there was the hint of an opening for the midfielder as he drifted left. Proving that his nickname of *Canhotinha de Ouro* (Golden Left Foot) didn't only apply to his passing ability, he took aim and then fired across Albertosi into the far corner of the net. Gérson ran, arms aloft and with a beaming grin, towards the Brazil bench. The first man to catch up with him was Brito, before substitute goalkeeper Ado and a coterie of coaches, followed by an avalanche of yellow engulfing the goalscorer.

In marked contrast to the chaotic delirium of his celebration, Gérson's play had been calm and assured throughout and the finish was no different, as Sam Kunti described, '[Gérson's] brain raced to conjure up a goalscoring matrix, sculpting the perfect arc for his shot.'[89] It was his only goal of the World Cup, but probably the most important of the 19 that the *Seleção* amassed, and it divided the final into two distinct halves. Before the goal, Italy had at first matched and then contained Brazil. After it they increasingly looked like a team struggling, and largely failing, to keep up with the opposition. Theirs was beginning to look like a lost cause as they teetered on the edge of a precipice. If Italy were a Puccini opera, the culmination of *Tosca* would have been appropriate. Cavaradossi now lay dying and the eponymous heroine had

89 Kunti, Sam, *Brazil 1970: How the Greatest Team of All Time Won the World Cup* (Worthing, England: Pitch Publishing Ltd, 2022)

hurled herself from the battlements of Castel Sant'Angelo. The fat lady wasn't singing yet, but Italian dreams were dying and their hopes plunging.

As if to emphasise the frustration now coursing through Italian veins, Domenghini lashed out at Pelé as the Brazilian tackled back to prevent the Cagliari forward launching a counterattack. The contact may have been relatively minimal, but should have surely brought a caution from the referee. Glöckner thought otherwise and, once more, even refused permission for the floored Pelé to receive attention from the medical staff. A couple of minutes later, Brazil exacted revenge of their own as the lead was doubled and the game definitively settled.

Another foul by Domenghini on Pelé around halfway gifted Brazil possession, and a further indication that Italian composure was being tested to the limit came as Bertini petulantly lashed the loose ball at Rivellino. The free kick was tapped short to Gérson, who advanced half a dozen steps before hoisting a ball into the Italy penalty area. It looked like a lazy, hopeful punt forward, but such descriptions are ill-suited to the talents of Gérson. With laser-like accuracy, the ball homed in towards the corner of the six-yard box where Pelé was being marked by Bertini. Defeated by the flight, the Italian initially hesitated, seduced into thinking he could head clear, then turned with alarm to see Pelé calmly nodding across goal in response to a call from the onrushing Jairzinho.

As the ball arrowed towards his team-mate's head, Jairzinho had taken a couple of steps away from the penalty area before turning sharply and sprinting into the box. The move briefly broke the shackles imposed by Facchetti and the winger met up with Pelé's header on the six-yard line, as the Italian captain desperately lunged to recover and block. It was a forlorn effort and Jairzinho stabbed the ball beyond an advancing Albertosi to add the third goal, and become the first player to score in every round of a World Cup.

Many years later, reflecting on his moment of immortality, he claimed, 'I scored what I considered the title-winning goal. It was 3-1 and they basically gave up.'[90] If the first claim can be considered as understandable hubris, the second was fully merited. Two goals in five minutes had taken the game well beyond reach of the Italians. Brazil knew it, Italy knew it, and the watching millions knew it. The cake was complete. It had a wonderfully individual taste of its own. There was no need to place a cherry on the top. Commenting on the consequences of the goal in FIFA's commentary, David Pleat's claim that Italy 'now have a mountain to climb' was outlandishly understated. Sam Kunti eloquently described the release felt by the team now surely destined to claim the *Seleção*'s third World Cup in 12 short years, 'The Brazilians were now liberated, a levity filling their souls, a gaiety suffusing their play ... A superhuman team indulging in a joyous game – and they were about to display a final, brilliant spark of artistry.'[91]

For the following 15 minutes Brazil were the strolling players, in more ways than one. Their play was now conducted at a walking place as they passed the ball around with unruffled ease, probing for a gap to add a fourth goal but in a way devoid of any urgency. This despite an admittedly hugely unlikely second Italian goal potentially

---

90 Donald, Michael, *Goal!* (London: Hamlyn, 2017)

91 Kunti, Sam, *Brazil 1970: How the Greatest Team of All Time Won the World Cup* (Worthing, England: Pitch Publishing Ltd, 2022)

bringing a measure of drama to the concluding minutes. They were the star performers on their own stage, and this was a curtain call, a joyful encore, even before the finale had been enacted. Valcareggi removed Bertini to add some creative impetus, but it wasn't Rivera entering the field. Instead, Napoli's Antonio Juliano trotted on for his only appearance in the tournament. There were 15 minutes left to play and all thoughts of the *staffetta* had been abandoned.

Or had it? With six minutes to play, Rivera made his belated entrance to the final. It wasn't Mazzola leaving, however. The AC Milan midfielder took the place of Boninsegna instead. The *Azzurri* now had the creative talents of Mazzola, Juliano and Rivera on the pitch at the same time, but there wasn't long left for them to have any meaningful effect. The change did, however, ensure that Rivera had a ringside seat for probably the most famous World Cup goal of all time.

The clock said 86 minutes had been played as Tostão chased Juliano all the way into the Brazil half, harrying him out of possession, powered by an energy bank filled to the brim with the adrenalin of being on the very cusp of a glorious victory. The ball broke to Piazza, who rolled it forward to Clodoaldo. On it went with first-time passes, through Pelé and then Gérson, then back to Clodoaldo. Two steps forward, a jink left, another in the same direction, a step-over and third move to the left, before a fourth, and a quartet of blue shirts were left floundering in the young midfielder's wake. Rivera, Domenghini, De Sisti and Juliano, each in turn, were compelled to contemplate their impotence to intervene. A pass out to the left completed the party piece as Rivellino collected and sauntered forward, sliding the ball down the line to Jairzinho, once again appearing on the opposite flank to his regular position with Facchetti in attendance.

The winger cut infield with the *Azzurri* captain shadowing, but unable to get a challenge in. Cera lunged forward from the back to launch a tackle but Jairzinho easily skipped past the weary effort, and pushed the ball on towards Pelé on the edge of the area. Burgnich closed him down but the brightest star in Brazil's firmament calmly controlled, moved the ball between his feet and then rolled it off into the open space to his right.

Carlos Alberto knew that in a few minutes' time the Jules Rimet Trophy would be handed to him and he could raise it aloft to salute the *Seleção*'s triumph. It would be the crowning glory of his career, and the moment that he would be remembered for across the years to come. In that second, however, as Pelé's perfectly executed pass rolled wide of Burgnich and gently crossed the white line into the penalty area, Carlos Alberto would trump that moment of raising the golden trophy on high. Arriving with precise timing, the ball sat up invitingly for him and, with both feet clear of the ground, he reached for the heavens, crashing an unstoppable shot past Albertosi. If Italy were Blue Thunder, this was Yellow Lightning and all Brazilian dreams were instantly cast into shades of *Canarinho*.

Do you recall that a cherry on top of this cake wasn't necessary? Well, here it was and, whether necessary or not, it was magnificent.

It was a time to give free rein to all the superlatives within reach and, commentating, Alan Parry did so, going into raptures.

'Oh, my word,' he screamed.

'It's magnificent!' See. I told you so.

'That's not just a goal,' he continued. 'That is a thing of beauty!' It was.

'How many Brazilian players were involved in that attack?' he queried. Well, if you count the number of yellow shirts it was ten, although Everaldo participated twice. 'How brilliant was the technique? How wonderful was the finish?' Parry continued, persisting with the rhetorical questions.

Then finally a statement, 'It was a goal that summed up Brazil!' Quite right, sir. Quite right.

'That goal will go into the memory banks of millions and millions of people who love football,' chipped in David Pleat, not wanting to be left out. It did, and there it lives to this day.

'Football is yellow and green again,' screamed a Brazilian radio commentator. No one would argue.

The last couple of minutes were played out but the game was done. Nothing could top that. There was even a strong claim for a penalty as a scything challenge felled Rivellino in the Italy area, but Glöckner waved away the appeals. Italy were already on the floor and well beaten. Reflecting on the final many years later, Italian journalist Amedeo Di Sora summed up the feelings of sad resignation at the time by admitting, 'We weren't used to being beaten in such a way.' It was true. Italy hadn't conceded four goals in a game since 1957. 'We have to be honest. Brazil was playing "champagne soccer" at times,' Di Sora concluded accurately.[92]

Fully wrapped up in the moment, Roger MacDonald in *The Times* described the scenes of a minute or so later, 'With the result never in doubt, Brazil's supporters could hardly

---

92 *CHAMP10NS*, Netflix

contain themselves until the final whistle and the touchline was a human wall of fans and photographers before the referee bowed to the inevitable and cut short the time added on for injuries. Then, in a moment, the pitch was a seething mass of humanity engulfing the Brazilian players while the Italians trooped sadly to the dressing rooms.'[93] Now it was official. 'And then it's a big party,' Pelé recalled.[94] In truth, it had been a party since Brazil first stepped on to the pitch against Czechoslovakia on 3 June. It was Brazil's 1970 World Cup Samba Party – and it wasn't over yet.

After eventually escaping the mob of fans, the triumphant team made its way into the stands to collect the trophy that would now forever be owned by Brazil. Then came Carlos Alberto's second-most famous moment. 'Soon, I was standing there as captain,' he reminisced wistfully. 'Lifting the Jules Rimet Trophy, representing my team-mates and my country. A lot of things go through your head – family, friends and the fans – it's indescribable. I was 25, the youngest captain in all World Cup history. Even now, no one calls me Carlos Alberto, they call me *O Capitão* – "The Captain!"'[95]

Writing in *The Times* the following day, Geoffrey Green's article was full of typically flamboyant praise for the *Seleção*. Under the heading 'Brazil dance their way to victory', he suggested, '[Brazil] achieved a perfect identity. In six matches, at the end of today they had won them all and scored 19 goals against the best of the rest of the world. That alone tells its story. No one has been able to live with

---

93 'Brazil win World Cup', *The Times,* 21 June 1970

94 Donald, Michael, *Goal!* (London: Hamlyn, 2017)

95 Donald, Michael, *Goal!* (London: Hamlyn, 2017)

them. They have won because their football is a dance full of irrational surprises and Dionysiac variations. There has been no fog or fear about their game, with everybody watching for everybody else's blunders. Blunders there have been, certainly, but they made them good. Everyone who saw them will recognise the skill factor of these Brazilians that was devastating. They were not corrupted by over usage. Best of all, perhaps, was the unshadowed enjoyment they enjoyed in their own pleasures and their own successes. They have shown the green light to the whole field of football over the past 20 years.'[96]

In 1966, so many things had combined to deny Brazil a hat-trick of triumphs, but 1970 proved to be the perfect redemption. The 1970 World Cup Samba Party was the culmination of multiple different threads being woven together with precision. Any party is only as good as its contingent parts and this time they had got the organisation right. The haphazard and over-long preparation of 1966 was rectified by applying a modern and scientific approach targeted at delivering the fittest team to Mexico. It worked. In so many games throughout the tournament, while opponents flagged in the heat and suffered from the effects of altitude, Brazilian party time was largely unaffected. The Samba rhythm was maintained. The right people were invited. All the way through from Zagallo to the players the guest list ensured that Brazil were not only the fittest and best-prepared team in Mexico, they were also the most talented.

In 1958, Brazil had won the World Cup when a teenage sensation introduced himself to the world. Four years later,

---

96 'Brazil dance their way to victory', *The Times*, 22 June 1970

without the presence of Pelé for much of the tournament, the trophy had been retained. In 1970, however, Zagallo's team had eclipsed every previous winner and, for many, each of those who have since followed them. The reason had little to do with the margins of victory they achieved – notwithstanding that the 4-1 win over Italy was the largest of any World Cup Final. It was their style of play. Brazil had won the World Cup, but football was also the winner. *O Jogo Bonito*, the Beautiful Game, had triumphed.

Part 5 – After the Gold Rush[97]

---

97 'After the Gold Rush', *After the Gold Rush,* Neil Young (Reprise, 1970)

Celebrations and Gatecrashers

If the celebrations in Mexico had been as chaotic as they were joyous, back in Brazil those levels were raised even higher. President Médici had decreed that a full-on carnival should be held in Rio to welcome the players home, regardless of the result in the final, with a two-star general put in charge of the operation and 4,000 military police at his disposal to maintain something at least passably resembling order. Even before that, Médici was anxious to ensure that he and his government could claim their share of the glory and use it to promote their vision of Brazil.

The whole party – players, coaches, medical staff and administrators – were keen to get back to Brazil, but the journey home was not free of problems. The plane carrying them took off from Mexico City on a planned direct flight to Brazil, but was soon forced to land in Acapulco due to a problem with one of the engines. It could have been a time for concern but, as so often had been the case when the group were feeling nervous, Samba came to the rescue and an impromptu party broke out at the rear of the plane. The delay meant that by the time the now repaired aircraft touched down on Brazilian soil, it was many hours after its scheduled arrival and many on board wondered if the expected crowds may have drifted away. The reality was very different.

After returning from Mexico, the triumphant group's first call was not to Rio but to Brasilia for a meet-and-greet luncheon with the president and his highly placed comrades at the government palace, accompanied by the inevitable photographers. On the way to the banquet, the streets were lined with cheering fans. If the players had harboured any doubts about how their exploits had been received back home, then they were quickly dismissed.

At the palace, the snappers did their work and the following day images of the president together with the players filled the front pages of popular newspapers. Governments wrapping themselves around sporting success, especially with football, is nothing new. Mussolini ensured that his Partito Nazionale Fascista was intrinsically linked with the success of the *Azzurri* at the 1934 World Cup, and used their triumph to glorify the fascist doctrine he promoted. Very much the same was true of Franco, both with the glory of Real Madrid's early domination of the European Cup and Spain's victory in the 1964 European Championship. Neither dictator had much interest in the game for aesthetic reasons, but both were quick to gatecrash the success of teams that could enhance their political fortunes.

Somewhat the same was true of Médici when he addressed the nation, as a section from his welcoming speech to the returning heroes illustrates, 'I feel profound happiness at seeing the joy of our people in this highest form of patriotism. I identify this victory won in the brotherhood of good sportsmanship with the rise of faith in our fight for national development. I identify the success of our [national team] with ... intelligence and bravery, perseverance and serenity in our technical ability, in physical preparation and moral being. Above all, our players won because they know how to ... play for the collective good.'[98] It reads like something from a straight-to-video B-movie script even Hollywood screenwriters would cringe at, but no one was likely to call Médici on it. The words were meant for public consumption, not to convince those already aware of a different reality.

Marx's oft-quoted assertion, 'Die Religion ... ist das Opium des Volkes' (Religion is ... the opium of the People), is in fact merely a part of a sentence, rather than a complete statement. In full, it translates as 'Religion is the sigh of the oppressed creature, the heart of a heartless world, and the soul of soulless conditions. It is the opium of the people.'[99] If one transposes the word 'football' for 'religion', the German political philosopher's words could be described as apposite to the attitude of Médici following the World Cup triumph.

The military government's slogan, 'Ninguem mais segue esta pais!' (Nothing can stop this country now!), was coined to project the much-trumpeted economic booming of Brazil since the coup but, as Dr Pete Watson of the University of Leeds cautions, 'You have to be a little bit careful about the economy "booming".' As in so many cases of, particularly, extremist governments boasting of economic booms, a gentle scratching of the surface can quickly reveal holes in the claim.

---

98 Mason, Tony, *Passion of the People?: Football in South America (Sport & Latin American Studies) (Critical Studies in Latin American Culture)* (Brooklyn USA: Verso 1995)

99 Marx, Karl, *Critique of Hegel's Philosophy of Right*, 1874

Dr Watson explained his position, 'What was certainly booming and very impressive was the rate of growth, which was around ten per cent for several years and increased slightly over the early part of the '70s. There was heavy economic growth of 10.4 per cent in 1970, 11.3 per cent in 1971, 12.1 per cent in 1972, 14.0 per cent in 1973.[100] Certain sectors of the economy were doing well, but not necessarily benefitting the population as a whole. There was also more of a focus on industrialising and that sector, as part of a political crusade towards industrial development and modernisation – the agricultural sector, traditionally the bulwark of the Brazilian economy through sugar, coffee, etc., was less of a focus and indeed some historians say that it was disregarded and relatively unsupported. The dictatorship obviously made the most of the publicity for these figures, stoking a sense of national economic optimism, but it is very questionable about whether the population as a whole (particularly lower classes) actually saw any real benefits.'

The benefits to the ordinary Brazilian were limited, as Dr Watson added, 'The main issue was that the dictatorship opened the economy up to foreign investment and stripped away certain restrictions (for example over environmental concerns and the disposal of waste products) to attract that non-domestic capital in order to industrialise. Wages were also low, attracting foreign business, and the crackdown on trade unions and workers by the dictatorship meant there was little improvement in wages, workers' rights, etc., meaning businesses did very well, but poorer families did not necessarily. This meant that foreign companies did come

---

100 Statistics taken from Schneider, Ronald M, *Order and Progress: A political history of Brazil* (Boulder, Colorado, US: Westview Press, 1991)

in and did very well, but also that most of the money and profits were leaving the country and not necessarily going back into the Brazilian economy.

'Consequently, large swathes of the Brazilian population, particularly lower classes, did not benefit at all from the impressive figures in economic growth. Economic growth and gaining favour with foreign capital and capitalists, and an obsession with those figures, was prioritised over national development, in terms of reinvesting in education, health, living conditions, etc. This is part of the "myth" of the Brazilian economic miracle. The benefits went more towards the economically successful sectors of the Brazilian population, and not those in greatest need of support, to the extent that the gap between rich and poor increased significantly. Apparently, the richest ten per cent of the population received 75 per cent of the benefits. Foreign debt also increased, given the onus on industrialising. Only certain areas really benefitted, like the south-east (other areas such as the north were left behind). You can also pinpoint this time as when deforestation started to become a serious issue in Amazonian areas with mining, logging, agricultural demands etc. A lot of the companies behind this were foreign ones. So basically, propaganda and so on might have helped the poorer think that their situation might be improved by the government given the economic miracle, but they saw few benefits. Wages didn't rise, there was no real investment in housing etc., so the benefits of economic growth did not really ever touch those most in need.'

For most of the population of the country, and particularly the sections from which football fans were mainly drawn, headlines proclaiming economic progress were, as Dr Watson described it, largely a 'myth'. Triumph on the football pitch was very different, however. In that particular field Brazilian success was unquestioned. They not only led the world but captured its heart as well. Médici was keen to exploit the moment, to use it to warm the 'heart of a heartless world' and apply it as a balm to the soul of those who lived in 'soulless conditions'. He was administering a carefully planned dose of the 'opium of the people'. Pelé later recalled that Cláudio Coutinho, himself a military man and one of Zagallo's coaches in Mexico, during preparation for the tournament told the squad that 'winning was important because it would calm the people.'[101] As Médici spoke, that suggestion was now made live.

Did the players feel used, political pawns in the regime's PR campaign, with the sheen of their triumph tarnished by political manoeuvring? Some prominent members of the party seemed ambivalent, at least in public. Ado and Carlos Alberto felt that way, with Mário Zagallo, 'It's delicious to note that the president of the republic is as human as everyone else.'[102] The image of Pelé was used extensively across the following months in government propaganda, ensuring that the link between World Cup glory and the ruling military government were stitched together as an undeniable part of the social fabric. The player was aware of the situation but was also apparently unworried by it. In his autobiography, published many years after the fall of the dictatorship, when any subdued regret at a nodding acquiescence could be addressed, he said, 'It was good PR for the country and [Médici's] government too – but

101 do Nascimento, Edson Arantes, *Pelé – The Autobiography* (London: Simon & Schuster UK Ltd, 2006)

102 Downie, Andrew, *The Greatest Show on Earth* (London: Arena Sports, 2021)

it was obvious that he was also a football lover.'[103] It was an approach more akin to the one taken by the Argentina players in 1978 who broadly claimed no knowledge of the excesses of the military junta in power there at the time, and less like the Iranian players who resolved not to sing the country's anthem at the 2022 tournament, as a protest against the repression taking place back home.

It's an approach Dr Watson offers a few explanations for, 'A lot of players were not well-educated, not greatly aware of politics or interested and did not read newspapers regularly. A lot of players came from poor, working-class backgrounds, had not got beyond primary-level education and just didn't have the interest, time or inclination to become politicised. Also, jobs were precarious.' Even World Cup-winning footballers' jobs? Apparently so. 'Given the precarity of contracts and how players could be sidelined or sold quickly, it wasn't in a player's interests to be overtly critical or stand up for his rights, either at a club level, or more politically … I think you have to consider the hopes and dreams of the players, the economic potential of a win, as being more important than standing up to the military and voicing opposition … There is a general sense that none of the players had a particular interest in politics or a will to criticise them.'

A quote from Tostão's autobiography adds support to Dr Watson's assertion, 'Some extremists criticise the players for not having rebelled against the dictatorship, as if we were political activists and that we should have abandoned the *Seleção*. We were all young, dreamers, ambitious, committed to your careers and desperate to be world champions. There

---

103 *Do Nascimento, Edson Arantes, Pelé – The Autobiography* (London: Simon & Schuster UK Ltd, 2006)

is nothing more human than that.'[104] Although, in the same book, Tostão later offered a slightly different perspective, 'After arriving in Brazil, we went to Brasilia to be welcomed by President Médici. It was the peak of the dictatorship which I so loathed, and I did not want to appear. I thought about it a lot, and I rationalised that I need to go, and that I couldn't confuse politics with sport. I repent of having gone, as it was the opportunity to show my indignation as a citizen.'

There were some dissenting voices at the time, but not from the players. Even when the tournament was taking place some opponents of the military confessed to hoping that the *Seleção* would lose, it being a lesser sadness than seeing the government profit from the team's success. As author Matthew Shirts suggested, their fear was that 'the cheers of the fans [would] drown out the screams of the torture victims.'[105] For most of the time, however, that's precisely what happened.

And yet – given the catastrophic and haphazard preparations that had blighted Brazil's attempt to secure a third successive World Cup triumph in 1966, would the transformation from fallen idols to globally acclaimed heralds of the beautiful game have occurred without the authoritarian control of a military dictatorship? It feels strange and almost blasphemous to consider apportioning, albeit perhaps begrudgingly, credit for the creation of something so worthy to such a brutal system.

And yet – the question of whether Brazil would still

104 TOSTÃO, 2016, p.50 apud Cornelsen; Marinho, 2020a
105 Shirts, Matthew. 'Playing Soccer in Brazil: Sócrates, Corinthians, and Democracy.' *The Wilson Quarterly 13.2* (1989): 119-23. JSTOR. Web. 6 May 2014

have won the 1970 World Cup if there hadn't been a military dictatorship in the country at the time requires consideration. Seeking the solace of another's opinion, the author posed it to Sam Kunti. His response was both frank and convincing, if not also a little dispiriting in its conclusion.

'No, the military, while ruling with an iron first, deployed faceless technocrats to run the country,' he replied, before going on to explain that football was approached in a similar way. 'They built dams, expanded the electricity network and did things that can be considered as progressive. Those technocrats also invaded sports and football – first DaCosta and then Carlos Alberto Parreira and captain Cláudio Coutinho in the backroom staff of the 1970 team. Taking a different approach, they measured everything, a clipboard in hand. In that sense Brazil's victory in 1970 was profoundly technocratic, the result of a careful scientific preparation devised by DaCosta, and enacted by Parreira and Coutinho, with Brazil taking their professional physical preparation from 1958 to a new level 12 years later – really applying science. This also dispelled the myth that Brazil simply picked players off the beach, danced their way past opponents and won in exuberance. It's a myth that still survives until today and the irony of Brazil's 1970 victory – their greatest, most feted win was so well prepared, so technocratic and so scientific that it prompted a new direction in Brazilian football and those heights of the Azteca Stadium were never reached again. Gradually, Brazilian football began replacing artists with bulky athletes.'

The consequence of Kunti's analysis is that the very glory of *O Jogo Bonito* was also destined to be its doom, as will be expanded upon in later pages.

Whatever the merits of the case that Kunti persuasively offers, and the government's attempts to gatecrash the *Seleção*'s party, there's little doubt that, for ordinary Brazilians, the success in Mexico was a reason for massive celebration. When the plane from Brasilia to Rio de Janeiro landed, an outburst of rain was expected to have diminished any welcoming committee of fans, but no. Disembarking, the players were taken on a three-hour ticker tape parade through the former capital on the back of a fire engine. According to some reports, it was attended by fans numbering up to a million, despite the pouring rain. Each of the squad had received a bonus reported to be $18,500, a princely sum at the time, but the adulation of the fans surely meant just as much, if not more. A ferocious round of receptions, banquets, interviews and appearances, in the capital and across the country's various states and cities, would dominate the next weeks. All of the country wanted contact with the men who had not only delivered on Brazil's own Holy Grail, but surely set in train a future for the country's football that was as bright as their *Canarinho* shirts. Or so everyone believed.

Part 6 – It's my party and I'll cry if I want to [106]

---

106 From the song 'It's my Party', Lesley Gore (Mercury, 1963)

Legacy – Triumph fills all spaces, but glorious failure allows room for dreams

When Brazil won the 1970 World Cup with their exciting mixture of ebullient skills, laid out before the footballing world to the background of an intoxicating Samba rhythm, it should have been merely an overture, a tantalisingly inviting foretaste, for a magnum opus that was bound to follow. The pattern had been set. A new paradigm of how football should be played had its own living, breathing, and hugely breathtaking, template. But it wasn't to be. What felt like the beginning of a new era in Brazilian football was in fact its zenith. There would be a brief flaring again a dozen years later but, after that, despite a startling run of World Cup successes, things were never quite the same again. Sadly, the Samba magic quickly faded into the distance. The party was over, but what a party it had been.

There's no other country in the world, no other team more associated with the phrase 'the beautiful game' than Brazil. But, even more specifically than that, the label belongs primarily to the 1970 vintage of the *Seleção*. As the journalist John Carlin argued, 'Brazil's mythical status in football is owed entirely to the Pelé generation of players."[107] It's not an isolated view. The importance of football – and a certain type of football – to Brazilians, such as that displayed in Mexico, is well documented. When asked how important to Brazilians is it that their team not only wins but also honours the legacy of *O Jogo Bonito*, Alex Bellos was in little doubt. 'It's very important,' he confirmed. 'They would probably prefer to win the World Cup ugly than lose it playing beautiful football; however, whenever Brazilians see their team play in a classically Brazilian way it makes them feel proud in a way that no other nation feels, since beautiful football is part of national identity.'

Bellos neatly captures the essence of the matter, how that 'mythical status' referred to by Carlin persists, and is not only cherished in the country itself but also finds a place in the heart and soul of all lovers of football, of the beautiful game. Even when other teams excel – the Dutch in 1974 for example – whether successfully winning tournaments or not, often they are granted the accolade of being compared to Mário Zagallo's *Seleção* of 1970. Artists before artisans. Poetry before prose. The glorious beauty of Pelé's extravagant step-over in the semi-final that left Uruguayan goalkeeper Ladislao Mazurkiewicz baffled and bewildered is not diminished in any way by the fact that a goal failed to follow. If anything, it only adds to the majesty as there is nothing so mundane as a mere goal to distract from it. The same applies to his attempt to chip the ball over Ivo Viktor from the halfway line in the group game against Czechoslovakia. There's an abundant joy in the audacity alone.

For all that non-Brazilians may believe they understand, and indeed some cherish, such an approach, it's surely best to

---

107 *CHAMP10NS*, Netflix

turn to a native of the country and allow them to capture its essence. Marcos Natali is an associate professor in Literary Theory and Comparative Literature at the University of São Paulo and, in his paper 'The Realm of the Possible: Remembering Brazilian Futebol', he offered this illustration, 'What other schools of football consider superfluous moves, irresponsible showmanship and irreverent flair, in Brazilian *futebol* is essential. Garrincha, considered by many to have been the most faithful incarnation of the Brazilian way of playing, is remembered for many plays without any immediately apparent objective – such as dribbling past the same player more than once, returning after having past him – rather than for goals scored … The value of the game, then, is judged by the pleasure and joy it elicits, far from the 19th-century English schools where football was considered a means of instilling moral values in boys, encouraging discipline, respect for rules and dedication to the Protestant work ethic. The idealised way of playing celebrated in Brazilian culture recognises the possibility that the disciplinary and pedagogical impulse of English sports might be for a moment dribbled by a body which seeks to be the site of pleasure … The player and the audience derive pleasure from the beauty of the moment, regardless of its consequences.'[108]

There is, therefore, a question to be addressed. How differently would the 1970 team be perceived if they had failed to deliver that third World Cup? Would their play still have claimed the affection of Brazilians 'regardless of its consequences' as Natali's stance suggests may have been the case? If it sounds a little fanciful, with too great

108 Marcos Natali (2007) 'The Realm of the Possible: Remembering Brazilian Futebol', *Soccer & Society*, 8:2-3, 267-282, DOI: 10.1080/14660970701224491

an indulgence dripping in romantic caprice to assert that it would be the case, then consider this. The only other *Seleção* in Brazilian footballing history, despite five subsequent World Cup triumphs, that rivals the 1970 vintage is the one that played in the 1982 World Cup in Spain, and was eliminated in the second group stage. More of that later.

There's a strange, but adverse, symmetry between what had led Brazil to the success of 1970 and what then followed. After winning their first World Cup in 1958, it took a further 12 years to complete the hat-trick. It would take another period of a dozen years before that new *Seleção*, the 1982 iteration, one truly worthy of the legacy of 1970, arose – and a further 12 years from there until Brazil reached their first World Cup Final since 1970. If 12 years seems to be the key period of time in this story, then the protagonists facing Brazil in the key games on each occasion are also consistent.

Success in 1970 came at the expense of Italy in that magnificent final. The *Azzurri* were once again the opposition as the acclaimed 1982 Brazil of Telê Santana failed in a glorious endeavour to repeat that triumph. Finally, in 1994, completing the 12-year cycle, the *Seleção* of Carlos Alberto Parreira triumphed in the USA to lift the World Cup for the first time in 24 years, again defeating Italy in the final. In a reversal of roles from 1970, this time it was Zagallo as subordinate to Parreira. But as we shall see later, that was a different, a very different, Brazil to that of 1970, as was the team that was sent to West Germany in 1974 to defend the World Cup.

Any supporters of the particular vintage whose soul carries a love of the game and were blessed to have experienced how Brazil's 1970 World Cup Samba Party redefined how football should be played would concur. Others, of more tender years, who may only have experienced that *Seleção*'s magic thanks to video screenings and the rambling, misty-eyed recollections of those who saw it live will have been denied the experience of spontaneous thrills but will still be convinced of their splendour. Sam Kunti was moved to title his book about the team as *Brazil 1970: How the Greatest Team of All Time Won the World Cup.*

As with so many others, Kunti's undiminished admiration is clear. And yet, in Brazil that is less the case, as Alex Bellos explained to the author, 'There is more of a legacy outside Brazil than in Brazil. It is not Brazil's most fondly remembered team within Brazil. But outside of the country it is probably the most famous national side of all time.' It feels a little strange to read that the team that won the World Cup in such style has been usurped in the affections of many Brazilians. Perhaps the passage of time and the accumulation of other World Cups since have dimmed the *Canarinho* light that shone so dazzlingly in Mexico. Writing for the *Daily Mail* in June 2022, Oliver Holt related how some of the stars of the 1970 World Cup squad seemed to think that may be the case, 'Some of Brazil's 1970 team feel they have been forgotten. They feel overlooked compared with the great entertainers of 1982, who are still adored here … "We get a health plan from the Brazilian Football Federation and 1000 euros a month for being former players but it's too little," says Paulo Cézar, "Caju", a member of the 1970 World Cup squad. "We were the most brilliant football generation ever. The public don't give us the credit we deserve."'[109]

---

109 https://www.dailymail.co.uk/sport/football/article-10953065/
    OLIVER-HOLT-Brazils-1970-World-Cup-heroes-feel-dishonoured-
    did-shun-Boys-66.html

There's a clear message of disappointment in the words of Paulo Cézar but, just as there is plenty of justification to laud the 1970 team as the greatest of all time, Brazil has been blessed with other exceptional iterations of *Seleção* too. After all, for a country that has won the World Cup on no fewer than five occasions, how could it be different? And yet it is the team that failed to even get beyond the groups 12 years after the glories of Zagallo's *Seleção* in Mexico that is the greatest rival for the affection of Brazil's football-loving public.

While appreciating all of this, Tostão made the case for the 1970 side when, during an interview with FIFA, he was asked if he thought that was the best national side in history. His reply was smoothly diplomatic, but also exuded an understandable pride in the achievement of his team in 1970. 'I don't know because there have been other great national teams, including in Brazil,' he said. 'In '58 there was Garrincha, Pelé, Nílton Santos, Didi. But I think '70 was a spectacular side, a revolutionary side in that era, and we were champions. The *Seleção* was spectacular in '82, but they didn't win. We won and we played spectacular football. We were revolutionary because we played modern football – you didn't see that back then. And we had amazing players – Pelé, Gérson, Jairzinho, Rivellino. I think it was an exceptional side. I think we enchanted the whole world.'[110]

Tostão was polite enough to exclude himself from the roster of attacking talents he listed in his answer, when he deserves to be ranked alongside them, but – as with Paulo Cézar – his referral to the 1982 *Seleção* is significant. This

110 https://www.fifa.com/fifaplus/en/articles/tostao-interview-brazil-fifa-world-cup-pele-maradona-cristiano-messi

is the Brazil that Alex Bellos refers to as being the 'most fondly remembered team' within the country. It's the team of Zico, Sócrates, Edu, Falcão, and Júnior, *et al.*, under Telê Santana, eliminated in the second group stage after losing 3-2 to Italy in what was perhaps a small measure of revenge for the *Azzurri*.

On this occasion they overcame the team acclaimed for its dash and daring, whereas they had succumbed to the *Seleção*'s Samba 12 years earlier. Perhaps, however, there shouldn't be a rivalry between the teams of 1970 and 1982. For without the Samba Party in Mexico there would hardly have been a legacy for Santana's team to live up to. Before considering how the heights of 1982 were the rekindling of the 1970 flame, a consideration of how that fire had dimmed in 1974 and 1978 is necessary.

It's fitting that the success in 1970 had been built on the combination of *Ordem e Progresso* (Order and Progress), the national motto of the country as displayed on its flag. Order in the preparation and organisation had allowed the progressive football of the *Seleção* to flourish. Yet partnerships are always prey to splinter – especially ones created by political expediency – with one ultimately assuming dominance. Given that the country was governed by a military dictatorship, one that had wrapped the glory of World Cup triumph around itself as a symbol of its success, it's perhaps of little surprise that following the success in Mexico it was *Ordem* that assumed the dominant position in Brazilian football thinking, with *Progresso*, progressive football, sadly sidelined. In 1974, the team sent from Brazil to defend the World Cup was very different to the one that had triumphed in Mexico, not only in personnel but, more importantly, also in approach. A team that had bewitched and bedazzled four years earlier had become one that besmirched the legacy of *O Jogo Bonito*. It certainly wasn't the beautiful game, as journalist Graham Hunter recalled, 'Brazil played in a way I didn't recognise, and I didn't like.' But what caused such a change?

Zagallo returned from Mexico as the undoubted leader of Brazilian football but, as the military had elbowed their way into ownership of the team as well, moving forwards, government influence would shape the coach's approach. With both parties apparently unable to recognise the contradictions between the straitjacketed and jack-boot approach of the government, and the joyous, free-flowing Samba play, *O Jogo Bonito* was the lamented victim of the alliance as Médici's government unwittingly set about destroying the opiate it had used 'to calm the people' after the triumph in Mexico.

Euclides de Freitas Couto is a professor at the Department of Social Sciences at the Graduate Program in History at the Federal University of São João del-Rei. He has written widely on topics such as the political repercussions of sport during the period of totalitarian governments and in one of his articles, he explained, 'Throughout the 1970s, the entrance of the military in the Brazilian football scenery introduced a varied set of authoritarian practices ... Such actions, combined with the development and modernisation of Physical Education, inspired radical shifts in the daily routine of football teams: from then on, physical and tactical training, sports medicine, nutrition and psychological preparation should work together to form and "maintain" the "football athlete". In the specialisation of professionals connected to football, there was a growing stiffening of disciplinary rules that were imposed to the working and personal routines of players. Those rules were supported by official discourses and by the major part of the press, giving legitimacy to the embodiment of the authoritarian ethos in Brazilian football.'[111]

As an example, he goes on to cite the case of Botafogo midfielder Alfonsinho, who just a couple of months after the Mexico triumph turned up for training at the club with his hair slightly longer than was permitted, and sporting a beard. By now, Zagallo had returned to his club duties at Botafogo's training ground, the renamed General Severiano training facility. In a further example of the government taking control of football, it had apparently been awarded the military rank in its name. As De Freitas Couto put forward in the article, the events that followed suggest, 'The club became the army and the footballer was the soldier.'[112]

Zagallo immediately banned Alfonsinho from training. It was the beginning of a long and bitter dispute between club and player that led to a case in Brazil's Supreme Court. Alfonsinho eventually prevailed in 1971, allowing him to change clubs as he wanted without the agreement of his former employer. In 1974, a documentary about the case, *Passe Livre*, was made by Oswaldo Caldeira telling Alfonsinho's story. The player triumphed legally but that hardly convinced the government-controlled press. As De Freitas Couto concluded, 'It is interesting to notice how

---

111 Euclides de Freitas Couto (2014) 'Football, Control and Resistance in the Brazilian Military Dictatorship in the 1970s', *The International Journal of the History of Sport*, 31:10, 1267-1277, DOI: 10.1080/09523367.2014.922069

112 Euclides de Freitas Couto (2014) 'Football, Control and Resistance in the Brazilian Military Dictatorship in the 1970s, The International Journal of the History of Sport', 31:10, 1267-1277, DOI: 10.1080/09523367.2014.922069

the press legitimated the disciplinary discourse of the trainer. The great exhibitions of the Brazilian team in the Mexican pitches not only represented the return of the artistic football, but also served to validate the new models of training and team formation implanted by Zagallo.'[113] It also highlighted the danger flagged up by Dr Pete Watson about the precarity of a player's contract, and the dangers of challenging authority.

It's surely too simplistic to say that the increasing militarisation of Brazilian football was the only cause of the *Seleção*'s decline from the majesty of 1970 to the hugely dispiriting defence of their title four years later in West Germany. As Andrew Downie points out, the players, or lack of them, at Zagallo's disposal would surely have had a significant impact on how the team performed. 'The key for me was players,' Downie insisted. 'How many can you remember from that 1974 team? Clodoaldo wasn't there. Carlos Alberto wasn't there [both were ruled out by injury]. Tostão wasn't there. Gérson wasn't there. Pelé wasn't there [for various reasons, all three had retired]. They'd lost a lot of their top stars and the guys who came in were not as good or certainly did not play as well as they could, Paulo Cézar for example, and Jairzinho as well.'

Downie's point is both well made and indisputable, as only seven of the 1970 squad made the trip to defend the trophy. There's no doubt that shorn of so many first-choice players from Mexico, the team's star quality had been denuded. That said, ahead of the 1970 tournament,

---

113 Euclides de Freitas Couto (2014) 'Football, Control and Resistance in the Brazilian Military Dictatorship in the 1970s', *The International Journal of the History of Sport*, 31:10, 1267-1277, DOI: 10.1080/09523367.2014.922069

Clodoaldo had only seven international appearances to his name and Everaldo eight. Plus both Piazza and Rivellino were dropped into unfamiliar roles at the 11th hour. There seemed little such inspiration in Zagallo's selection in West Germany. The issue with players was arguably as much to do with who wasn't there as it was with who replaced them and how the survivors from 1970 performed or, more accurately, failed to do so. There's also a sizeable chunk of irony in the fact that Zagallo, the man who had launched *O Jogo Bonito* just four years earlier, had prescribed a dose of pragmatism and physicality as the remedy for the ills of the team caused by the absence of some players. It was the first step on the road of Brazil abandoning their ownership of the beautiful game.

As holders of the title, Brazil were excused the rigours of qualification for the 1974 finals. While automatic qualification is a boon, the absence of competitive fixtures hardly helps a coach to battle-harden his team with only friendlies to bed them in. The situation wasn't helped by the South American Championship not awakening from its eight-year hibernation until 1976. With no continental trophy to compete for and qualification assured, preparation for the defence of the World Cup was undoubtedly compromised.

A further factor was that Zagallo had bitter memories of seeing how Brazil had been brutally treated by opponents in the 1966 tournament, while receiving little protection from the referees. With the 1974 World Cup back in Europe, there was an understandable fear for the coach that a repeat may be on the cards, and there was a need to play with a high level of physicality in order to address the matter. This was 1974 though, not 1966, and such an attitude had become outdated, largely rendered redundant by his own team's success four years earlier. That Brazil played with overly excessive physicality in West Germany was less to do with a reaction to European tactics of eight years previously, and more to do with compensating for the lack of stellar talents in their squad.

The team limped through the first group section, edging into the second phase by finishing second to Yugoslavia thanks to the fact that they scored one goal more against Zaire than Scotland had. They then beat East Germany 1-0 and Argentina 2-1 in a typically febrile encounter to set up a last game against the Netherlands to see who would reach the final. In sharp contrast to Brazil, the Dutch had been flamboyant and hugely impressive. A game between the Brazil of 1970 and the Dutch of 1974 would have been a feast, a delight, an encounter for the ages. With the 1974 version of the *Seleção* taking part instead though, that was far from being the case. A team featuring just Rivellino, now wearing Pelé's number ten shirt, plus Jairzinho from the 11 that had contested the final in Mexico seemed to readily concede that they could not compete with the Dutch, and resorted to deep defence and physical excesses in equal measures.

Somewhat fittingly, in this game Brazil wore a two-tone blue ensemble rather than the mesmeric *Canarinho* and blue that represented their heritage. At least the yellow shirt was spared the ignominious performance. The Dutch, somewhat appropriately, wore white. With just 40 seconds of the game played, defending on the edge of his own penalty area, Rivellino tumbled Johan Neeskens to the turf. It set the pattern for the game. Pelé was watching from the stands and later lamented, 'We have suddenly become too defensive-minded ... Perhaps it is only an uncharacteristic phase that will pass in due course. I hope so at least.'[114]

The Dutch won 2-0. Graham Hunter reflected, 'That was emblematic to me of what was going on. This beautiful team in white was playing the way I'd seen that amazing Brazil team play four years earlier.' Brazil were eliminated, and lost the third-place play-off to Poland. Later, Rivellino conceded that fourth place was the limit of what the team deserved, 'Suddenly Holland comes with revolutionary soccer. Poland, Holland and Germany were better than Brazil.'[115] It was a harsh reality check. Many years later, writing in *The Times*, Brian Glanville said, 'The team Zagallo took to West Germany largely tried to compensate for its inadequacies with a bruising approach.'[116] From the Samba-dancing heights of 1970, Brazil had plummeted downwards to become clog-dancing outliers, pale imitations of what had been, unworthy heretics, wantonly discarding a legacy of the true faith.

It was a sad, almost apologetic way of conceding their title of world champions. The game against the Netherlands was a touchstone. Two teams on diametrically opposed trajectories passing each other on the way. The Dutch ended it full of hope and expectation, while for the *Seleção* the emotions were of disillusion and regret. When posed the question as to whether he thought that the rise of the Dutch in 1974 brought the decline of Brazil into sharp contrast, Sam Kunti had little doubt, 'It did. The contrast between

---

114 'Rensenbrink's injury looks like putting him out of the final', *The Times*, 5 July 1974

115 *CHAMP10NS*, Netflix

116 'Abysmal Brazil defence explodes myth of Zagallo', *The Times*, 13 July 1998

the flamboyant, unkempt, hippie-looking-like Dutch and the brutal Brazilians of 1974 was enormous. The team of coach Rinus Michels were the darlings of the tournament whereas everyone was wondering where the Brazilians of old had gone. They were criticised for almost being the worst team in the tournament, playing such economic and uninspiring football.

'Of course, it wasn't easy; they were defending their title on European soil, their preparation was protracted again, divisions between Carioca and Paulista players festered and some of the great stars of 1970 had retired. It was a decimated Brazil without Pelé, Carlos Alberto, Gérson, Clodoaldo and Tostão. Rivellino and Jairzinho were shadows of themselves and Paulo Cézar, Pelé's heir apparent, failed to deliver. It was disappointing for those kids who had been told by their fathers and uncles how extraordinary it was to watch. And this was the first World Cup when TV really became prevalent. Brazil at their best were indeed a spectacle, but in Germany they were pragmatic even if their side was still talented enough.

'Not helping matters and deepening the contrast was their brutality against the Dutch in the de facto semi-final. They had their moments in the match, but ultimately looked like a side unhappy to be there, much in the image of the rest of their tournament. But Brazil had now taken the technocratic direction, underlined by Cláudio Coutinho leading the team at the 1978 World Cup.'

Kunti's answer provoked a follow-up question in the author's mind. Is it too simplistic to say that the way the Dutch played enthralling football in 1974 made them the 'New Brazil 1970'? Kunti was quick to dismiss the notion, and explained why, 'Yes, it is simplistic and also a misnomer.

A match-up between Brazil 1970 and Netherlands 1974 would have been fascinating but of course we will never know the result, but both teams were profoundly different. Would the 1970 Brazilians have coped with Holland's high press and swarming style? Would the 1974 Dutch have coped with the sheer talent and firepower of the *Seleção*? Brazil 1970 were perhaps the last great side of individuals with names that until this day roll off fans' tongues whereas the Netherlands 1974 were the first real system team. By 1974, club football had overtaken the international game and, in a way, the Dutch national team were a club team. They played *totaalvoetbal*, a style that is deeply interwoven with Dutch identity and how the Netherlands dealt with space, architecture and urban planning in a country that lies below sea level. The back four aside, Brazil never really invented great systems. They brought artists to the game.'

Four years later, the World Cup was back in South America as Argentina hosted the tournament. Cláudio Coutinho, the man who had counselled Pelé about the importance of success in 1970 when part of Zagallo's coaching team, had also been part of the setup in West Germany as technical coordinator, following a period working with the Peruvian national team. After a less-than-encouraging qualification process featuring two wins and two draws in a group that also included Colombia and Paraguay, his military background – a former army captain – marked him down as the favoured candidate to take the *Seleção* to the World Cup.

By this time, Brazilian football had gone through a period of revision, hastened by the debacle of 1974. The traditional emphasis on flair and individuality had now been accepted as outdated with a European 'collective' model of play the dominant paradigm, with the Netherlands being held up as the ideal model. As a technocrat though, his favoured methods of play, with organisation and defined roles at its core, clashed noisily with the required free expression required by the Dutch model. It led to a crisis of identity for the team and Brazil again disappointed.

A single win by the only goal of the game against Austria accompanied by two draws saw them qualify from the initial group stage, finishing as runners-up. The second stage saw some improvement with a 3-0 victory over Peru and a 3-1 triumph against Poland. A goalless draw against the hosts, however, left them vulnerable, and a raft of shenanigans and sleight of hand culminating in a 6-0 win over the Peruvians took Argentina to the final, relegating Brazil into the third/fourth play-off, where they defeated Italy – of course – to collect the bronze medal.

It was a consolation prize but, as Sam Kunti explained, 'Brazilian football's golden age was over. The new direction was clear: Brazil wanted to win in a different way and replaced artists with bulky athletes.'[117] Brazilian football felt like it needed to catch up with the rest of the world, especially Europe, despite the fact they were the vanguards of a new and beautiful enchantment of the game in 1970. The likes of Coutinho and, later, Carlos Alberto Parreira who, despite saying of the 1970 team that 'We like to keep the ball. We like the Samba!'[118], were adherents to the new school of technocrats at the head of Brazilian football who had only a nodding regard for the glories of the past, and

117 Kunti, Sam, *Brazil 1970: How the Greatest Team of All Time Won the World Cup* (Worthing, England: Pitch Publishing Ltd, 2022)
118 *CHAMP10NS*, Netflix

were committed to vain pursuit of a new scientific, highly polished and gleaming future. Coutinho would be no part of it though. He left his post in 1980, for a brief spell in the USA taking charge of Los Angeles Aztecs. The following year, while on holiday back in Brazil before taking up a new post in Saudi Arabia, he was tragically killed in a diving accident. He was just 42 years old.

The new man heading up the *Seleção* was Telê Santana, then coach of Palmeiras. For a brief and glorious passage of time the hold of the technocrats was broken. Santana had a reputation for attacking play and was once described on Brazilian television as the 'last romantic of Brazilian football'.[119] He had enjoyed success with previous clubs Fluminense, Atlético Mineiro and Grêmio, securing the Campeonato Brasileiro Série A in 1971 with Mineiro. Since then, however, his only success had been to win the Campeonato Gaúcho with Grêmio six years later. Nevertheless, it was an inspired appointment and in 1982 Santana would lead 'the most fondly remembered team' alluded to by Alex Bellos and the one that Oliver Holt earlier described as the 'great entertainers' to the World Cup in Spain.

Some may suggest that the acclaim offered to Santana's 1982 version of the *Seleção* had much to do with them reigniting the memories of the 1970 Samba Party in Mexico, offering a hope of a return to *O Jogo Bonito* following the stagnation of technical control. After Brazil fans had endured two disappointing and largely dispiriting World Cups, the desire for a return to the play of 1970 was hugely understandable. It must have been a significant factor. For

---

119 *Roda Viva*, TV Cultura, 22 June 1992

more informed explanations I conscripted the help of Stuart Horsfield, author of both *1982 Brazil: The Glorious Failure: The Day Football Died* and *España 82: A Hazy Shade of Summer,* and Aidan Williams, who wrote *The Nearly Men: The Eternal Allure of the Greatest Teams that Failed to Win the World Cup.* Both had studied the 1982 *Seleção* as part of the research for their books, and I set them the task of explaining how a team that fell short of even reaching the last four in Spain could be regarded favourably when compared to the triumphant Brazil of a dozen years earlier.

Horsfield has a self-confessed emotional attachment to the 1982 vintage, and it bubbles to the surface in his answer, but there's a reason why that is true even though in cold, hard statistical terms, they fell well short of regaining the World Cup. Do you recall the thoughts of Professor Marcos Natali concerning Brazilian footballing culture wherein he emphasised how the pleasure and beauty of the game is regarded as paramount?

Horsfield's comments mesh perfectly with this expression, 'The Brazilian side of the 1982 World Cup remain that favourite child, the one who maybe underachieves compared to their siblings, but they are the one who are the most engaging and funny – the one that everybody in the family secretly likes the most. That Brazil side who went to Spain as favourites returned, essentially as losers. Yet as time progresses and heals, they have become global icons and the embodiment of what football used to be and can be. Led by a manager whose mantra was that he would rather "Lose beautifully than win ugly": Telê Santana was the conductor of the most beautiful symphony.

'Arguably the fact that the 1982 Brazil side was essentially comprised of Brazilian-based players meant

344

that this was the last national side that the fans could truly identify with and legitimately wave off from Brazilian shores. The magnificent Falcão at AS Roma and the tragic Dirceu at Atlético Madrid were the only players plying their trade outside of Brazil. Santana's obsession with players practising passing in training produced a brand of football unlike anything seen before at a World Cup. An attacking formation that has never been conclusively defined allowed for an instinctive brand of football that was, mesmerising aesthetically beautiful and yet effortless.

'The 1982 side was brimming with natural attacking talent, containing arguably the best player in the world at that time, Zico, and a captain who was a political idealist and a man of the people. This side scored 15 goals in five games, by seven different players. They were the absolute embodiment of a *Jogo Bonito* renaissance. Not only did this side enchant the Brazilian population, they enchanted the world. For a side that didn't even make the semi-finals, they are more celebrated and lauded than other Brazilian sides who have won the World Cup. They are lamented by Brazilians for failing to achieve their destiny, and they are lamented by the rest of the world because they are the last Brazilian side who truly encapsulated what Brazilian football is truly about.'

Williams was clearly of the opinion that the similarity in outlook between the team of 1970 and that of 1982 went a long way to explaining the lauding of the latter. 'After the disappointments of 1974 and 1978, Brazil's 1982 side represented a return to what many Brazilians felt was their true footballing identity,' he asserted. 'It was a team that played in the manner the Brazilian people saw themselves: carefree, expressive, exuberant, extravagant.

It was a refreshing return following the more cynical and conservative approaches Brazil had taken since 1970. They had failed more with tactics rather than technique, and so by 1982 they reverted back to their roots, becoming more *arte* than *força*.

'The 1970 winners cast a huge shadow over the teams which followed, but there has, to date, still not been a successor to them in Brazilian yellow as worthy as the wonderful team of 1982. Brazilians love the mythology of their natural skill and flair, emerging untrained from the shanty towns to take Brazil to glory on the grandest stage. More than any other, the 1982 team, with a purity on a par with that of 1970, captured that ideal to perfection. They represented the very essence of Brazilian character and folklore, earning them a rare and enduring place in Brazilian hearts for a team who lost, but beautifully so.' Once more, the echoes with Professor Natali's writings are clear.

Sam Kunti agreed, 'In terms of honouring the beautiful game with their style, yes [the 1982 *Seleção* of Telê Santana were probably the true heirs of Zagallo's 1970 *O Jogo Bonito* team]. It is possibly the last great Brazilian side.' He added, however, that they should not be regarded as better than the team that lifted the World Cup 12 years earlier, 'Brazil 1982 are revered, admired and remembered more fondly perhaps than Brazil 1970, but they are not rated more highly. Ultimately, defeat is more compelling than victory – for all the drama and for everything that didn't materialise. There is almost something romantic about losing. Defeats reverberate forever whereas very few victories do that in fact. That's why the *Maracanazo* and the day that football died, in Zico's words, remain so fascinating. In 1950, Brazilians got their inferiority complex confirmed on the global stage while in 1982 it seemed that the Italians' victory demonstrated that Brazil could no longer play their own kind of football to win the World Cup. 1970 was football in transition – on the cusp of professionalism, commercialism, etc. – whereas in 1982 the World Cup was already the main global sporting event. So, the context was very different. In 1970, football was by and large still romantic whereas in 1982 that notion was beginning to fade. In that sense, Brazil's elimination was perhaps even more painful because they reminded the audience of times gone by.'

Borrowing the words of Zico, as referenced by Kunti above, Horsfield subtitled his *1982 Brazil: The Glorious Failure* book as *The Day Football Died.* His passionate adulation of the 1982 *Seleção* and lament over their defeat offer clear reason for that summation. It's an assessment that would echo in the words of former Brazilian sports journalist Marcos Uchoa, when interviewed by Oliver Holt for the *Mail on Sunday* and recalling the 3-2 defeat to Italy which eliminated Brazil on the 'day football died'. 'It was on that day that, morally, we lost the role as custodians of beautiful football,' Uchoa lamented. 'We had four great midfielders in that team and we have never really had a great midfielder again. We became scared of creativity. It was the end of a golden era in Brazil. Our players started to leave for Europe and spent their best years abroad and we lost what made us unique.'[120]

Santana was also granted a second chance to emulate 1970 when he returned to take control of the *Seleção* in 1985, guiding them to the 1986 finals. With the World Cup

---

120 https://www.dailymail.co.uk/sport/football/article-10953131/Brazils-
   1982-World-Cup-team-feted-heroes-Zico-claims-Italy-defeat-scarred-
   game.html

returning to Mexico once more, and Brazil again playing their group games back at the Estadio Jalisco in Guadalajara, a potential 'Back to the Future' scenario brought renewed hope. After winning all three group matches, however, and comfortably disposing of Poland 4-0 in the last 16, Brazil missed out on a semi-final slot when losing to France on penalties after a 1-1 draw in the quarter-final.

Given that Santana and many of the players from the Spain tournament were still in place for 1986, it may be more accurate to say that it was mortally wounded in 1982, with the *coup de grâce* ironically being delivered back in Mexico where *O Jogo Bonito* had been born. Had Santana's 'entertainers' triumphed, Brazilian football may well have taken a different path moving forwards but, as Uchoa described, any road back towards the enthralling play of 1970 was now lost forever, and Brazilian teams would continue to become increasingly less Brazilian.

Back in 1970, every member of Zagallo's squad played their club football in Brazil and even by 1982 only two of Santana's players were attached to clubs outside of the country. For 1986 the number was again two. Skipper Edinho and Júnior were both playing in Italy, the former with Udinese, with the latter joining Torino.

Four years later, Sebastião Barroso Lazaroni was in charge of the squad that contested Italia '90. With more than half of the players selected now attached to European clubs, it was of little surprise that the coach attempted to play a Europeanised system with a sweeper deployed in his defence. Elimination in the last 16 suggested that the increasing European influence was hardly proving beneficial. The *Seleção*'s identity was ebbing away without gaining anything in exchange. Sand running through fingers and being blown away by the winds of change.

That process had run its course by the time of the 1994 World Cup held in the USA. Lazaroni's brief tenure was doomed after the poor showing in Italy and the CBD turned to Falcão, their former player and hero of 1982. After returning to Brazil from Roma, he had played briefly for São Paulo before retiring. Now he was entrusted with rejuvenating a jaded *Seleção* in search of itself. For a first-time coach, the task was surely too big and certainly too soon. After a run of just nine wins in 16 games he was replaced by a caretaker, Ernesto Paulo, whose single match in charge, a home defeat against Wales, ruled out any possibility of an extended stay. Instead, after trying a rookie coach, the CBD opted for the opposite extreme and appointed someone who had not only already served as part of the coaching staff in previous World Cups but had also taken other countries to the finals.

Carlos Alberto Parreira had coached the Kuwait side that qualified in 1982, and was also in charge of the UAE at Italia '90. Neither had excelled – Kuwait's 1-1 draw with Czechoslovakia was the only game in which either of Parreira's teams hadn't been defeated – but two decades of coaching and tournament experience was in his favour and, after Falcão's sad failure, experience looked to be an essential asset for the new man.

Taking over in October 1991, his first game was a 3-0 victory over Yugoslavia. From there he took the *Seleção* through qualification, losing just a single game when late goals from Etcheverry and Peña gave Bolivia a home victory in La Paz that had never looked on the cards up to that point. Arriving in the USA, a 2-0 victory against Russia, a three-goal romp against Cameroon, and a 1-1 draw against Sweden were enough to top their group. It took them into a knockout game against the hosts where a solitary goal was sufficient for a place in the last eight. Successive single-goal margins against the Netherlands and then Sweden took Brazil to the final at Pasadena's Rose Bowl. As in 1970, Italy provided the opposition. There was no sweeping aside of the blue-shirted Italians this time, though. Ninety minutes of fairly stilted play, and a further 30 when defences dominated even more, took the final to a penalty shoot-out. Three Italians failed to convert and Brazil subsequently became the first team to win the World Cup courtesy of a 12-yard lottery.

The World Cup would return to Brazil for the first time in 24 years, but across the country the success was hardly met with the same joyous outburst as 1970, or the lament for the glorious failure of 1982. The less-than-satisfactory denouement may well have served to take a little of the shine from the triumph, but other factors weigh heavily in the way that many Brazilians regard the 1994 victory. Paulo Cézar spoke for many of them. 'I haven't rooted for Brazil for years,' he told the *Daily Mail*. 'I don't like the philosophy. It's too defensive. It's pragmatic. No charm. No art. Brazil played in 1982 and they lost but who cares? It was fantastic. Nobody talks about the 1994 side that won the World Cup. We don't celebrate that. Brazilian football has paid a high price right until now for what happened in '82 in terms of the quality of the football we play. The beautiful football has gone. It's gone. It's very sad.'[121]

---

121 https://www.dailymail.co.uk/sport/football/article-10953131/Brazils-1982-World-Cup-team-feted-heroes-Zico-claims-Italy-defeat-scarred-game.html

It has, and it is. As if to illustrate that the 1994 *Seleção* had little connection to the one that bewitched the world in Mexico, no fewer than nine of the 11 players who began the final were playing for European clubs. And, of the two playing club football in Brazil, Mazinho had only recently returned from a couple of years in Italy and after the tournament would move to Spain where he would play for three different clubs across a seven-year stretch. The remaining player, midfielder Zinho, would depart for the booming J.League and Yokohama Flügels. A year after the tournament, none of the 11 players on the pitch at the start of the final would be playing in Brazil.

Parreira's *Seleção* had won the World Cup in the manner of a European team. Yes, they still wore the *Canarinho*, but that was the only true link between them and Zagallo's 1970 Samba Party team. Sam Kunti had said that 'Brazil wanted to win [the World Cup] in a different way'. In 1994 they found that way, but it was anything but truly Brazilian as had been defined in 1970.

A further World Cup was added in 2002 when Brazil beat Germany 2-0 in Yokohama, Japan. It gave the country its fifth title, more than any other nation. And yet the price paid to achieve such success may well be considered too expensive by fans who hold dear to the memory of the 1970 World Cup Samba Party.

Earlier, I quoted the words of Professor Marcos Natali, 'The idealised way of playing celebrated in Brazilian culture recognises the possibility that the disciplinary and pedagogical impulse of English sports might be for a moment dribbled by a body which seeks to be the site of pleasure … The player and the audience derive pleasure from the beauty of the moment, regardless of its consequences.' Such beliefs now seem to have been dismissed in the Brazilian national team, sacrificed on the altar of success valued above the professor's idea of 'Brazilian culture', and it's difficult to believe that will ever return.

The party was over.

It was Brazil's party. Let them cry if they want to.

The only things remaining are memories and the aching sadness of a hangover.